THE PASSION TRANSLATION

THE BOOK OF

ISAIAH

the vision

BroadStreet
PUBLISHING

CONTENTS

ISAIAH

ABOUT THE PASSION TRANSLATION

The message of God's story is timeless; the Word of God doesn't change. But the methods by which that story is communicated should be timely; the vessels that steward God's Word can and should change. One of those timely methods is Bible translation. Bible translations are both a gift and a problem. They give us the words God spoke through his servants, but words can be poor containers for revelation because they leak! The meanings of words change from one generation to the next. Meaning is influenced by culture, background, and many other details. Just imagine how differently the Hebrew authors of the Old Testament saw the world three thousand years ago from the way we see it today!

There is no such thing as a truly literal translation of the Bible, for there is not an equivalent language that perfectly conveys the meaning of the biblical text. It must be understood in its original cultural and linguistic settings. This problem is best addressed when we seek to transfer meaning, not merely words, from the original text to the receptor language.

The purpose of The Passion Translation is to reintroduce the passion and fire of the Bible to the English reader. It doesn't merely convey the literal meaning of words. It expresses God's passion for people and his world by translating the original, life-changing message of God's Word for modern readers.

You will notice at times we've italicized certain words or phrases. These highlighted portions are not in the original Hebrew, Greek, or Aramaic manuscripts but are implied from the context. We've made these implications explicit for the sake of narrative clarity and to better convey the meaning of God's Word. This is a common practice by mainstream translations.

We've also chosen to translate certain names in their original Hebrew or Greek form to better convey their cultural meaning and significance. For instance, some translations of the Bible have substituted Jacob with James and Judah with Jude. Both Greek and Aramaic leave these Hebrew names in their original form. Therefore, this translation uses those cultural names.

God longs to have his Word expressed in every language in a way that would unlock the passion of his heart. Our goal is to trigger inside every English-speaking reader an overwhelming response to the truth of the Bible. This is a heart-level translation, from the passion of God's heart to the passion of your heart.

We pray this version of God's Word will kindle in you a burning desire for him and his heart, while impacting the church for years to come.

Please visit ThePassionTranslation.com for more information about The Passion Translation.

ISAIAH

Introduction

AT A GLANCE

Author: Isaiah the Seer-Prophet
Audience: Originally Israel, but these revelations speak to everyone
Date: 740–700 BC
Type of Literature: Prophetic literature
Major Themes: The Bible in one book; judgment for rebellion; vindication for
God's people; redemption hope; the Messiah unveiled
Outline:

Yahweh's Vision concerning Judah and Jerusalem — 1:1–5:30
The Vision and Prophetic Call of Isaiah — 6:1–13
Yahweh's Signs, Judgment, and Deliverance — 7:1–12:6
Yahweh's Judgments of the Nations — 13:1–23:18
Yahweh's Victory Over the Nations — 24:1–27:13
The False Hope of Trusting the Nations — 28:1–33:24
Enemies Judged, the Redeemed Return — 34:1–35:10
The Vision concerning Hezekiah — 36:1–39:8
The Vision concerning God's Promises — 40:1–48:22
The Vision concerning Redemption and Restoration — 49:1–55:13
Yahweh, Our Judge and Redeemer — 56:1–66:24

ABOUT ISAIAH

Isaiah, the first of the major prophets, was the prophet of Zion. He was not just
a teacher or preacher but a seer and intercessor for God's people. Zion is not
simply a spiritual place; it is a spiritual people. It is a realm of glory, a realm of
vision. Zion is also a term used to describe a supernatural people who live in the
reality of a supernatural vision. This vision is for all those who long to live as
God's people from Zion, the realm of supernatural glory.

You are about to enter a vision-zone of heaven descending upon the earth.
Let's study the vision of a man who saw the glory of God and now speaks with
burning lips. True prophetic ministry flows from this vision until it grows into
a burden. With a blast of newly released Spirit-wind,[a] Isaiah now speaks for

---

a All of the Word of God is inspired or "God-breathed." See 2 Tim. 3:16.

God with fire-touched lips. He speaks about the supernatural reality of Yahweh breaking into the reality of this world in order to impart to his people insights into his loving heart and wise plan.

The book of Isaiah is one enormous collection of prophecies (the longest in the Bible) described as the *vision* (Heb. *chazown*). This word is a descriptive term for the entire supernatural revelation given by God to Isaiah. It is not simply teaching or an historical record; it is the overarching vision of the heart of God revealed to his seer-prophet. This vision spans the plan of the ages. It becomes a collective overview of all that God has planned. It takes us beyond the days of Isaiah, even beyond our own times, bringing us into the council chambers of eternity, revealing the unfolding plan of an all-wise God. The vision did not belong to Isaiah; it is the Lord's vision for a people raised up on the earth who will reflect his glory.

The documents of Isaiah are among the most reliable of all the Old Testament. We even have a copy of the book that dates to 100 BC thanks to the discovery of the Dead Sea scrolls. They predate the next oldest extant copy by nearly one thousand years, and very little variation in the manuscripts was found. So we can be confident as we read Isaiah's inspired prophecies that we are gazing upon the truth of the ages.

The apostle John writes, "Isaiah said these things because he had seen and experienced the splendor of Jesus and prophesied about him." (John 12:41). Isaiah was taken into heaven's throne room and saw the Son of God as the Lord on the throne. The "Lord high and exalted" is Jesus Christ before he became a man. Here's how Peter described the ministry of the prophets, including Isaiah:

> This salvation was the focus of the prophets who prophesied of this *outpouring of* grace that was destined for you. They made a careful search and investigation of the meaning *of their God-given prophecies* as they probed into *the mysteries* of who would fulfill them and the time period when it would all take place. The Spirit of the Anointed One was in them and was pointing prophetically to the sufferings that Christ was destined to suffer and the glories that would be released afterward. God revealed to the prophets that their ministry was not for their own benefit but for yours. And now, you have heard these things from the evangelists who preached the gospel to you through the power of the Holy Spirit sent from heaven—the gospel *containing wonderful mysteries* that even the angels long to get a glimpse of. (1 Peter 1:10–12)

The poetic message of Isaiah is the glorious message of overcoming, hope, comfort, and the restoration of all things. Because of Christ's appearing with love for all the world, Isaiah's words are now seen as clear prophetic insights into the death, resurrection, and glory of our King. To see him in every chapter of Isaiah will be the key to unlocking its deep prophetic mystery to our hearts. Read it with joy and passion to discover the Beloved—you will find him!

PURPOSE

The scope of this book touches every nation on the earth today. The prophecies of Isaiah are addressed not only to the citizens of the eighth century BC but to the inhabitants of the whole earth—"with all of us who are alive here today" (Deut. 5:3). He was commissioned by the Lord through supernatural revelation to proclaim the vision containing divine insight into impending judgment for sins, coming comfort for future destruction, and the hope of eventual redemption. Significant to the church in these last days is his prophetic insight into the person and work of Jesus—the Faithful Servant, Chosen Servant, Teacher-Servant, and Suffering Servant.

With panoramic insight, Isaiah preaches about the virgin birth of Christ and the virgin Bride of Christ. We read prophecies of the new thing God delights in doing and the New Jerusalem God delights to dwell in. We see Christ Jesus as the Man of Sorrows and the Conquering King. Isaiah's burning message is not only for the future, it is for *now*.

With their vast and grand themes, Isaiah's prophecies are unrivaled in all of Scripture. They present to us a description of cataclysmic judgments, the survival of a holy remnant, and the canopy of glory that is coming to earth. A cleansed, holy people will emerge in Zion. They will be the outgrowth of the one called the Branch, and they will possess his glory and his beauty. These revelation insights assure us that we can trust Lord Yahweh with our present suffering and future restoration.

AUTHOR AND AUDIENCE

Isaiah, an educated and prominent man in the nation of Israel, was married to a prophetess (8:3) and had two sons, named She'ar-Ya'shuv, meaning "a remnant will return" (7:3) and the younger, Maher-Shalal-Hash-Baz, meaning "Quickly—to the plunder! Hurry—to the loot!" (8:3).

Historian and church father Jerome says of Isaiah, "He was more of an evangelist than a prophet because he presented the mysteries of the church of Christ so vividly."[a] How true! In Isaiah 53 Isaiah brings us a clear presentation of Jesus as the Savior and the crucified one. John Wesley concluded, "Undoubtedly he was the prince of all the prophets."[b] About Isaiah's prophetic book he wrote, "He so evidently and fully describes the person, and offices, and sufferings, and kingdom of Christ, that some of the ancients called him the fifth Evangelist."[c]

Isaiah the seer-prophet is indeed a fifth evangelist, making his prophetic work a fifth gospel, for he reveals the hidden mysteries of Lord Yahweh's good news. These mysteries were unveiled first before the people of God, at once confronting them and the nations with future doom and encouraging them with future glory. Ultimately, Isaiah's evangelistic prophecy is meant for all the world, unveiling before it the beauty and majesty, hope and expectations, of Messiah Jesus.

---

a *The Lives of the Holy Prophets*, Holy Apostles Convent, 101.

b *John Wesley's Notes on the Whole Bible (Wesley's Notes)*, derived from an electronic text from the Christian Classics Ethereal Library, ccel.org.

c Ibid.

MAJOR THEMES

The Bible in One Book. Isaiah is like the entire Bible in that there are sixty-six books of inspired Scripture and sixty-six chapters in Isaiah. The first thirty-nine books of the Bible comprise the Old Testament, or what our Jewish friends call "the Covenant." The first thirty-nine chapters of Isaiah parallel the first thirty-nine books of the Bible. Both include woes, judgment, and promises; there is a focus on the Hebrew people and their history; and the destined future of God's people is unveiled. The last twenty-seven chapters of Isaiah in many ways mirror the last twenty-seven books of the Bible, what we call the New Testament—beginning with Isaiah 40 and the prophecy of John the Baptizer as a "thundering voice shouting in the desert" (John 1:23), heralding the coming of the Messiah, who brings the message of life and hope. You could consider your journey through Isaiah like taking a journey through the entire Bible, for both end with God making all things new, including giving us a new heaven and a new earth (Isa. 66:22; see also Rev. 21–22).

If you were to take the whole Bible and squeeze it into one book, you would end up with the prophecy of Isaiah. It is truly the Bible in miniature. Both Jesus and Paul quote Isaiah more than any other Old Testament book. If you really want to know your Bible, read Isaiah!

Judgment for the Rebellious. From the beginning, the vision unveils a major theme that courses throughout this prophetic work: judgment for the rebellious. All are corrupt, having stubbornly continued in their rebellion from the bottom of their feet to the top of their heads. Lord Yahweh, Commander of Angel Armies, has issued prophetic utterances of judgment against human beings, from the leaders of Sodom to the people of Gomorrah, from the Philistines to the Moabites, from Egypt to Babylon. In stirring, graphic language, Isaiah prophesied the day of Lord Yahweh, a period when he would punish the world for its evil and the wicked for their sins. In the day of his fierce anger, the heavens will shudder and the earth will shake from its foundations.

This outpouring of corrective wrath is reserved not only for the nations who have turned their backs on Lord Yahweh but for God's people who have despised the Holy One of Israel. Israel and Judah had become estranged and alienated from God, offering defiled sacrifices and tainted worship. More significant, they exchanged worship of the Holy One of Israel for worthless idols of wood and stone. The covenant Israel entered into with Yahweh was broken by their idolatry and unbelief. It was as though God's children disowned their Father. And destruction was promised for such arrogance. Yes, God is love and longs to pour out his love upon his people, those he has chosen and established as his own. Yet God is holy, and although in mercy he may delay judgment, he will judge his people.

Remarkably, even during devastation and judgment, God calls his people the "daughter of Zion" (Isa. 1:8). God's people are his daughter, born out of Zion, the holy realm. Instead of being his dwelling place, they became like a flimsy hut. The work of God, as seen in the book of Isaiah, was to restore this "hut" to a dwelling place of divine shelter through his refining fire. Even the besieged city will one day become the New Jerusalem, where God and humanity mingle as one.

The Hope of Vindication and Redemption. Favor and mercy always triumph over judgment. God will excel in grace toward his people and give them back even more than what sins spoiled and Satan stole. There is coming a day when Lord Yahweh will wield his massive, mighty sword and take up our cause, slaying the serpent of confusion and working a mighty work of vindication from enemies and redemption from sins in the lives of his people. He is our Kinsman-Redeemer, the Mighty One who unveils to us his cherishing love like a relative coming to the aid of his next-of-kin in trouble to redeem and rescue them. He loves us so much that he took upon this role of family protector, becoming the sacrifice to rescue us from danger and return us to God.

God is a God of restoration, even for those who have miserably failed him. He has always had a remnant people, a "holy seed" of survivors who will spring up through his mercy, even in a time of judgment. Today, true believers have the holy seed of Christ within us, for we have been born from above. The remnant is an important theme found in the messages of the prophets, especially Isaiah. The theology of God preserving a remnant meant so much to Isaiah that he named one of his sons Shear-Jashub, "a remnant will return" (7:3). The remnant of the lovers of God who have taken hold of one Man (Jesus) will be sheltered and protected, even in a time of judgment.

This vindication and redemption is encapsulated in three songs in the book of Isaiah: the Song of Praise for the Redeemed (ch. 12), the Joyful Song of the Redeemed (35:1–10), and the Song of Salvation (52:7–12). In each, the children of God are invited to praise Lord Yahweh for turning away his anger and offering tender comfort; for breaking through and giving us victory, avenging our enemies with the salvation of divine retribution; for the beautiful message announcing peace and happiness; and for the unveiling of Lord Yahweh's saving power before all the nations. Praise is a vital component of Isaiah's teachings on redemption. If we ourselves don't praise, creation will in our place!

The Hebrew word for salvation is *yĕshuw'ah*, and it is found in Isaiah twenty-eight times. It is similar to the Hebrew name of Jesus: Yeshua. Redemption is God's last word, not judgment. To know Jesus is to know the God of salvation who sent him (John 14:9). Through him, the Suffering Servant, our salvation was accomplished as he was rejected and mocked, pierced and crushed, bruised and punished. "Like wayward sheep, we have all wandered astray," Isaiah writes prophetically. "Each of us has turned from God's paths and chosen our own way; even so, Yahweh laid the guilt of our every sin upon him" (53:6), unlocking the door of hope leading to redemption.

Unveiling the Messiah. Finally, the vision offers us prophetic insights into the most important theme of Scripture: the Messiah. More than any other place in God's Word, divine revelation concerning Lord Yahweh's Anointed One is poured out here for the benefit of God's people. Just consider all of the mysteries unveiled before us through this seer-prophet:

Isaiah 7 promises the world a sign from Lord Yahweh himself: "The virgin will conceive and give birth to a son and will name him God Among Us" (v. 14). There is nothing miraculous about a young woman having a baby; it happens every day. However, Matthew quotes this prophetic word for the virgin birth of the Messiah (Matt. 1:23). No child with a human father could be the fulfillment of Immanuel, *God among us.*

In chapter 9, Isaiah is prophesying the ministry of Jesus that would reverse the curse through the radiance of his light shining upon the places where devastation has robbed us of hope. This glorious light includes Jesus' teachings, his miracles, and the pure life he lived before the Father. Jesus Christ is a light of rescue for the lost, comfort for the hurting, wholeness for the broken, and escape for the captive. He is the light of joy, the light of revelation, the light of deliverance. Isaiah prophesied that as the light of Jesus shines on the earth it will bring in a harvest of joy and rejoicing.

The first five verses of chapter 11 unveil several aspects of the Messiah. He would be from David's lineage. He is the stump of Jesse, the fruitful Branch. He would have the sevenfold Spirit of God resting upon him: the Spirit of Yahweh, the Spirit of Extraordinary Wisdom, the Spirit of Perfect Understanding, the Spirit of Wise Strategy, the Spirit of Mighty Power, the Spirit of Revelation, and the Spirit of the Fear of the Lord. His government would be equitable and full of righteousness, and it would demonstrate his loyalty to God. Jesus fulfills all of these attributes completely as the long-awaited Branch-Messiah of Lord Yahweh.

Isaiah 42 introduces to us the Lord Jesus, the Messiah, as the chosen servant of the Lord, sustained by Yahweh, sent on a divine mission to bring light and freedom to the hearts of his covenant people. Starting with chapter 42, Isaiah gives us four Servant Songs: (1) This chapter presents him as the Faithful Servant who brings light to the nations. (2) In 49:1–13 he is the Chosen Servant to bring salvation to the nations and to restore Israel. (3) In 50:4–9, we have the song of the Obedient Servant who reveals the Father. (4) In 52:13–53:12 we find the Suffering Servant. These songs comprise a capstone of divine revelation unveiling the Messiah.

All of the prophetic writings have the power to change you. They change our outlook toward the future, they give us prophetic meaning for the past, and they empower us to live holy lives today. Read Isaiah to be transformed and watch God change your life.

ISAIAH

The Vision

1 Here is the vision*a* that Isaiah,*b* the son of Amoz, received by divine revelation concerning what was going to happen to Judah and Jerusalem during the times of Uzziah, Jotham, Ahaz, and Hezekiah, kings of Judah.*c*

A Nation in Rebellion
2 Listen, O heavens! Hear,*d* O earth!
  For the Lord Yahweh has spoken:*e*
  "I tenderly nurtured children and made them great,*f*
  but they have rebelled*g* against me!

---

a 1:1 Or "prophecy." This refers to the entire book as a divine revelation from God. The Hebrew word *chazown* means to see spiritually, to have a revelation or dream, or to receive an oracle. This word was commonly used to describe how the prophets received divine communication.

b 1:1 It is believed that Isaiah was an aristocrat, a member of the royal family and the nephew of King Uzziah. His father, Amoz, was the brother of King Amaziah.

c 1:1 Even the names mentioned in v. 1 have something to teach us. Isaiah means "Yahweh is salvation (victory)." Amoz means "to be made strong or courageous." Judah means "praise." Jerusalem means "the teaching of peace (wholeness)." Isaiah prophesied during the reign of Uzziah ("the power of Yahweh" or "mighty is Yahweh"), Jotham ("the one Yahweh makes perfect" or "Yahweh is upright"), Ahaz ("possessor" or "to lay hold of"), and Hezekiah ("strengthened by Yahweh" or "the one Yahweh makes firm"). Here is what the meanings of the names of v. 1 teach us: We can see that prophetic vision from a courageous prophet imparts the power of Yahweh, which releases those whom Yahweh makes perfect to maturity. They will be possessors and those who lay hold of heaven's promises until they are strengthened by Yahweh and made firm in all their ways! All of this will take place in the land of praise and in the teaching of peace.

d 1:2 The Hebrew is literally "ear me."

e 1:2 God summons into his courtroom his two witnesses (Deut. 19:15), the heavens and the earth, concerning God's seven-count indictment against Israel for breaking covenant with him. See Deut. 4:26; 30:19; 31:28; 32:1; Ps. 50:4; Jer. 2:12.

f 1:2 Or "raised them up high (exalted)." The words translated as "nurtured" and "made them great" are two Hebrew synonyms that could be translated "exalt, advance, set on high, mature, increase, magnify, promote, raise up, and cause to grow." This is what Father God will do for his children. In the book of Isaiah, God's love toward Israel is displayed in a threefold way: He is Father (Isa. 1:2–3; 63:16; 64:8), a nursing Mother (66:12–13), and a Husband (54:5). God was Israel's Father, Mother, and Husband.

g 1:2 The Hebrew word for "rebelled" (*pasha`*) indicates the breaking of a contract. The covenant Israel entered into with Yahweh was broken by their idolatry and unbelief. It was as though God's children disowned their Father.

³Even a dumb ox instinctively knows its owner
  and the stubborn mule knows the hand that feeds him,ᵃ
  but Israel does not know meᵇ
  nor do my people understand."ᶜ

Isaiah's Indictment

⁴Oh,ᵈ how this nation keeps sinning!
  See them dragging the heavy burden of their guilt!
  They are corrupt children, descendants of evildoers.
  They have turned their backs on the Lord God
  and despised the Holy One of Israel!ᵉ
  They have cut themselves off from the help of God!ᶠ
⁵Why would you seek to be injured further?
  Why would you stubbornly continue in your rebellion?ᵍ
  Your whole head is sick,ʰ
  and your heart and your will are weak and faint.
⁶You are corrupt from the bottom of your feet
  to the top of your head. There is no integrity—ⁱ
  nothing but bruises, putrefying sores, and raw open wounds!
  They have not been drained or bandaged or soothed with oil.ʲ

---

a 1:3 Or "where to find its master's feeding trough (crib)." God is showing that "dumb" animals have more devotion to their masters than God's people have toward him.

b 1:3 Although implied in the Hebrew, both the Latin Vulgate and the Septuagint (LXX) have "know me." The Hebrew word for "know" is *yaḏa'* and refers to having a personal, intimate relationship with someone. God's people had no intimacy with God, seemingly unaware of the incredible opportunity to be intimate with the God of heaven. At least the donkey knows where his master will feed him, while God's people do not understand where they can be fed and strengthened by the Word and by the Spirit. It is time to know the Master and his manger. Isn't it interesting that Jesus was laid in a donkey's manger at his birth? The "owner's manger" is the birth of our Lord Jesus Christ, who has come to feed us his living Bread.

c 1:3 That is, "My people neither understand my ways nor how kind I am."

d 1:4 Or "Alas" or "Woe." The Hebrew word (*hoy*) was used at funerals as a lament.

e 1:4 This is Isaiah's favorite title of God; he uses it twenty-six times in this book. Twenty-six is the numerical value of the Hebrew name for God, YHWH (Yahweh).

f 1:4 Or "They are utterly estranged (alienated from God)" or "They have gone backward (running away from God)."

g 1:5 Or "Why, knowing you'll be beaten again, do you rebel again?" This is more the lament of a loving father than the indictment of a judge. The broken heart of God toward his wayward people is revealed.

h 1:5 The "head" speaks of at least two things: the leadership of the nation and the thoughts that have turned from God.

i 1:6 Their wounded "feet" speak of their walking away from God; the top of the head represents their thought life that crowded out God.

j 1:6 Yet, if we turn to God, he will bandage our wounds and bring us healing (Luke 4:18; 10:34). Jesus was wounded from head to toe, bruised and beaten, to bring us life and healing. Jesus took all the punishment described in this chapter, and he took it all for us.

[7]Your country is devastated
and your cities burned to the ground;[a]
foreigners plunder your crops before your eyes—
with nothing but devastation and destruction in their wake![b]
[8]And the daughter of Zion[c] is left as helpless as
a deserted shack in a vineyard or
like a flimsy shelter in a field of cucumbers—
in every way like a city besieged![d]
[9]If the Lord of Angel Armies[e] had not left us survivors,
our fate would have been the same as Sodom and Gomorrah![f]

Justice, Not Hypocritical Worship

[10]Hear the word of Yahweh:[g]
"You leaders of Sodom, heed the correction[h] of our God!
People of Gomorrah, you'd better listen to his rebuke."
[11]And Yahweh keeps saying:
"Why such countless sacrifices—what use are they to me?
I've had my fill of your burnt offerings of rams
and your fattened animals.[i]
I find no delight in the blood of bulls, lambs, or goats!
[12]When you come before my face,
who asked you to come trampling on my courtyards?

---

a This was literally fulfilled about 175 years after this prophetic declaration with the invasion of Babylon in 586 BC. See Jer. 25.

b 1:7 God's judgment takes the form of military invasion and destruction.

c 1:8 Even during devastation, God calls his people the "daughter of Zion." God's people are his daughter, born out of Zion, the holy realm. Instead of being his dwelling place, they have become like a flimsy hut. The work of God, as seen in the book of Isaiah, is to restore this "hut" to the place of the divine shelter or dwelling place (see Isa. 66). Even the besieged city will one day become the New Jerusalem, where God and humanity mingle as one.

d 1:8 Isaiah may be prophesying of the coming Assyrian invasion of Judah under King Sennacherib. See Isa. 36–37.

e 1:9 Or "the Lord of every sort of host" or "Yahweh, who is hosts."

f 1:9 But mercy won and took dominion over judgment (James 2:13). God will leave survivors, a remnant in the land. A "holy seed" (Isa. 6:13) will spring up. The "remnant" is an important theme found in the message of the prophets (Isa. 6:13; 10:20–22; 11:11–13, 16; Jer. 6:9; 23:3; 31:7; Mic. 2:12; Zech. 8:12) and Paul (Rom. 9:27–29; 11:5). The theology of God preserving a remnant meant so much to Isaiah that he named one of his sons Shear-Jashub, "a remnant will return" (Isa. 7:3).

g 1:10 Isaiah uses this command twenty-three times in this book.

h 1:10 Although the Hebrew uses the word *torah* ("law, instruction"), it is used in the context to mean "correction or rebuke."

i 1:11 Outward sacrifices are empty if there is no inward reality (Ps. 51:16–17; Mic. 6:6–8; Matt. 23:23). God cannot be bought. He looks at the heart and requires offerings given in holiness and truth. The sacrifice of a fattened animal is an outward picture of what God wants to do inside of us. He wants to kill that "fattened" part of us that is stuffed only with the letter of the Word but not the humility taught by the Word (Deut. 8:2–3; 2 Chron. 7:14; Isa. 66:2; James 1:21).

¹³Stop bringing your meaningless offerings.*ᵃ*
Your burning incense stinks!
Your sin-stained celebrations,*ᵇ*
your new moon festivals, Sabbaths,
your various pious meetings—I can't stand them!
¹⁴With all my soul*ᶜ* I hate
your new moon festivals and your feasts;*ᵈ*
they are nothing but a burden
that I'm sick and tired of carrying.
¹⁵When you stretch out your hands to pray,
I will hide my eyes from you.*ᵉ*
Repeat your prayers all you want, but I will not listen,
for your hands are stained with innocent blood.
¹⁶Wash yourselves and make yourselves clean.
Remove your evil actions from my sight
and stop sinning!*ᶠ*
¹⁷Learn what it means to do what is good
by seeking righteousness and justice!
Rescue the oppressed.*ᵍ* Uphold the rights of the fatherless
and defend the widow's cause.*ʰ*
¹⁸Come now and let's deliberate over the next steps to take together.*ⁱ*
Yahweh promises you over and over:*ʲ*
"Though your sins stain you like scarlet,*ᵏ*
I will whiten them like bright, new-fallen snow!
Even though they are deep red like crimson,*ˡ*
they will be made white like wool!*ᵐ*

---

a 1:13 Or "your gifts of nothing."

b 1:13 Or "iniquity and obligatory assemblies," a likely hendiadys. See also Jer. 7:11.

c 1:14 God has a soul with emotions and desires. He is perfect throughout.

d 1:14 God calls them "your feasts," not his (Lev. 23:2). Their celebrations had become so shamefully sin-stained that God didn't even want his holy name associated with their sinful conduct on those sacred days. See Amos 5:21–24.

e 1:15 See 1 Tim. 2:8; Ps. 66:18.

f 1:16 This was also the message of John the Baptizer (Matt. 3:8).

g 1:17 Or "Vindicate the victim."

h 1:17 See Ps. 9:18; Isa. 58:7; Jer. 22:16; James 1:27.

i 1:18 Or "Come now and let us argue it out together." This is taken from the Hebrew word *yākah*, which has clear judicial overtones with an implication of a verdict in court.

j 1:18 Instead of pronouncing judgment to the guilty, Judge-Yahweh, in his grace and mercy, offers complete forgiveness.

k 1:18 The Hebrew for "scarlet" is taken from a root word for "double (dyed)" or "twice (dipped in scarlet dye)," making a permanent color.

l 1:18 The word for "crimson" (Heb. *tola*) is also the word for a worm that, when crushed, bleeds a deep crimson color and is then used to dye fabric a permanent color. Jesus called himself a "worm (*tola*)" while on the cross, as one who was crushed and bleeding crimson blood. See Ps. 22:6.

m 1:18 Snow and wool are both naturally white. The Lord will not only deal with our outward sins but he will cleanse our nature, changing us from the inside out. Grace includes full amnesty.

¹⁹If you have a willing heart to let me help you,
and if you will obey me, you will feast on the blessings
of an abundant harvest.ᵃ
²⁰But if you are stubborn and refuse to obey,
the sword will eat you instead."ᵇ
The mouth of Yahweh has spoken."

The Collapse of Society
²¹Look how the once faithful city
has become as unfaithful as a prostitute!
She who was once the "Center of Justice,"
where righteousness made its home,
is now the dwelling place of murderers!ᶜ
²²She was once like sterling silver, now only mixture;
once so pure, now diluted like watered-down wine.ᵈ
²³Your rulers are rebellious and companions of crooks.
They are *self-centered* racketeers
who love a bribe and who chase after payoffs.
They don't defend the fatherless
or consider the rights of a *helpless* widow.
²⁴Therefore, here is what the Sovereign One decrees,
the Lord God of Angel Armies, the Mighty One of Israel:
"Ah,ᵉ I will get relief from my adversaries
and avenge myself on my foes!ᶠ
²⁵I will bring my fiery hand upon you
and burn you and purify you into something clean."ᵍ

---

a 1:19 Or "the best of the land." For the believer today, this is the land of grace that the meek inherit. The best of the land is the fruit of the life of Jesus (Gal. 5:22, the harvest of the Spirit). The devouring sword is the flashing sword of the Word, exposing and piercing us to the innermost part of our being (Heb. 4:12).

b 1:20 The Hebrew text contains an obvious wordplay. "If you listen, you will *eat* the harvest; if you rebel, you will be *eaten* by the sword."

c 1:21 Or "those who cause to execute," a possible indictment of judges who condemned the innocent to death.

d 1:22 What was silver (redemption) has now become dross. The choice wine (fullness and gifts of the Spirit) has become watered down and unintelligible. The gifts of God have been diluted by fleshly lives that did not measure up to the standard of holiness—the choice wine of the Spirit ruined (watered down) by the works of the flesh.

e 1:24 Or "Woe!" The Septuagint reads "Woe to those who have power in Israel."

f 1:24 Sadly, because the once faithful people and their leaders turned away from what is right, God now calls them his "adversaries" and his "foes." To fight against the sovereign God means that he may turn and fight against you.

g 1:25 The Septuagint adds a sentence not found in Hebrew: "I will destroy those who refuse to obey and remove the lawbreakers from your midst." The Hebrew is "I will turn my hand against you and smelt away all your dross and remove your alloy."

God Promises Deliverers

[26]"I will restore deliverers as in former times
and your wise counselors as at the beginning.[a]
Only then will you be called the Righteous City
and the Faithful City!"[b]
[27]Yes, Zion will be redeemed with justice
and her repentant converts with righteousness.[c]
[28]There will be a shattering of rebels and sinners together,
and those who forsake the Lord will be consumed.
[29]You will reap shame from the idols you once delighted in
and you will be humiliated by your *cultic* sacred groves,[d]
where you chose to worship.
[30]You will be like an oak tree with faded, fallen leaves
and like a withered, waterless garden.
[31]The "powerful elite" will become like kindling
and their evil deeds like sparks—both will burn together
and no one will be able to put out the fire.

The Mountain of the Lord's Temple

2 This is the word revealed to Isaiah, son of Amoz, concerning Judah and Jerusalem:

[2]In the last days,[e] the mountain of Yahweh's temple
will be raised up[f] as the head of the mountains,
towering over all the hills.[g]

---

a 1:26 God promises a restoration of deliverers (Obad. 21) or "judges" and "wise counselors." Apostolic judges and prophetic counselors are on their way. They are sent to challenge the status quo and make us consider our ways. The result of their needed ministries is that God's people will become the Righteous City and be restored to be the City (Church) of Faithfulness. This is Isaiah's glimpse of the New Jerusalem, the Bridal City coming to the earth. It will be a "City of Righteousness," for God will dwell with his people.

b 1:26 See also Gal. 4:26.

c 1:27 The Septuagint uses the word *mercy*.

d 1:29 The Hebrew word for "sacred groves" (or "terebinth") rhymes with the Hebrew word for "false gods." It is a play on words that is common to the prophets. The Baal cult worshiped at the groves of sacred oaks. See Ezek. 6:13; 20:28; Hos. 4:13.

e 2:2 This phrase, often used by the prophets of the Old Testament, speaks of our current time in human history between Pentecost and the coming again of Christ. See Heb. 1:2; 1 John 2:18.

f 2:2 Or "prepared." See Eph. 1:21–22.

g 2:2 This is a contrast from ch. 1 to ch. 2 of Isaiah. No matter how despicable our past, God's grace will fully establish his people as the mountain rising above every other mountain. Mountains in the Bible are often used metaphorically for kingdoms. Kingdoms and governments are like mountains and hills on the landscape of history. The mountain-kingdom of God is in view here. It will be the chief of all mountains, the highest of all hills. The secular world sees Christ's kingdom as irrelevant and powerless. But one day the kingdoms of the earth will be leveled and the King's mountain will be high and exalted. With no rival, Jesus will sit enthroned. This prophetic outlook is the backdrop for all that Isaiah preaches. See Isa. 25:6–8; Mic. 4:1–5.

A sparkling stream of every nation will flow into it.[a]

[3]Many peoples will come and say,

"Everyone, come! Let's go up higher to Yahweh's mountain,
to the house of Jacob's God; then he can teach us his ways
and we can walk in his paths!"

Zion[b] will be the center of instruction,[c]
and the word of Yahweh will go out from Jerusalem.

[4]He will judge fairly between the nations
and settle disputes among many peoples.[d]

They will beat the swords they used *against each other*
into plowshares and their spears into pruning hooks.[e]

No nation will take up weapons against another,
nor will they prepare for war anymore.

[5]O house of Jacob, come let us walk
in the *wonderful* light of Yahweh![f]

The Judge of the Nations

[6]*Lord*, you have abandoned your people, the house of Jacob,
for they are full of divinations from the east,
like the land of the Philistines, with diviners everywhere;
they are pleased with what is false and foreign.[g]

---

a 2:2 Or "All the nations will flow as a river to it." The Hebrew word *nahar* can be translated "stream (river)" or "to sparkle, to be cheerful." In Isa. 60:5 it is translated "radiant." A cheerful, sparkling stream of people will come into divine radiance as they come up the mountain of the Lord. This speaks of the uphill flow of the river of God—a supernatural magnetism bringing the nations into the kingdom of Christ. This is the reversal of the dispersion of the people at Babel (Gen. 11).

b 2:3 Zion is more than a location; it is a realm where God is enthroned (Ps. 2:4–6; 87:5). Zion is a synonym for the people of God, the dwelling place of his Spirit (Ps. 9:11; 74:2; 76:2; Heb. 12:22–24). The perfection of beauty is in Mount Zion, where the light of God shines (Ps. 50:2). Perfected praise rises to the Lord in this place of perfect rest (Ps. 65:1–2). The Mountain of Zion is where the Lord is known in his greatness (Ps. 99:2; Isa. 12:4–6). It is the hope of all the afflicted (Ps. 102:16–22; Isa. 14:32; 51:11).

c 2:3 Although the Hebrew word *torah* is used here, it means more than "the law." It also can be translated "instruction" or "teaching." This is not the law of Moses, for that came from Sinai. This is revelation of the gospel and the instruction of God out of the Zion realm that overcomes every work of darkness within us and around us. From Jerusalem the gospel light and the twelve mighty apostles went forth to change the world.

d 2:4 The wisdom of the Lord will resolve ethnic conflicts and international disputes.

e 2:4 Or "sickles" (LXX). Weapons that were turned on one another will now be used for the harvest.

f 2:5 The Hebrew concept of the light of the Lord includes his ways, favor, presence, blessings, and revelation.

g 2:6 That is, since they don't seek the true light of the Lord and his true prophetic word, they end up with Eastern mysticism, *the false and the foreign*. Arguably, this is one of the more difficult verses to translate in Isaiah, with multiple possibilities. The last clause can be rendered "They clasp hands with foreigners (unholy alliances)" or "They are with the children of foreigners."

⁷Their land overflows with gold and silver;
  they are wealthy beyond measure.
  Their land is filled with horses and innumerable chariots!
⁸Worthless idols are everywhere, and they worship
  the work of their own hands, what their fingers have made.ᵃ
⁹The people bow down low *before the "no-gods,"*
  and the leaders lie down flat before them *in worship,*
  so do not spare them!ᵇ
¹⁰Enter into the rock and hide in the dust
  from the dreadful presence of Yahweh
  and from his majestic glory.ᶜ
¹¹The arrogantᵈ will be humbled
  and the pride of man brought low.
  Only one will be exalted in that day: Yahweh!
¹²The Lord of Angel Armiesᵉ
  has a day of humiliation in store for all the high and mighty,
  for all who are proud and self-exalting.
  They will be brought low.ᶠ
¹³His judgment is coming against all the
  lofty cedars of Lebanonᵍ and all the oaks of Bashan,ʰ
¹⁴against all the high mountains and all the lofty hills,ⁱ
¹⁵against every high towerʲ and every fortress wall,ᵏ

---

a 2:8 Isaiah condemns what the people were trusting in: their broadminded tolerance, financial
  security, military might (horses and chariots), and the idols they themselves had crafted. See
  also Deut. 17:14–17.

b 2:9 Or "Do not raise them up again."

c 2:10 Everyone on earth will seek to hide in a rock. Those who love the Lord will find shelter
  in the rock of salvation. Those who deny the Lord will make the rocks and caves their hiding
  places from the face of God (lit. "hide in the dust from the face of the terror of the Lord").

d 2:11 Or "the eyes of the haughty."

e 2:12 Or "Jehovah-Sabaoth," the Lord of hosts.

f 2:12 See Zeph. 2:3; Mal. 4:1.

g 2:13 Isaiah uses the metaphor of trees to symbolize humanity. Lebanon is used metaphorically
  as a symbol of beauty in the Scriptures. The tall and lofty cedars of Lebanon are a picture
  of the cultural elite, those of high standing in society. Men are like trees who stand tall and
  upright, only to be cut down in death. Jesus stands as the fairest of all the trees, like an apple
  tree in the forest of humanity (Song. 2:3).

h 2:13 These oaks were known for making oars (Ezek. 27:6). They speak of the military captains
  and soldiers surrounding Jesus on the cross, who were like the savage bulls of Bashan (Ps. 22:12).
  The word *Bashan*, although the area was known as a fertile land northeast of the Sea of Galilee, is also the word for "serpent." Oaks of Bashan may also represent great global leaders
  empowered by demonic spirits.

i 2:14 Governments and kingdoms of this earth are like hills and mountains. Even the highest
  of men's governmental authorities will bow to the one called the Lord Almighty.

j 2:15 *High towers* could also represent godless academia that towers intellectually above
  others.

k 2:15 This could refer to the strongholds in the mind of man, thoughts of self-importance that
  exalt themselves against the knowledge of God (2 Cor. 10:3–6). Towers and walls served as a

¹⁶against all the *trading* ships of Tarshish^{*a*}
and all the impressive sailing vessels.^{*b*}
¹⁷People's arrogance will be conquered and brought low,^{*c*}
and those proud of heart will be humiliated.
Only one will be exalted in that day: Yahweh!
¹⁸Every worthless idol will utterly pass away.^{*d*}

The Coming Dread of God

¹⁹People will hide in caves and holes in the ground
from the dreadful presence of Yahweh
and from his majestic glory when he rises
to mightily shake the earth.
²⁰In that day,^{*e*} people will throw away the worthless idols
their hands have made from gold and silver.
They will fling their treasures to the rodents and bats
²¹as they crawl into the clefts of the rock *to hide* from the
dreadful presence of Yahweh
and from the majesty of his glory
when he rises to shake the earth mightily!^{*f*}
²²So *once and for all*, stop trusting in man,
who is but one breath *from death*—frail and puny man!^{*g*}

When God Rises to Judge

3 Behold—Yahweh, the Sovereign One,
the Commander of Angel Armies, is about to cut off
from Jerusalem and Judah every source of their
support and security,^{*h*} including all food supplies and water.

---

refuge during an attack. Rebels against God built a tower in Babylon (Gen. 11:1–9), seeking
to be independent of God.

a 2:16 The ships of Tarshish were the largest of ships, able to take the longest voyages and the
greatest cargoes. They typify the great commercial empires built by man (Ezek. 28:2–5). The
economic system, the commerce of earth, will be brought to the feet of Jesus as he establishes
an eternal kingdom where righteousness and justice rule.

b 2:16 The last clause is difficult to translate with accuracy. Some scholars believe the Hebrew
word *śākâ* may be an Egyptian loan word for something like "yacht" or some impressive sailing vessel or "ship of pleasure." Others translate it as "splendid palaces, works of art, pleasant
pictures, images of desire."

c 2:17 Isaiah taught that those who bowed low before idols (2:11) will one day bow low before
the true God.

d 2:18 The Hebrew has only three words: "Nothings to nothingness!" See 1 Cor. 8:4.

e 2:20 The phrase "in that day" is used fifty times by Isaiah.

f 2:21 See Heb. 12:25–29; Rev. 6:15–17.

g 2:22 Or "who has but breath in his nostrils—of what account is he?" Man's life is fragile and temporary. His breath is in his nostrils, ready to stop at any moment. With all our boastings and with
all our ingenuity and marvelous inventions, man is but a poor, vain creature. In all our littleness
and helplessness we must turn away from the answers of men and ask for the breath of God.

h 3:1 "Support and security" is a play on words similar to "bag and baggage" or "house and home."

²*He will remove* their heroes and soldiers,
  prophets and judges, their fortune-tellers and statesmen,
³their respected military leaders,
  pillars of the community,*ᵃ*
  their counselors, skilled craftsmen,*ᵇ*
  and those professional charmers.*ᶜ*
⁴I will make *inexperienced* youth their rulers,
  and children*ᵈ* will govern them.
⁵Everyone will take advantage of everyone else,
  and neighbor will struggle against neighbor.
  The youth will not respect their elders,
  and the dishonorable will sneer at those worthy of honor.
⁶One man will even seize a relative
  right in his father's house *and say,*
  "*At least* you own a coat; you be our leader!
  You can oversee this heap of ruins!"
⁷In that day he will cry out,
  "I have no remedy *for this mess!*ᵉ
  I don't have any food or clothes either,
  so don't make me your leader!"*ᶠ*
⁸Jerusalem has stumbled and Judah has fallen
  because their words and their works
  are defiant before the face of the Lord's glorious presence.*ᵍ*
⁹The look on their impudent faces says it all,
  for they publicly flaunt their sin like Sodom,
  not even trying to hide it.*ʰ*
  Woe to their souls, for they invite
  disaster upon themselves.
¹⁰Yet reassure the righteous; it will go well with them!
  They will fully enjoy the reward of their deeds.*ⁱ*

---

a 3:3 Or "the ones lifted up with respect to their faces"; that is, their respected elite.

b 3:3 See 2 Kings 24:14. The Hebrew word *charashim* is a homonym that can be translated either "skilled craftsmen" or "magicians."

c 3:3 Or "eloquent orators, clever enchanters, intelligentsia" (LXX).

d 3:4 Or "mockers" (LXX).

e 3:7 Or "I will not be a healer" or "I will not be your leader" (LXX).

f 3:7 Ignoring leadership is the definition of anarchy. As they ignore the one who is our true leader, they are left with those who have no remedy. The righteous King has a cloak of righteousness to give them if they would only turn to him.

g 3:8 Or "provoking the glance of his glorious eyes" (see Hab. 1:13). Sin provokes the glorious eyes of God. This is the opposite of finding favor in his eyes.

h 3:9 See Jer. 3:3.

i 3:10 The lovers of God, even in a time of difficulty, can enjoy the sweet fruits of seeking God and serving his kingdom. They will reap the good seeds they planted, for seeds turn into fruit. The fruit of their deeds is the holy confidence that God is with them, even in a season

[11]But woe to the guilty,[a]
for they will get fully what they deserve!
[12]My people, mockers exploit you
and creditors[b] rule over you.
My people, your leaders mislead you
and confuse you with their guidance.[c]

The Judge in His Courtroom

[13]Yahweh is taking his rightful place in court;
he is rising to judge his people.
[14]Yahweh comes to issue the guilty verdict
of the elders and leaders of his people, saying:
"You are the ones who have ruined the nation![d]
Your houses are full of what you've stolen from the poor!
[15]What gives you the right to crush my people
by shoving the faces of the poor into the dirt?"[e]
Yahweh, the Sovereign One, Commander of Angel Armies,
has spoken.

Cleansing the Daughters of Zion

[16]Here is what Yahweh says:
"The daughters of Zion are proud,
walking about arrogantly with their noses in the air.[f]
Their eyes are seductive as they skip along
with jewelry jingling on their ankles.[g]
[17]So the Lord[h] will afflict the foreheads
of the daughters of Zion with scabs;[i]
Yahweh will make the front of their heads bald in that day."

---

of judgment. We can know it will go well with us, for the message of hope is this: "Tell the righteous they can still be joyful and it will be well with them."

a 3:11 Isaiah uses the phrase "woe to the guilty" twenty-two times. (One time he used it about himself.)

b 3:12 Or "women."

c 3:12 As translated from the Septuagint. The Hebrew appears to read "My people, his oppressors he deals with severely, and women rule over them. My people, your guides oppress you and confuse (a homonym for "swallow up") the way of your paths." It is difficult to understand the correct meaning of the text, and it is debated among scholars.

d 3:14 Or "the vineyard," which is a metaphor for God's vineyard, the nation of Israel. In the New Testament, God's vineyard is the church, the source of joy and blessing to the nations. To be leaders in God's kingdom means being examples of purity, avoiding every form of corruption.

e 3:15 Or "by grinding the faces of the poor." See Prov. 22:22–23.

f 3:16 Or "with an outstretched neck."

g 3:16 Metaphorically, these "daughters of Zion" could represent churches today that walk in pride, flirting with the world. In ch. 4, they lay hold of one man, Jesus Christ.

h 3:17 The Hebrew is the name Adonai; also in v. 18.

i 3:17 A scab would make them unclean and unable to come before God as priests (Lev. 13:2–6). Scabs are unhealed wounds. Our thoughts (foreheads) must be clean and healed from any past wounds.

¹⁸⁻¹⁹In that day, the Lord will strip away *their vanity*—
their beautiful ankle jewelry, necklaces, crescent pendants,
earrings, bracelets, and veils of shimmering gauze.
²⁰*Gone will be* their elaborate headdresses and ankle chains,
their sashes, sachets,ᵃ and charms.
²¹*He will snatch away* their signet rings and nose rings,
²²their stately gowns, capes, shawls, cloaks, and purses,
²³hand mirrors, fine linen garments *interwoven*
with gold and purple, turbans, and long veils.ᵇ
²⁴A stench will take the place of *seductive* perfumes;
a rope will take the place of a sash,
baldness for braided hair, rags instead of a fine robe,
and the brand of a captive instead of beauty.
²⁵Your men will fall on the battlefield
and your heroes will die in war.
²⁶Cries of mourning will be heard at the city gates;
with the anguish of such great loss,
she will sit down and *grieve* in the dirt.

One Man

4 Seven women will take hold of one man in that day, saying, "We will eat our *own* food and wear our *own* clothing; just take away our disgrace and let us be called by your name."ᶜ

The Branch of the Lord

²In that day, the branch of Yahweh
will be beautiful and glorious,ᵈ

---

a 3:20 Or "perfume boxes" (lit. "houses of breath").

b 3:23 When we put our emphasis on what is outward and ignore purity within, we stand in danger of losing it all. God looks upon the heart, not the outward appearance (1 Sam. 16:7).

c 4:1 This chapter should be viewed as a continuation of ch. 3 regarding the women of Zion. The women of Zion can also be a metaphor for the churches. There is coming a day when the church will become so destitute of answers that she will turn to one man, the Lord Jesus, and take hold of him. We have taken hold of the world, and we have taken hold of clever ideas, but the "seven women" (seven churches of Rev. 2 and 3) are about to lay hold of their Beloved. The church will long for him, that he would feed us his bread and we would wear his garments. We will want to be called by his great name. The shadow of his beauty will remove our disgrace.

d 4:2 Although the Hebrew word used here for "branch" is somewhat ambiguous, it is clearly a Messianic term (see also Isa. 11:1; 53:2; Jer. 23:5; 33:15; Zech. 3:8; 6:12). Jesus defines himself as the "Vine," and we who are joined to him by faith are the branches (John 15:1–6). Today, Jesus has branched out through us to bring forth the fruit of his Spirit. This is the Immanuel ("God with us") character of Christ that increases and grows like a branch carrying his life (Isa. 9:6–7). Our "family tree" is the branch of the Lord in his beauty. The branch of Lord that is magnificent (or "beautiful") and glorious reveals Christ's divine nature; the fruit of the earth is his human nature (man was formed from the earth). Jesus is the fruit of the earth, the fruit of the womb of Mary, and the fruit on the Tree of Life. Heaven gave its beauty and the earth its fruit for you and me.

and the fruit of the earth will be the pride and glory
of the remnant of Israel.
³Then the remnant in Zion and Jerusalem,ª
those who are written for lifeᵇ in Jerusalem,
will be called holy.
⁴And the Lord has washed away
the filthᶜ of the daughters of Zionᵈ
and cleansed the bloodstains of Jerusalem
by a Spirit of justiceᵉ and by a Spirit of burning.ᶠ

A Cloud and a Glow
⁵Then Yahweh will create over all of Mount Zion
and over every gathering a cloud *of smoke* by day
and a glow of flaming fire by night.ᵍ
And all this manifestation of dazzling glory
will spread over them like a wedding canopy.ʰ

---

a 4:3 See Isa. 37:31–32.

b 4:3 The Aramaic is "written for eternal life." Some see a reference here to a Book of Destiny, which has written in it the names of those made holy. Perhaps this is the same book Daniel wrote about in Dan. 12:1, or it could be the book David mentioned (Ps. 139:16). Moses spoke to the Lord about his "book" (Ex. 32:32). We also read of the "Book of the life of the Lamb" (Ps. 69:28; Phil.4:3; Rev.20:12) that belongs to the Lamb (Rev. 13:8). For those who fear the Lord, there is kept a "scroll of remembrance" with their names written in it (Mal. 3:16). Jesus reminded his disciples that their true source of joy was not that they could cast out demons but that their names were written in the journals of heaven (Luke 10:20).

c 4:4 The Hebrew word for "filth" is also translated in the Old Testament as a drunkard's vomit (Isa. 28:8) and human excrement (Isa. 36:12). The daughters of Zion were haughty in ch. 3. Now they have become humble and repentant, needing the cleansing of the Lord. See Zech. 13:1.

d 4:4 This is a prophetic metaphor for the churches, Zion's daughters. God's people dwell in the Zion realm (see footnotes Isa. 2:3 and 10:24). The Zion realm is a synonymous term for the New Jerusalem (Heb. 12:22).

e 4:4 Or "judgment."

f 4:4 By the Judging Spirit and by the Burning Spirit, the Lord (Adonai) will wash away the filth from the churches of Christ—even bloodstains. The Hebrew word for "Spirit" can also be translated "breath" or "blast." The blast of justice and the blast of fire are coming to cleanse God's people. This Spirit of Judgment releases holy vision to see things as God sees them. Decisions will be made by the justice of God, not the prejudices of men. It is not that he merely executes judgment but that he demonstrates perfect discernment to see what is holy and what is not. This Spirit of fire (a possible reference to the baptism of fire, Matt. 3:11) will thoroughly cleanse God's remnant and make them holy by refining fire (Mal. 3:2–4). A fire of passionate love for Jesus Christ will cleanse the church. The fire of love as a seal over our hearts will keep us pure from temptation and end-time distractions (Song. 8:6).

g 4:5 See Ex. 13:21–22.

h 4:5 Or "nuptial chamber." The Hebrew word *chuppâ* always denotes the marriage chamber. As part of a Jewish wedding ceremony, the bride and bridegroom would be overshadowed by a canopy (*chuppâ*). This marriage chamber will provide peace, rest, and security for the bride of Christ.

⁶It will be a tabernacle*^a* as a shade
 from the scorching heat of the day
 and a safe shelter to protect them from the storm and rain.*^b*

Isaiah's Love Song

5 Let me sing a song for the one I love, called*^c*
 "My Lover and His Vineyard":
 My beloved *planted* a vineyard on a very fertile hill.
²*First* he dug up its ground and hauled away its stones*^d*
 so he could plant within it the choicest of vines.
 He built a watchtower in the middle of it
 and carved a winepress out of its rock.*^e*
 He fully expected it to bear good grapes,
 but instead it produced only worthless wild grapes.
³So now, you residents of Jerusalem and people of Judah,
 you be the judges!

---

a 4:6 The overshadowing tabernacle points to the Lord Jesus Christ, who "tabernacled" among us (John 1:14). This is the same Hebrew word (*cukkah*) used in Amos 9:11 to describe the "tabernacle (tent) of David" that God promises to restore on the earth with night-and-day worship before the unveiled presence of God.

b 4:6 The remnant of the lovers of God who have taken hold of one man (Jesus) will be sheltered and protected, even in a time of judgment, just as Goshen provided a refuge for Israel during the plagues of Egypt.

c 5:1 It is proper, even as we honor God for his transcendence and holiness, to love him and sing about his love. Divine romance never diminishes God's glory; it elevates and extols it. Isaiah is a singing prophet, as many prophets are. This chapter contains three prophetic songs: The Song of the Vineyard (vv. 1–7), the Song of Woes (vv. 8–23), and the Song of Judgment (vv. 24–30). What a variety of methods God will use to awaken his people and bring people to repentance! The prophet sings this song to the glory of his Beloved. Maybe it was sung by Isaiah at the Feast of Tabernacles when the grape harvest was brought in. Or perhaps Isaiah walked through the streets of Jerusalem or the hillsides of Israel singing to God's people this prophetic message. Or perhaps the Lord Jesus himself sang this over Jerusalem as he stood on the hillside overlooking the city, weeping (Luke 19:41).

d 5:2 Israel is the vineyard of the Lord (Jer. 2:21). The parable is an obvious picture of how God planted and loved his vineyard, Israel. He cleared it of stones, removing all that would make his people stumble (Isa. 62:10). With the stones, he built a wall of protection around them (5:5). For Israel, these stones would represent the Canaanites, those inhabitants of the land who made them stumble. Then he planted and established his people, calling them the choicest ("noblest") of vines, with everything they needed to grow and be fruitful. In John 15, his vineyard is described as God's redeemed people, the church. He has removed our stony hearts and given us hearts of flesh to respond to his voice. Throughout the Gospels, we see the people of the Lord compared to a vineyard (Matt. 20:1; 21:28-41; Mark 12:1; Luke 13:6; 20:9–16; John 15:1).

e 5:2 For Israel, this watchtower would be Jerusalem, the place where the owner of the vineyard dwelt and cared for his vineyard. For the church, the watchtower is the Zion-realm, the place of his presence. He not only planted us as his vineyard, he dwells among us (2 Cor. 6:16). The winepress or wine vat is the sacrificial system that God gave to his people to provide them with access to himself. For believers today, the wine vat is the privilege of open access that the Holy Spirit (our wine) provides for us as we gather together.

⁴"What more could I have done for my vineyard?
  When I expected it to bear luscious grapes,
  why did it produce only wild, worthless grapes?
⁵So let me tell you what I am about to do to my vineyard.
  I will tear down its fence and it will be plundered.ᵃ
  I will break down its wallᵇ and it will be destroyed!
⁶I will make it a wasteland, and no one will cultivate the land.ᶜ
  It will grow only weeds and thorns!
  I will command the clouds
  and they will not drop their rain upon it!ᵈ
⁷For Israel is this vineyard of Yahweh,
  the Commander of Angel Armies,
  and the people of Judah are the garden of his delight.ᵉ
  When he waited for *a crop of* justice,
  he got a *harvest of* bloodshed!
  When he waited to *reap* fairness,
  he heard only the cries of victims.ᶠ

Isaiah's Song of Six Woes

#1 – *Grasping Materialism*

⁸Woe to those who *in their greed* buy up
  house after house to make one grand estate
  until there is no place for anyone else
  and only the landowner is left!ᵍ
⁹This is what Yahweh, the Commander of Angel Armies,
  said in my ears:ʰ
  "Truly, many of your houses will become devastated
  and your large, impressive mansions
  will have no one living in them!
¹⁰Indeed, even a vast vineyardⁱ
  will produce only a few gallons of wine,

---

a 5:5 As translated from the Septuagint. The Hebrew *ba'ar* is a homophone that could be translated "(a place of) grazing" or "burning."

b 5:5 Or "I will break through its wall."

c 5:6 Or "It will not be pruned or hoed." We would become a wasteland if God were to lift his favor and blessings from our lives.

d 5:6 Clouds giving rain is a metaphor for blessing. Rain is often a picture of revelation teaching that falls on our hearts like rain.

e 5:7 Or "the planting of his pleasantness."

f 5:7 There are remarkable plays on words found in the Hebrew. The Hebrew word for "justice" is *mishpat*, and "bloodshed" is *mishpakh*. "Fairness" is *zedakah*, and "cries of distress" is *zeakah*.

g 5:8 This verse is not a prohibition on real estate endeavors but the greedy accumulation of houses and land at the expense of the poor. This is the first of six woes found in this chapter (vv. 8, 11, 18, 20, 21, 22).

h 5:9 Or "For the ears of the Lord of Hosts heard these things" (LXX).

i 5:10 Or "a ten-yoke vineyard," the amount of land ten yoke of oxen could cultivate.

and several bushels of seed will produce only
a bushel of harvest!"[a]

#2 – Drunken Pleasure-Seeking

[11]Woe to those who start drinking early in the morning,
lingering late into the night to get drunk with wine.
[12]Their lavish parties are complete with
the music of harps and flutes—and the wine flows!
Yet they have no respect for what Yahweh has done,
nor do they contemplate the work of his hands![b]
[13]Therefore, my people go into exile for lack of understanding.[c]
Their leaders[d] are starving,
their multitudes parched with thirst.[e]
[14]The *shadowy* realm of death[f] grows thirsty for souls
and opens its mouth even wider *to drink in* the people!
It gulps down the leaders of Jerusalem,
along with their noisy, boasting crowds![g]
[15]The people will be humiliated, all of humanity humbled,
and the arrogant will be brought low.[h]
[16]With justice the Lord Yahweh,
Commander of Angel Armies, displays his greatness,
and righteousness sets him apart as the holy God.
[17]Then lambs will graze, as if in their own pastures,
and the refugee will eat in the ruins of the rich.

#3 – Defiant Sinfulness

[18]Woe to those who drag behind them their guilt
with ropes made of lies—[i]
straining and tugging, harnessed to their bondage![j]
[19]They say, "May *God* hurry up and bring his judgment[k]
so that we can see it *once and for all*!
Let the prophetic plan of the Holy One of Israel
quickly come to pass so that we can see what it is!"[l]

---

a 5:10 Or "A homer of seed will produce only an ephah." The land-hungry people will go hungry.
b 5:12 See 1 Sam. 12:24.
c 5:13 See Prov. 10:21; Isa. 1:3; Hos. 4:6.
d 5:13 Or "men of glory."
e 5:13 How ironic! Their thirst for strong drink was their downfall; now they have nothing to drink at all.
f 5:14 Or *Sheol*, a poetic term for the underworld.
g 5:14 See Hab. 2:5.
h 5:15 Or "The eyes of pride are brought low."
i 5:18 Or "cords of emptiness."
j 5:18 Or "pulling your sins with cart ropes." See Ps. 129:4; Prov. 5:22; Rom. 6:16.
k 5:19 Or "his work," which, in the immediate context, is his judgment.
l 5:19 See Jer. 17:15; Ezek. 12:22–25; 2 Peter 2:3–7.

#4 – Perversion of Values

²⁰Woe to those who call evil good and good evil,
  who replace darkness with light and light with darkness,
  who replace bitter with sweet and sweet with bitter.[a]

#5 – Arrogant Conceit

²¹Woe to those who are wise in their own eyes
  and see themselves as clever and shrewd.[b]

#6 – Injustice

²²Woe to the champion wine drinkers
  who are heroes in mixing strong drinks—
²³*judges and politicians* who acquit the guilty for a bribe
  and take away the rights of the innocent.[c]

Isaiah's Song of Judgment

²⁴Therefore, just as tongues of fire
  lick up the straw and dry grass,[d]
  they will be destroyed, just as a plant with decaying roots
  and blossoms dries up like dust and is blown away in the wind.[e]
  For they said, "No!" to the teachings of Yahweh,
  the Lord of Angel Armies,
  and have despised the word of the Holy One of Israel!
²⁵For this reason Yahweh's anger burned against his people,[f]
  and he struck them down with his holy hand!
  The mountains trembled,[g] and dead bodies were littered
  like garbage left in the streets.

---

a 5:20 Their moral code is reversed as sin is accepted as something good. Not content to abandon what is good, they must label it as evil. Those who abandon the absolute standards of God's Word will find a reversal of every true virtue. Good is mocked and evil is embraced. Light is ridiculed and darkness is worn like a cloak. The sweetness of God is called bitter; the bitterness of sin is called sweet.

b 5:21 See Prov. 3:7; Isa. 29:14. Who will outwit Eternal Wisdom? Who can outsmart Infinite Intelligence? God will resist the proud of heart. The wisdom that comes from above is without pride (James 3:13–16).

c 5:23 Or "The righteousness of the righteous they take from them." Verses 22 and 23 are Isaiah's use of sarcasm, pointed to the leaders of the nation. The ones who should be champions and heroes are only "great" in their self-indulgence. With perverted justice, they corrupt the nation instead of safeguarding society.

d 5:24 See Num. 22:4.

e 5:24 Some see the roots and flowers (blossoms) as a metaphor for parents and children.

f 5:25 God's anger is a righteous anger. It is the necessary vindication of the honor of his holiness and authority. There is no reason to make an apology for God's anger. It is not a blemish on his divine character nor inconsistent with his mercy and grace. His anger is as pure and holy and good as his mercy or his love. Everything about God is holy and perfect. See Deut. 32:39–41; Ps. 7:11–13.

g 5:25 This could be a reference to the days of King Uzziah and the great earthquakes that took place during his reign. See Amos 1:1; Zech. 14:5.

Even with this, his anger has not turned away
and still his hand is heavy upon them!
²⁶He will lift up a banner to *signal* the distant nations;
he whistles^{*a*} for them to come from the ends of the earth.
Look! Here they come, running swiftly and speedily!
²⁷Not one *warrior* stumbles or grows weary—
not even stopping to rest or sleep; they are battle ready!^{*b*}
²⁸Their arrows are sharpened and every bow strung.
Their horses' hooves are hard as flint
and their chariot wheels turn like the whirlwind.
²⁹Their shout is like a lion's roar,
the roar of strong lions growling as they seize their prey.
They carry away *captives,* and none can rescue them.
³⁰They will roar and roar on that day
like the roaring of crashing waves,
and if you look back across the land
you'll see only darkness, disaster, and distress;^{*c*}
daylight itself will be obscured by thick clouds.^{*d*}

The Throne Room

6 In the year that King Uzziah died,^{*e*} I clearly saw the Lord.^{*f*} He was seated on his exalted throne, towering high above me.^{*g*} His long, flowing robe *of splendor* spread throughout the temple.^{*h*} ²Standing above him were the angels

---

a 5:26 Or "hisses."

b 5:27 Or "Their belts don't come loose, nor are their sandal straps broken." This is a metaphor for being prepared and ready for action. Eastern people of that day wore long, loose garments that left them unprepared for action. But a belt (girdle) fastened meant they were ready for war. Their sandals unbroken meant that nothing would hinder them.

c 5:30 Much of this verse is uncertain in the Hebrew. The Septuagint reads, "And these will look up to the heaven and down to the earth."

d 5:30 Or "the gloomy vapor" (Syriac and Vulgate). There is a sense in which Jesus endured all the judgments of this chapter for us, becoming our Savior to set us free. Even the sun hid its face from the suffering Christ while he was on the cross.

e 6:1 King Uzziah died a leper (2 Chron. 26:23). It is likely that the prophecies of Isaiah chs. 1–5 were given before Uzziah's death in 740 BC. The prophet realized that God would judge even a king if he sinned. Isaiah saw the holiness of God in the judgment of the leprous king and knew that if his uncle Uzziah would be judged, he would be too. When we see the way he deals with sin, our eyes are opened and we see the Lord as he really is.

f 6:1 Although the word for "Lord" here is *Adonai* ("Sovereign or Master"), we see from vv. 3 and 5 that it was "the Lord God, Commander of hosts." Long before Jesus was born, Isaiah saw his glory (John 12:41).

g 6:1 Isaiah mentions this throne seven times (6:1; 9:7; 14:13; 16:5; 22:23; 47:1; 66:1). Transported into the throne room, Isaiah overheard the solemn chanting of the seraphim. He felt the trembling of the very foundations of the temple, and he witnessed the rainbow glory robe of almighty God. He also saw an altar, fire with burning coals, antiphonal singing, and flying seraphim.

h 6:1 This very robe of glory has touched us in Christ, for we are his temple. When we "put on Christ," we are robed in his splendor before God and angels. Just the seam/edge of his robe fills the temple. This is a picture not just of the majesty of God but of his incomparable size.

of flaming fire,*a* each with six wings: with two wings they covered their faces *in reverence*, with two wings they covered their feet, and with two wings they flew.*b* ³And one called out to another, saying:

"Holy, holy, holy is the Lord God,
Commander of Angel Armies!*c*
The whole earth is filled with his glory!"*d*

⁴The thunderous voice of the fiery angels caused the foundations of the thresholds to tremble*e* as the cloud of glory*f* filled the temple!

Isaiah's Seventh Woe
⁵Then I *stammered and* said, "Woe is me! I'm destroyed*g*—doomed as a sinful man! For my words are tainted and I live among people who talk the same way.*h* King Yahweh, Commander of Angel Armies! My eyes have gazed upon him!"

⁶Then *out of the smoke*, one of the angels of fire flew to me. He had in his hands a burning coal he had taken from the altar with tongs. ⁷He touched my lips with it and said, "See? The burning coal from the altar has touched your lips. Your guilt is taken away; your sin is blotted out."*i*

---

a 6:2 Or "seraphim (burning ones)," the fiery custodians of the holiness of God. The seraphs were a class of angels stationed around the throne of God. *Seraph* comes from the Hebrew word for "burn." Some have equated the seraphim with the living creatures mentioned in Rev. 4:6–9. They were on fire, burning with the adoration of God.

b 6:2 With wings folded upward and wings folded downward, they appeared to Isaiah as huge flames of fire. What Isaiah saw is still taking place today in heaven's throne room.

c 6:3 Almost every Jewish commentator speaks of the threefold repetition of the word *holy* as a reference to the way God manifests his holiness (1) in heaven, (2) in this world, and (3) in the ages to come. Today we can see the triune God being praised: Holy (Father), Holy (Son), Holy (Spirit). Throughout church history this sacred chant has been heard in liturgy, worship, and song. Fifty times Isaiah calls him "the Holy One of Israel."

d 6:3 Isaiah saw the sinfulness of man; the seraphim saw the glory of God. Isaiah had to see what the angels see. Every true voice for God must have the revelation of glory filling the earth. Without this vision, we are only seeing part of the truth. What fills the earth is his glory, not our sinfulness. This is occurring now, not just in the future.

e 6:4 What caused this shaking? The celestial praises of God, sung to their highest, caused the foundations to shake.

f 6:4 Or "(holy) smoke." This cloud (smoke) is mentioned seven times in Isaiah: 4:5; 6:4; 9:18; 14:31; 34:10; 51:6; 65:5.

g 6:5 The Hebrew word *nidmêti* can be translated "finished, cut off, pierced through, devastated, destroyed, doomed, undone, silenced, ruined." See also Judg. 13:22; Job 42:5–6. Isaiah pronounces his seventh woe upon himself.

h 6:5 Isaiah was a prophet who made his living from speaking, yet he calls himself a man with unclean lips. He declares himself a sinner who has offended with his words. He has offended others, and he has offended the holiness of God. Polluted with sin, his words (and ours) are "unclean" (foul, defiled, polluted, contaminated).

i 6:7 Or "Your sin is atoned for." Instead of the seraph throwing him out of the sanctuary, he brought God's cleansing coal. It was a coal, for when God judged sin, only coals of fire

[8]Then I heard the Lord saying, "Whom should I send *to my people*? Who will go to represent us?"

I spoke up and said, "I will be the one. Send me."[a]

Isaiah's Message

[9]Then he said, "Go and tell the people:

'You keep listening but understand nothing.

You keep watching but learn nothing.'

[10]Go and preach a message that will make their hearts dull,[b]

their ears plugged, and their eyes blind.[c]

Otherwise, their eyes will begin to see,

their ears will begin to hear,

their hearts will begin to understand,

and they will return to me for healing and be healed."[d]

[11]Then I asked, "O Lord, for how long?"

He answered,

"Until their houses and cities are destroyed and uninhabited

and their land a desolate wasteland.

[12]Until the Lord has exiled them all to a distant country

and the entire land lies deserted."

[13]Yet if even a tenth[e] remains there,[f]

it will be burned again.

It will be like a fallen oak or terebinth tree when it is felled;

the stump still lives to grow again.[g]

Now, the "stump" is the holy seed.[h]

---

were left; it speaks of a finished sacrifice. The fires of wrath were spent on Christ. The word for "coal" is *ritzpah* and means "ceremonial stone." In the temple, incense was poured upon the *ritzpah* stone. Then the stone was placed in the fire, creating the fragrance of the burning sacrifice of the Lamb of God. This white-hot stone that was placed on Isaiah's lips is perhaps the "shining white stone" given to the overcomers (Rev. 2:17).

a 6:8 No prophet or servant of the Lord answered God's call more swiftly than Isaiah.

b 6:10 Or "make fat (calloused) their hearts." Light rejected hardens the heart. See Ex. 8:15.

c 6:10 Or "plaster over their eyes." Isaiah's message is to those who practice idolatry. As they worship idols of wood and stone with no eyes or ears, they become like that which they worship. See also Jer. 10:14.

d 6:10 To those who have an ear for God and a heart to receive revelation, more will be given. To those who do not have a heart to hear God, even the little revelation they have will be taken from them (Matt. 13:11–15). Jesus came speaking in parables. He longed for the open heart to receive more while the closed heart would be blinded further. The paradox of these verses is in the way God's Word closes the hearts and minds of the rebellious but opens the ears and eyes of the hungry seeker.

e 6:13 *The tenth* could be the tenth reign of a king or the tenth part of the people.

f 6:13 See 2 Kings 25:12, 22.

g 6:13 The two trees mentioned here (terebinth and oak) grow in the Middle East. They both have the power to produce new shoots even when cut down to a stump.

h 6:13 Or "The seed of holiness is its stump" or "The stump is the sacred seed." Isaiah uses the word *seed* twenty-five times. This is not the end but a new beginning. God always has remnant

God's Message for Ahaz

7 During the reign of Ahaz,^a the son of Jotham and grandson of Uzziah, two kings launched an attack against Jerusalem: Rezin, the king of Syria,^b and Pekah,^c the son of Remaliah, the king of Israel. But they failed to conquer it.^d

²When the royal court^e was told that Syria had formed an alliance with *the northern kingdom of* Israel,^f the heart of King Ahaz and all his people trembled with fear, like trees swaying in the wind.

³Then Yahweh spoke to Isaiah and said, "Go and meet with King Ahaz. You'll find him on the road to the Washerman's Field^g at the end of the aqueduct where it empties into the upper pool.^h Take with you your son, *whom you named* a Remnant Will Return.ⁱ ⁴Give him this message: 'Stay calm! Be quiet and guard your heart! Don't panic or be discouraged over these two smoldering stubs of firewood, because of the rage of Rezin and Aram the son of Remaliah.^j ⁵Syria has plotted with the northern kingdom of Israel^k and the son of Remaliah to come against you. ⁶They are saying, "We will attack Judah and cut off

---

people, even in a time of judgment. Today true believers have the "holy seed" of Christ within them, for they have been born from above. Note the seven requirements of the divine call: (1) a revelation of God, high and lifted up (vv. 1–4), (2) a revelation of holiness (vv. 1–4), (3) a revelation of our uncleanness (v. 5), (4) divine cleansing (vv. 6–7), (5) a personal call—the voice of the Lord (v. 8), (6) abandonment to God (v. 8), and (7) divine commissioning (vv. 9–13).

a 7:1 Ahaz was the king of Judah, whose capital was Jerusalem. He took the throne at the age of twenty and reigned sixteen years. He was a young leader facing his first major test as king. See 2 Kings 16. This section of Isaiah (chs. 7–11) is known as the "Book of Immanuel."

b 7:1 Or "Aram," which is modern-day Syria. Rezin means "wicked pleasure," a picture of the life of the flesh.

c 7:1 *Pekah* means "open-eyed, seeing," a picture of human reasoning. This unholy alliance of the two kings threatened to invade if King Ahaz did not agree to surrender. Two kings (two principalities), Rezin and Pekah, rose up against the king of Judah. The northern kingdom of Israel (Rezin) and Syria (Pekah) joined each other to overthrow Ahaz and put "the son of Tabeel" on the throne in his place. The pressure was on King Ahaz to join this united front against the Assyrian expansion.

d 7:1 This verse is a summary statement of what is unfolded in the following verses.

e 7:2 Or "the house of David."

f 7:2 Or "Ephraim," a metonym for the entire ten tribes of the northern kingdom of Israel. They are collectively called "Ephraim," for their first king (Jeroboam) was from that tribe (1 Kings 11:26).

g 7:3 Or "Fuller's Field," where cloth was washed and bleached. In Mark 9:3, the Greek text uses the phrase "whiter than any fuller can make them." See also Mal. 3:1–3.

h 7:3 Ahaz was likely inspecting the city's vulnerable water supply. It is good to be vulnerable and on the road to being purified and made ready for God to use "on the road to the Washerman's Field." The heavenly Washerman wants to cleanse our hearts from unbelief, hiding in false belief systems that close our hearts from a true work of the Spirit. God wants to make you an aqueduct or "channel" of the upper (heavenly) pool.

i 7:3 Or Shear-Jashub, which in Hebrew means "A remnant will return." Isaiah was married and had at least two sons (8:1–4). Shear-Jashub was a walking oracle of hope, with a promise in his name: God will preserve a "holy seed" as a remnant (6:13).

j 7:4 Both Pekah and Rezin were dead within two years of their hostilities against Ahaz.

k 7:5 Or "Ephraim."

Jerusalem—we will terrorize and conquer it for ourselves and install the son of Tabeel as king!"""

⁷Now hear what the Lord Yahweh says:
"They will not succeed—it will never happen!
⁸For the head of Syria is Damascus,
and the head of Damascus is Rezin.
Sixty-five years from now the northern kingdom of Israel
will be shattered, with nothing left of it.ᵃ
⁹The head of the northern kingdom of Israel is Samaria,
and the head of Samaria is the son Remaliah.ᵇ
If you do not stand firm in your faith,
you will not be able to stand at all!"ᶜ

God with Us
¹⁰Again Lord Yahweh spoke to Ahaz:
¹¹"Go ahead—ask for a sign from Yahweh, your God.ᵈ Ask for something big, so miraculousᵉ *that you will know only God did it*!"

¹²Ahaz answered, "I will not ask. I won't attempt to test the Lord Yahweh."

¹³So Isaiah said, "Pay attention, family of David. It's bad enough to try the patience of a prophetᶠ but even worse when you try the patience of my God as well! ¹⁴The Lord himself will give you a sign.ᵍ Behold—the virginʰ will conceive

---

a 7:8 Or "shattered and no longer a people." Some scholars see this sentence as a scribal commentary that got merged into the text. M. Scott, "Isaiah 7:8," *ExpTim* 38 (1926/1927), 525–26.

b 7:9 By implication, the head of Judah would be Jerusalem and the head of Jerusalem would be David's son, Ahaz. Notice that God sees a city as the head of a nation and the head of a city to be a human leader. This is the principle of the stronghold/strongman. If the chief city of a nation is taken, the nation will fall. If the chief leader/spirit in a city is taken, the city will fall. See Mark 3:27.

c 7:9 Or "If your faith does not hold, you will not be able to hold it together." We must be willing to take God at his word and lay our fears to rest or we will be insecure, unstable, and unable to stand against our foes. Sadly, Ahaz did not heed the words of God and sought help instead from the king of Assyria, even using the gold of the temple to buy his favor (2 Kings 16:7–8). Ahaz was one of the worst of Judah's kings, yet he had the living God standing ready to help him if he would turn back to the Lord.

d 7:11 This would be a sign to Ahaz proving that God is trustworthy and can keep his word. God is willing to prove himself to Ahaz and to us.

e 7:11 Or "as deep as sheol or as high as heaven"; that is, something so outside human experience that only God can do it.

f 7:13 Or "men." The Targum reads "prophet."

g 7:14 This is a double sign. There is the sign of the Virgin Mary and the virgin bride of Christ of the last days. See 2 Cor. 11:2.

h 7:14 Although the ambiguous Hebrew word for "virgin" (*'almah*) is more often translated "a girl of marriageable age," the context is God performing a miracle sign (v. 11). This sign is not merely for Ahaz but for the family (house, including descendants) of David. There is nothing miraculous about a young woman having a baby; it happens every day. However, the Septuagint

and give birth to a son and will name him God Among Us.*ᵃ* ¹⁵He will eat curdled milk and honey,*ᵇ* and he will know enough to refuse the evil and choose the good. ¹⁶Yet even before that time comes for him to know good and evil, the lands of those two kings you dread will be deserted.*ᶜ*

The Whistler

¹⁷"The Lord Yahweh is going to bring days of catastrophic trouble—on you, on your people, and on the whole royal court—not seen since the northern kingdom of Israel broke off from Judah. He is going to bring the king of Assyria *with his great army*!"

¹⁸In that day, the Lord Yahweh will whistle and call for flies from Egypt's lower streams.*ᵈ* He will whistle for bees from the land of Assyria, ¹⁹and they will swarm *down upon* you and settle into the steep ravines, the crevices of the rocks, on every thorn bush and at every *stagnant* pool.*ᵉ*

The Lord's Razor

²⁰In that day, the Lord will take his "razor," the hired king of Assyria from beyond the Euphrates,*ᶠ* and he will shave your head, your legs,*ᵍ* and also your beard, *leaving you ashamed and exposed*!

---

translates this word as "virgin" here as well as in Matthew's quotation for the virgin birth of the Messiah (Matt. 1:23). No child with a human father could be the fulfillment of Immanuel, "God among us." However, some scholars view Isaiah's other son, "Maher-Shalal-Hash-Baz" (8:3), as the Immanuel referred to here.

a 7:14 Or "Immanu El ("God became one of us," Matt. 1:23)." A new nature is about to be planted in the soil of humanity. *Immanuel* is a term used for this new creation life coming down out of heaven. It will begin as a man but will soon become a company of men and women. Immanuel is the partnership of heaven and earth, God and humanity.

b 7:15 This coming "son" will be one who has the kingdom promises as his diet (John 4:32). Milk and honey represent the promised land, where God fulfills all of his promises. Jesus is the only one who has fulfilled the Father's desires. Feeding on the promises enabled him to choose the right. He resisted temptation by means of the Word of God dwelling in him. Strength to reject evil comes from feeding on truth. See Matt. 4:11.

c 7:16 This prophecy was fulfilled when Assyria defeated first Syria (732 BC) and then the northern tribes of Israel (722 BC).

d 7:18 Or "Niles," a reference to the flooding of the Nile that brought swarms of dog flies, which are known to buzz like bees and whose bite is extremely painful.

e 7:19 Or "every bush (possibly the stinkwood)." In this case, the flies and bees are the foreign warriors coming to invade. God's whistle brought them into the land. Experts tell us that beekeepers can persuade bees to come out of their hives or return from the fields by whistling. Like bees gathering to sting (the hill country of Assyria was known for its bees), these warriors will assemble into every compromise. The steep ravines are a picture of the slippery slopes of darkness that bring defeat into our hearts. These flies and bees are found where there is corruption and decay within the soul. Crevices of the rocks are where we hide our compromises. The thorn bushes are symbols of our flesh life, with its briars and offenses that do not yield to God (Matt. 13:7, 22). "Every stagnant pool" points us to the stagnant places in our lives that we have not allowed to be renewed and revived.

f 7:20 Or "the river." Ahaz had paid tribute and, in a sense, hired the king of Assyria to shave Syria and the northern kingdom. Instead, the king now serves God's purposes in bringing judgment and devastation to Judah.

g 7:20 Or "the hair of the feet." In ancient times, the feet were used euphemistically for genitalia. The hair of the head points to the king (Ahaz); the legs, his soldiers; the beard, the officials of

²¹In that day, *if* a farmer keeps alive only one heifer and two goats, ²²they will give so much milk that he will have more than he needs. And everyone left in the land will have all the milk and honey *they desire.*

²³In that day, the fine vineyards, each with a thousand vines and worth a thousand pieces of silver,*ᵃ* will be a wilderness overgrown with weeds, briars, and thorn bushes.*ᵇ* ²⁴People will hunt there with bow and arrow but will find nothing except thorn bushes and briars! ²⁵The once-cultivated hillsides where vineyards used to grow will be completely overgrown with thorns so that people will be afraid to go there. It will become a place where cattle graze and sheep trample.

A Son Becomes a Sign

8 The Lord Yahweh said to me, "Take a large tablet*ᶜ* and engrave upon it these words using the stylus of a man:*ᵈ* Quickly—to the Plunder! Hurry—to the Loot!*ᵉ* ²Then summon two reliable men, Uriah the priest*ᶠ* and Zechariah, son of Jeberechiah, to act as witnesses."*ᵍ*

³Then I slept with *my wife*, the prophetess;*ʰ* she became pregnant and gave birth to a son. Then the Lord Yahweh told me, "You will name him Quickly—to the Plunder! Hurry—to the Loot! ⁴For before the boy knows how to say 'my father' or 'my mother,' the wealth of Damascus and Samaria will be plundered and carried away by the king of Assyria!"

---

the land. Thus, "shaving" was a metaphor for the Lord stripping from them all that they had: their livelihoods, crops, and private ownership of their land. This supernatural "shaver" will be Assyria coming to cut off their pride, their glory, and their boasts. Often the victors would shave the heads of the vanquished. Mourners had their heads shaved (Isa. 15:2). So Judah will mourn over their ways as judgment falls. Shaving off the beard was an embarrassment to Hebrew men (2 Sam. 10:4–5).

a 7:23 See Song. 8:11–12.

b 7:23 See Isa. 5:1–7.

c 8:1 See also Hab. 2:2.

d 8:1 Or "in the form of a man" or "with an ordinary stylus." God can use what is written by man to touch man. Weak, ordinary, frail man has the grace to write and speak for God. It was with the hand of a man that God wrote on the wall for Belshazzar and all his guests to see. See Dan. 5.

e 8:1 This is the Hebrew name of Isaiah's soon-to-be-born son, Maher-Shalal-Hash-Baz.

f 8:2 See 2 Kings 16:10. *Uriah* means "Yahweh is my flame of light."

g 8:2 The prophetic act of Isaiah needed to be witnessed by men of stature so that when the fulfillment of the demise of the northern kingdom came to pass it would be impossible to deny Isaiah's prophetic message. Perhaps this scroll was unfurled like a banner outside Isaiah's house or placed over an entrance into the temple area. It would have been publicized in some visible fashion. As the people would pass by this sign, they would wonder what it meant. This was a vivid way to make known the prophecy.

h 8:3 Isaiah and his wife were a prophetic duo. Isaiah spoke the word of the Lord, then the prophetess "gave birth" to it. She would literally give birth to the word of God! At the birth of their son, God spoke again and told them the symbolic name of the child, the same message Isaiah had received earlier and had engraved for all to see. Maher-Shalal-Hash-Baz was a walking sign; a son became a sign.

A Flood or a Peaceful Stream

[5]The Lord Yahweh spoke to me again: [6]"Because these people have rejected the gentle flowing stream *of my loving presence*[a] and melt in fear[b] before Rezin and the son of Remaliah, [7]now, therefore, the Lord is about to bring against them the mighty, massive flood of the Euphrates. The king of Assyria and all his glory[c] will overflow on you like a river flooding its channels and running over all its banks! [8]It will flood into Judah, swirling over it, overflowing and reaching up to your neck, O Immanu El,[d] and spread out its wings[e] over your entire land!

[9]"You will be broken,[f] O nations, and will be shattered.
Listen, all you distant nations. Prepare for war,[g]
though it will backfire on you!
Prepare for war, yet you will be shattered!
[10]Go ahead, hatch a plot, but it will be foiled!
Go ahead, speak a word,
but it will not stand, for God is with us!"[h]

A Snare or a Sanctuary

[11]The Lord's mighty hand rested on me, and he warned me[i] with these words not to act like[j] these people:

[12]"Don't believe their every conspiracy rumor. And don't fear what they fear—don't be moved or terrified. [13]Fear nothing and no one except Yahweh, Commander of Angel Armies! Honor him as holy. Be in awe before him with deepest reverence![k] [14]He will become for you a holy sanctuary but for them a stone people trip over. He is a rock that causes the two houses of Israel to stumble—a trap[l] and a snare for the people of Jerusalem.[m] [15]Many will stumble and fall and be broken. Yes, they will be snared and taken away captive."

---

a 8:6 Or "Shiloah." Although some see this as a possible reference to one of the streams of the Gihon Spring, it is more likely a metaphor for the loving care, presence, and blessing of the Lord that flowed to them via David's monarchy. The rejected blessing contrasts with the overflowing flood of Euphrates (Assyria) that is about to sweep over the land. Because Euphrates is a figure of speech for Assyria, Shiloah becomes a figure of speech for God's loving care; a relational God seeks relationship with his people. He longed to be their "fountain" of peace, flowing within them like a gentle stream.

b 8:6 Or "rejoice," a Hebrew homophone for "melt in fear" or "rejoice."

c 8:7 That is, his vast armies.

d 8:8 Or "God with us."

e 8:8 Or "its wings" (a possible metaphor for the Assyrian armies spreading over the land). God once spread out his wings over the Hebrew people and carried them to Sinai. Now the Assyrian armies spread out their wings and overwhelm them with destruction.

f 8:9 Or "Unite (assemble) yourselves."

g 8:9 Or "Gird yourselves."

h 8:10 The Hebrew is *immanu el*.

i 8:11 Or "He turned me aside" (Dead Sea scroll 1QIsa[a]).

j 8:11 Or "walk in the way of."

k 8:13 Or "dread."

l 8:14 Or "a noose."

m 8:14 See 1 Peter 2:8.

Trust in the Hidden God

[16]Now, tie up the scroll and preserve it *as legal evidence.* Seal my instructions *for the future* for my disciples. [17]I will wait for the Lord Yahweh, who hides his face[a] from the family of Jacob. And I will place all my hope in him!

[18]Behold—here I stand, and the children whom the Lord Yahweh has given me are for signs and wonders[b] in Israel, sent from the Lord Almighty, Commander of Angel Armies, who is enthroned on Mount Zion![c]

Darkness or the Light of Dawn

[19]Now, suppose someone says, "Consult mediums and spiritists who moan and mutter their incantations in their ritual pits; after all, isn't it right for people to seek oracles from their gods[d] by asking the dead about the destiny of the living?"

[20]*You are to answer them:* "Listen to the teaching and instruction of the Lord! If their speech does not line up with his word, they will have no light of dawn![e] [21]They will wander here and there, distressed and hungry. And when they are famished, they will be enraged and begin to curse their king and their God.[f] If they look to the heavens [22]or to the earth, they will find only despair and darkness and fearful gloom, and they will be thrust into obscure darkness!"[g]

A Son Is Born

9 No more gloom for those who are in distress! Although the Lord greatly humbled the regions of Zebulun and Naphtali,[h] he will one day bestow upon

---

a 8:17 See Isa. 45:14.

b 8:18 Or "symbols." Isaiah's family was a living prophecy to all who discerned it.

c 8:18 This verse has a dual meaning. Historically, it refers to Isaiah and his sons: Shear-Jashub, "a remnant will return," and Maher-Shalal-Hash-Baz, "Quickly—to the Plunder! Hurry—to the Loot." But there is another meaning to all this. In this verse, Isaiah becomes a type or picture of Christ, who would come to the earth (Immanuel). Hebrews 2:13 quotes this verse about the Lord Jesus Christ and his children. Christ and his disciples (children) will be for signs and wonders (miracles). The Zion-realm is more than just a place. It is the realm where God and his people walk together in fellowship. God wants to dwell in Zion with his consecrated ones.

d 8:19 Or "from God."

e 8:20 Or "dayspring." The implication for the believer is that we *will* have a "dawn." The light of dawn is the hope of Jesus Christ that grows inside of us. The path of the righteous is like the light of a sunrise shining in the eastern sky. From dark to dim to bright, it increases (Prov. 4:18). In times of calamity, make sure you quiet your heart and seal up the Word of God in your soul. The dawning of Christ's glory is coming. For us, the early rays of morning light are already shining.

f 8:21 Or "gods."

g 8:22 Or "with no dawn." The exact meaning of the Hebrew phrase is uncertain.

h 9:1 This was the region that first went into captivity during the Assyrian invasion in 734–733 BC. Yet this land was the first to enjoy the blessings of the ministry of Jesus, for his works were done among them. Their "honor" would be to host the life and miracles of the Prince of Glory, the Messiah. Isaiah is prophesying the ministry of Jesus that would reverse the curse over that region. In the place where devastation had robbed hope, he will appear. He chooses them great honor—from the Mediterranean eastward to the other side of the Jordan*a* and throughout the Galilee of the gentiles.

²Those who walked in darkness*b*
have seen a radiant light *shining upon them.*^c^
They once lived in the shadows of death,
but now a glorious light has dawned!*d*
³*Lord,* you have multiplied the nation
and given them overwhelming joy!
They are ecstatic in your presence
and rejoice like those who bring in a great harvest*e*
and those who divide up the spoils of victory!*f*
⁴For you have broken the chains*g*
that have bound your people
and lifted off the heavy bar across their shoulders,
the rod the oppressor used against them.
You have shattered all their bondage,*h*
just as you did when Midian's armies were defeated.

---

the places in our lives where we have the most disgrace and shame, and there he shines his light. Our past failures become prophecies of a future victory.
a 9:1 That is, Gilead or Transjordan.
b 9:2 See Isa. 8:20; Ps. 82:5; 107:10.
c 9:2 Just as darkness and night have boundaries (Gen.1:4), so the Lord will cause gloom to end and the shadows to flee. He is the one who says, "It will last this long and not a day longer." God begins in darkness and brings darkness into the day. The darkest thing in us will be bathed in his glory-light.
d 9:2 See Isa. 55:8; Matt. 4:15–16; Eph. 5:8. This glorious light includes Jesus' teachings, his miracles, and his pure life lived before the Father. Jesus Christ is a light of rescue for the lost, comfort for the hurting, wholeness for the broken, and escape for the captive. It is the light of joy, the light of revelation, the light of deliverance. Jesus' birth signals an end of night and the beginning of morning.
e 9:3 As the light of Jesus shines on the earth, it will bring in a harvest of joy and rejoicing. The people of God are about to arise and spoil the kingdom of darkness, even as Israel spoiled Egypt and went out rejoicing. God will cause our joy to overflow like those distributing loot after a battle. Great will be the conversions, the increase, and our rejoicing. Many sons will be brought into glory as the increasing Light of Dawn appears (Heb. 2:10). With both harvest and victory in battle, people rejoice in what God has done.
f 9:3 The Masoretic text reads "You have magnified joy to everyone who receives the Light." A sign of the moving of God among us to fulfill this promise is an outbreak of joy! He fills our mouths with laughter as a sign that the great ingathering of the harvest is here (Ps. 119:162; 126). The phrase "They are ecstatic in your presence" refers to the heart of worship God is releasing today. The gospel will always bring joy, and those who receive good news will rejoice (Ps. 67:4; Acts 8:8). This is the joy of the Feast of Tabernacles. The two great joys of the human heart come at a time of harvest and a time of victory. Human celebration at these two times knows no bounds. As the increase is brought in, victory is experienced. What greater joy is there in heaven and earth than when souls are saved?
g 9:4 Or "burdensome yoke."
h 9:4 The words *chains, yoke,* and *rod* all represent oppression and bondage.

[5]Every boot of marching troops
and every uniform caked with blood
will be burned as fuel for the fire.

The Wonderful One
[6]A child has been born for us;
a son has been given to us.[a]
The responsibility of *complete* dominion
will rest on his shoulders, and his name will be:
The Wonderful One!
The Extraordinary Strategist!
The Mighty God![b]
The Father of Eternity!
The Prince[c] of Peace!
[7]Great and vast is his dominion.[d]
He will bring immeasurable peace and prosperity.[e]
He will rule on David's throne and over David's kingdom
to establish and uphold it by promoting justice and righteousness
from this time forward and forevermore.
The marvelous passion[f] that the Lord Yahweh,
Commander of Angel Armies, has for his people
will ensure that it is finished!

The Lord Judges Arrogance and Oppression
[8]The Lord decreed a word against Jacob, and it brought calamity upon Israel. [9]And all the people of Ephraim and Samaria knew of it. Their hearts filled with pride and they arrogantly boasted, [10]"Our brick walls may have crumbled, but we will rebuild them with dressed stones. *Invading armies* may have cut down our sycamore trees, but we will plant cedars in their place!"[g]

---

a 9:6 The "child" speaks of Christ's humanity, and the "son" points to his eternal deity. This son would be born in a time of darkness, but he will bring the light of a new day to the hearts of men.

b 9:6 Or "the God of battle" or "Champion-God." See Ps. 45:3.

c 9:6 The Hebrew word for "prince" is *sar*, formed from two Hebrew roots: a verb meaning "to wrestle, to fight" and another verb meaning "to rule or to govern (as royalty)." So combined, the Hebrew word *sar* is "warring prince." Sarah, the feminine version of Sar, can be translated "a princess who is a warrior." It is possible to render v. 6 as "A Wonderful Counselor is the Mighty God! The Everlasting Father is a Prince of Peace."

d 9:7 Or "His authority will continually expand." The Hebrew word *misrah*, found only here in vv. 6 and 7, can be translated "empire, governmental authority, dominion."

e 9:7 The Hebrew word *shalom* can be translated "peace, prosperity, wholeness, and success." Perhaps all of these concepts are included in the *shalom* Christ brings us.

f 9:7 Or "intense devotion." See 2 Cor. 11:2.

g 9:10 Their attitude is basically "Even if God sends judgment, we will start over and be stronger and more prosperous than before," not realizing that God will not lift his hand of judgment until they humble their hearts.

[11]So the Lord Yahweh stirred up their enemies and strengthened Rezin's foes,[a] and they came against the people. [12]Syrians[b] on the east, Philistines on the west—they came with bared teeth[c] and devoured Israel. Yet despite all this, his anger did not subside, and his hand *of judgment* is poised to strike them again. [13]For the people did not repent and turn to the one who struck them or seek the Lord Yahweh, Commander of Angel Armies.

Judgment Coming to the Leaders

[14]In a single day, the Lord Yahweh cut off from Israel both head and tail, palm branch and reed. [15]The elders and dignitaries are the head, and the prophet who teaches lies is the tail. [16]The leaders have led them astray, and the citizens are left in confusion. [17]That is why the Lord did not show pity to the young people or have compassion on their orphans and widows. For everyone was godless and did evil and each mouth spewed out wickedness. Therefore, the Lord's anger has not subsided, and his hand is poised to strike them again.

Israel's Tribes Turn Against One Another

[18]Surely wickedness burned like *an out-of-control* fire, consuming thorns and thistles. It set ablaze the thickets of the forest with flames swirling upward in columns of smoke. [19]The land was scorched[d] because of the anger of the Lord Yahweh, Commander of Angel Armies. The people themselves became fuel for the fire, and no one showed compassion toward another. [20]With their right hands they snatched what belonged to others, yet remained hungry. With their left hands they stole food, yet they were starving[e] and even ate their own offspring![f] [21]Manasseh devoured Ephraim, and Ephraim Manasseh, and together they turned against Judah.[g] Yet despite all this, the Lord's anger has not subsided, and his hand is poised to strike them again.[h]

Arrogant Assyria

10 Woe to those who legalize injustice and write oppressive legislation! [2]You rip away the rights of the poor and prey upon widows and orphans![i] [3]What will come of you on your day of visitation when disaster comes from afar?

---

a 9:11 That is, the Assyrians. The Septuagint reads "the enemies of Mount Zion."

b 9:12 Or "Arameans," a confederacy of Aramaic-speaking people known as Aram (modern-day Syria).

c 9:12 Or "with their whole mouth."

d 9:19 The Hebrew word *n'étam* is a hapax legomenon taken from an Arabic word for "dark." Its Hebrew meaning is uncertain and could be rendered "scorched," "shaken," or "darkened."

e 9:20 This is a figurative way to describe civil war. Although they all belonged to Israel's tribes, they are now turning against one another.

f 9:20 Or "They ate the flesh of their own arm." This could be a figure of speech for harassing and destroying one another. See also Jer. 19:9.

g 9:21 See 2 Chron. 28:6–15.

h 9:21 Or "his hand is still reaching out."

i 10:2 Or "You make widows your spoil and orphans your prey."

To whom will you run for help? And what will you do then with all your great wealth?[a] [4]You'll have no option but to cringe among the captives or fall among the corpses of the slain! Yet despite all this, his anger has not subsided, and his hand is poised to strike.[b]

[5]Woe to *arrogant* Assyria, the rod of my anger! The club I place in the *king's* hand is my fury. [6]I am the one who has sent him against a godless nation and ordered him to attack a people who anger me. I sent him to take the spoil and seize the plunder[c] and to trample them down like dust in the street. [7]But he has no clue what he's doing, and he has something else in mind. He plans on annihilating many nations [8]and thinks, "After all, I have made my executive commanders into kings. [9]Calneh[d] will be no different than Carchemish,[e] *whom I destroyed.* I'll destroy Hamath as I did Arpad[f] and Samaria like Damascus.[g] [10]Since I was able to seize kingdoms full of idols and images more powerful and more impressive than those of Jerusalem and Samaria, [11]won't I do the same thing to Jerusalem and Samaria and their idols?"[h]

[12]But when the Lord has carried out his purpose on Mount Zion and Jerusalem, he will punish the king of Assyria because of his overbearing arrogance and unrestrained pride![i] [13]He boasted, "Look what I have done by the strength of my hand and by my wisdom. See how clever I am! I have erased the borders of nations and plundered their treasures. I have been like a mighty conqueror, subduing those in strong fortresses.[j] [14]I seized their wealth as one who found an *unprotected* nest. As one who gathers eggs that have been left behind, so I gathered the wealth of the world. And the young birds could neither move a wing nor even open their mouths to peep!"

God Decrees Judgment on Assyria

[15]Is the axe greater than the one who wields it? Is the saw greater than the one who cuts with it? Can the axe strike without a hand to move it? Can a *lifeless* wooden

---

a 10:3 Or "glory" or "honor," a possible metaphor for their vast armies.

b 10:4 Or "his hand is still reaching out."

c 10:6 See Isa. 8:1.

d 10:9 Calneh or Calno, which means "(selfish) ambition," was a city in Shinar (Gen. 10:10).

e 10:9 Carchemish, which means "fortress of one who subdues," was a capital city of northern Syria, once known as the Hittite empire.

f 10:9 *Hamath* means "high walls" and was the principal city of northern Syria. *Arpad* means "I will spread out" and was a Syro-Hittite city north of Aleppo in northwestern Syria.

g 10:9 *Samaria* means "watch (guard) mountain." It was the mountainous region north of Jerusalem also known as the northern kingdom of Israel. Damascus is not a Hebrew word (likely Aramaic); it means "alert, active." Damascus is the major city of Syria and is viewed as the oldest continually inhabited city on earth.

h 10:11 In his blasphemous boast, he equates the Lord Yahweh with all the other gods and their idols that he had conquered. His arrogance will be his downfall. Although he became the rod of God's anger to punish Judah and Israel, that same rod is now poised to strike him down.

i 10:12 Or "the pride of his exalted eyes."

j 10:13 Or "brought down kings from their thrones." Assyria represents human reasoning, with its high thoughts and deceptive fantasies that exalt themselves against God (see 2 Cor. 10:1). The intellect of man falls short and is inferior to the wisdom and knowledge of God.

cane walk all by itself?[a] [16]Therefore, the sovereign Lord Yahweh, Commander of Angel Armies, will send a devastating plague among Assyria's proud warriors. Yes, the "glory"[b] of Assyria will be burned and go up in smoke! [17]For the Light of Israel will become a fire *in their midst*, and the Holy One will become a flame! He will consume the thorns[c] and thistles of the Assyrian king in one day! [18]The splendor of his forest and orchard[d] will be completely destroyed,[e] like a dying man fading away.[f] [19]The forest will have so few trees left[g] that even a little boy could count them.

Restoration Promised

[20]In that day, neither the remnant of Israel nor the survivors of the house of Jacob will lean anymore upon the one who abused them,[h] but they will lean fully[i] on *the faithfulness of* the Lord Yahweh, the Holy One of Israel. [21]A remnant will return, the remnant of Jacob's tribes to the mighty God. [22]Though your people Israel were as many as the sand on the seashore, only a remnant will return. Destruction has been decreed, and it will be overflowing with righteousness. [23]For the Lord Yahweh, Commander of Angel Armies, will complete the destruction he has decreed upon the whole land.

[24]So hear what the Lord Yahweh, Commander of Angel Armies, has to say: "My Zion-people, do not be gripped with fear over the Assyrians who oppress and abuse you,[j] as the Egyptians did long ago. [25]After only a brief moment, I will end my indignation against you, and it will fall upon them to their destruction!"

[26]The Lord Yahweh, who commands angel armies, will wield his whip against them, as when he struck Midian at the rock of Oreb.[k] And once again he will raise his rod over the waters, as he did in Egypt.

[27]In that day the Lord will remove the heavy burden from your shoulders and break off the yoke of bondage from your necks because of the heavy anointing *upon you!*[l]

---

a 10:15 Although God used Assyria as his "axe" and his "saw" to bring about his purposes, that doesn't mean they have reason to be proud. The same can be said of us. Although God may use us powerfully, we must give glory and credit to God and his grace. See Acts 12:23.

b 10:16 The "glory" of Assyria is a metaphor describing all their pomp and military might.

c 10:17 Moses knelt before the burning thorn bush, and God ignited a fire in his heart. Today God wants to light a holy flame in every heart that follows Christ.

d 10:18 The phrase "forest and orchard" is a metaphor for Assyria's armies (forest) and his noblemen (orchard).

e 10:18 Or "From breath to flesh, it will be destroyed," a metaphor for totality.

f 10:18 The Hebrew text of this last clause is uncertain.

g 10:19 The fire of the glory of the Lord will consume the armies of Assyria. One angel destroyed 185,000 Assyrians in one night. See Isa. 37:36–38; 2 Kings 19:35.

h 10:20 That is, Assyria.

i 10:20 Or "sincerely."

j 10:24 Or "who beat you with a rod and lift up their staff against you."

k 10:26 The rock of Oreb ("raven") is the place where Gideon killed two fleeing Midianite princes (Judg. 7:25). Isaiah mentions both the rock of Oreb and the victory at the Red Sea to illustrate how God will completely subdue his enemies.

l 10:27 Or "because of oil (anointing)." Oil is a frequent symbol of the anointing of God. Although the meaning of the Hebrew text of this clause is uncertain, some scholars see the imagery of

²⁸The Assyrian army*ᵃ* attacked Aiath;*ᵇ*
they passed over into Migron*ᶜ*
and stored their equipment at Michmash.*ᵈ*
²⁹They went through the pass
and spent the night at Geba.*ᵉ*
Ramah*ᶠ* was alarmed and trembled.
Those in Gibeah, the city of Saul, ran for their lives.
³⁰Cry aloud, O daughter of Gallim!*ᵍ*
Listen, O Laishah!*ʰ* Poor Anathoth!*ⁱ*
³¹Madmenah*ʲ* is retreating;
the residents of Gebim*ᵏ* are hiding.
³²This very day,*ˡ* standing at Nob,*ᵐ* he will shake his fist
at the mountain of the daughter of the house of Zion—
at the hill of Jerusalem.
³³Behold, the Sovereign Lord of Angel Armies
is about to cut off the branches with terrifying power.
He will cut down the exalted heights of the high,
and all the lofty will be brought low.
³⁴He will slash the thickets of the forest as with an axe,
and Lebanon will fall before the Mighty One.

---

an ox who grew so fat that it shattered the yoke over his neck. Assyria's yoke of bondage will be broken off Judah because they will grow fat, heavy with the anointing of God's restored favor.

a 10:28 Or "he." By implication and context, it is the king of Assyria with his armies.

b 10:28 Aiath (or Ai) was a city east of Bethel and near Jericho. It means "heap of ruins." In vv. 28–31, the Hebrew text contains no conjunctions and is in a very disjointed, short, hard-hitting style. There is much scholarly debate about when this invasion took place. Perhaps the names of the locations give us hints about the things God will "invade" inside of believers today. The "heap of ruins" could be an apt picture of our flesh life.

c 10:28 Migron means "threshing floor." God takes his chosen ones through the threshing floor of our hearts by the Holy Spirit.

d 10:28 Michmash is a city about ten miles north of Jerusalem, believed to be modern-day Mukhmas, and means "hidden." God will go after our hidden issues.

e 10:29 Or *Gibeah*, which means "uphill," a picture of striving in the flesh.

f 10:29 *Ramah* means "high place," an obvious metaphor for lofty and arrogant attitudes that are "raised up in defiance of the true knowledge of God" (2 Cor. 10:1).

g 10:30 *Gallim* means "heaps (of waves, stones, etc.)" or possibly "springs." It represents the flow of life that does not originate with God but with self.

h 10:30 Or *Laish*, the Hebrew word for "lion." The lion's den is a picture of the realm of demonic power (Song. 4:8).

i 10:30 Or "Answer (her), O Anathoth!" *Anathoth* means "answers to prayers."

j 10:31 *Madmenah* means "dung heap." See Phil. 3:8.

k 10:31 *Gebim* means "pits" or "ditches."

l 10:32 Or "while it is still day."

m 10:32 Nob was the city of priests, which the Talmud and Jerome's translation state was within sight of Jerusalem. *Nob* means "higher place."

The Branch of the Lord

11 The cut-off stump of Jesse*ª* will sprout,*ᵇ*
and a fruitful Branch will grow from his roots:*ᶜ*
²the Spirit of Yahweh will rest upon him,*ᵈ*
the Spirit of Extraordinary Wisdom,*ᵉ*
the Spirit of Perfect Understanding,*ᶠ*
the Spirit of Wise Strategy,*ᵍ*
the Spirit of Mighty Power,*ʰ*
the Spirit of Revelation,*ⁱ*
and the Spirit of the Fear of Yahweh.
³He will find his delight*ʲ* in living
by the Spirit of the Fear of the Lord.

---

a 11:1 That is, the royal family line of David. Jesse, the grandson of Boaz, was the father of King David. Jesse means "upright, firm, strong."

b 11:1 Or "Go forth." Notice the contrast with the arrogant "trees" that are cut down (10:33–34).

c 11:1 The Hebrew word for "branch" or "twig" is *netzer* (lit. "to grow green"), the root word for Nazarene, Nazarite, and Nazareth (Matt. 2:23). Christ is both the root and the offspring of David (Rev. 5:5; 22:16). This means that the "(scion) branch" that grows from the roots (his spirit/nature) points to the body of Christ, his church on the earth. Christ in us is the vine and we are his fruitful branches. Jesus Christ branches out through his people and grows from his root. Overcomers are the branches that bring forth the fruit of Christ's life. This sprout will grow to become the rod of God's power. See Jer. 23:5, 33:15; Zech. 3:8; 6:12; John 1:1–15; Rom. 15:12; Gal. 5:22–23.

d 11:2 The Spirit of Yahweh is the Spirit of prophecy, the manifest presence of God resting upon the Lord Jesus. In the Hebrew culture, to say "the Spirit of Yahweh rests upon" someone meant the Spirit of prophecy was upon them. See John 1:32–33.

e 11:2 Or "the Spirit of Skillfulness" (Ex. 31:2–4). This gives equipping ability for music, art, business, writing, creativity, and wisdom for judicial decisions. Paul prayed for the churches to receive this "Spirit of wisdom" (Eph. 1:17–19).

f 11:2 Or "the Spirit of Intelligent Insight." This imparts the ability to discern the truth, to know the meaning of riddles, and to decipher parables and allegories. This anointing was upon the prophet Daniel. See Dan. 1:17; 5:11–12; 9:21–23.

g 11:2 Or "the Spirit of Guidance." This is the Hebrew word *etsah* and is used numerous times in the Old Testament for "counsel, advice, or purpose." It is also used for steering (guiding) a ship. This anointing imparts the wisdom and counsel needed for spiritual leadership. See Ex. 18:19.

h 11:2 Or "the Spirit of a Mighty Warrior."

i 11:2 Or "the Spirit of Knowledge." This is not knowledge that is learned from books or study but knowledge that comes from experiencing intimacy with God.

j 11:3 Or "his smelling (sensing)," a Hebraic figure of speech for finding pleasure in something. The Septuagint reads "He will fill him with the spirit of the fear of the Lord (absolute loyalty to God)." The Aramaic can be translated "He will shine forth with the reverence of the Lord." The seven Spirits of God mentioned in these verses are also mentioned in Rev. 1:4; 4:4–5; 5:6. The Holy Spirit is one (Eph. 4:3–4) but revealed in seven dimensions. The golden lampstand in the tabernacle had seven branches. The sevenfold Spirit of God is the illuminating influence over God's people.

He will neither judge by appearances[a]
nor make his decisions based on rumors.[b]
⁴With righteousness he will uphold justice[c] for the poor
and defend the lowly of the earth.
His words will be like a scepter of power
that conquers the world,[d]
and with his breath[e] he will slay the lawless one.[f]
⁵Righteousness will be his warrior's sash
and faithfulness his belt.[g]

Christ Will Subdue All Things

⁶*Then* the wolf will be *subdued* and live with the *gentle* lamb,[h] and the leopard[i] will lie down[j] with the *gentle* lamb.[k] The young calf and the ferocious lion[l] will be together, *and as a shepherd drives his flock*, a small child will guide them along! ⁷The cow and the bear will graze alongside each other;[m] cubs and calves will lie

---

a 11:3 Or "by the glance of his eyes." Jesus, our Messiah, sees clearly into our hearts and knows our every motive. See James 3:16–17.

b 11:3 Or "by what is heard by his ears."

c 11:4 Or "by judging with righteousness." Isaiah uses this word (Heb. *tzedeq*) fifty-one times.

d 11:4 See Rev. 2:26–28.

e 11:4 Or "spirit."

f 11:4 See 2 Thess. 2:8.

g 11:5 That is, fairness and truth will be his clothing. The first five verses of this chapter show us that the Messiah would be from David's lineage and would have the sevenfold Spirit of God resting upon him. His government would be equitable, full of righteousness, and a demonstration of his loyalty to God. Jesus fulfills all these attributes completely.

h 11:6 The list of animals in this section represents various attributes and spiritual conditions within human beings (cf. Calvin). Some are clean and some are unclean; some are wild and some are tame. They typify aspects of human nature (e.g., the nature of a wolf, a lamb, a lion, a leopard) because elsewhere in Scripture they refer to human beings. Each reveals an aspect of the nature of Adam or of the nature of Christ. This figurative passage of Scripture points to the subduing power of the life of Christ within his people, taming the "wolf," the enemy of a lamb (John 10:12; Acts 20:29–30), to be subdued and to lie down with the lamb (Christ's nature within us). The Hebrew word for "lamb" (*kebes*) is taken from the root word "to subdue, dominate." There are fifteen natures (creatures) mentioned in this passage that are reconciled and rest together. Fifteen in the Bible is the number of rest.

i 11:6 The leopard is mentioned eight times in the Bible, and in every instance, it is used figuratively for an aspect of human beings or of spiritual powers of darkness. It is emblematic of an aspect of human nature that cannot be changed or tamed. See Song. 4:8; Jer. 5:6; 13:23; Dan. 7:6; Hab. 1:8; Rev. 13:2.

j 11:6 Or "stretch out."

k 11:6 Or "kid," meaning either a male lamb or a male goat (Song. 1:8). The Hebrew word for "kid" (*gĕdiy*) comes from the root word "cut off." As the Lamb of God, Jesus was cut off from the land of the living for our salvation.

l 11:6 See 1 Peter 5:8.

m 11:7 There is a subtle play on words found in the Hebrew. The word for "graze (feed)" is *tirʿêynâ*, and the word for "become friends" is *titrāʿêynâ*. So the cow and bear grazing together become friends.

down together. The lion, like the ox, will eat straw. [8]The nursing child will play *safely* near the rattlesnake's den, and the toddler will stretch out his hand and shine light over the serpent.[a] [9]On all my holy mountain of *Zion*,[b] nothing evil or harmful[c] will be found. For the earth will be filled[d] with the *intimate* knowledge of the Lord Yahweh just as water swells the sea![e]

The God Who Restores
[10]On that day, the root of Jesse[f] will be lifted up[g] as a *miracle*-sign to *rally* the people.[h] Gentiles will diligently seek him,[i] and his resting place will be glorious![j]

[11]On that day, the Lord will extend his hand a second time to restore[k] the remnant of his people from Assyria, Egypt, Pathros,[l] Ethiopia,[m] Iran,[n] Iraq,[o] Syria,[p] and the coastlands of the sea.[q] [12]He will lift up a banner among the

---

a 11:8 The Hebrew word for "hand" is *yad* and can also be translated "power." Although many translations render this "A child will put his hand over the serpent's den," the Hebrew text uses the word *meuwrah*, which means "an opening of light." Jesus told us that unless we become like little children we can never enter heaven's kingdom reality. Even little children in God's kingdom have power over the serpent and bring light into its hiding place. The Hebrew word for "toddler" is "weaned child." This word (*gāmûl*) is a homophone that can also be translated "ripe fruit, reward, deal bountifully, do good (to another)." This "weaned child" is the nature of Christ being produced in us. All is subdued and hostility removed in the kingdom of God. See Phil. 3:21.

b 11:9 See Isa. 2:1–5.

c 11:9 Or "destructive."

d 11:9 The Septuagint uses a present-tense verb, "is (presently) filled (to the brim)."

e 11:9 Or "as the waters form a covering for the sea." See Jer. 31:34; Hab. 2:14; Heb. 8:11.

f 11:10 That is, the royal family line of David (a metonymy). John took this phrase from Isaiah and quotes Jesus referring to himself as the Root of David. See Rev. 5:5; 22:16.

g 11:10 Or "standing up." Jesus was *lifted up* on the cross to bring us salvation (John 12:32).

h 11:10 The contemporary Hebrew word *nes* means "miracle," while the ancient Hebrew means "sign (signal)." The translation includes both concepts. The Septuagint is "He will arise to rule the nations (gentiles)."

i 11:10 Or "Gentiles will put their hope in him" (LXX). See John 12:21; Rom. 15:12.

j 11:10 Instead of saying "glorious," the prophet simply employs the noun *glory* (*kabod*). The bride of Christ is now his resting place (Song. 1:16–17). The Hebrew word *menuḥâ* is also found in Psalm 23:2, "He offers a resting place for me. . . . His tracks take me to an oasis of peace." He had nowhere to lay his head (headship), but the heart of a believer is now his resting place. Glory is found at the place where he rests.

k 11:11 God is a God of restoration, even for those who have miserably failed him.

l 11:11 Possibly a loan word from Egyptian indicating the region of Upper Egypt. *Pathros* means "desert dryness."

m 11:11 Or "Cush," which means "scorched" or "blackened."

n 11:11 Or "Elam," a nation-state in the southwestern region of modern-day Iran, whose ancient capital was Susa. *Elam* means "hidden" or "concealed."

o 11:11 Or "Shinar (Babylonia)." *Shinar* means "divided land" or "divided stream."

p 11:11 Or "Hamath," west-central Syria. *Hamath* means "walled-up fortress."

q 11:11 Possibly the "islands of the (Mediterranean?) sea." These eight regions are eight areas that Christ will restore within the hearts of those who follow him. Eight is the number of a new beginning.

nations and will gather the scattered Jews,[a] and assemble the outcasts of Israel from the four corners of the earth. [13]Then Ephraim will be cleansed of envy, and those who are hostile to Judah will be cut off. Ephraim will no longer be jealous of Judah, and Judah will no longer be hostile toward Ephraim.[b] [14]But they will swoop down on the slopes of Philistia[c] to the west; together they will plunder the people of the east. They will rule over Edom and Moab, and the Ammonites[d] will obey them.

[15]The Lord Yahweh will dry up[e] the gulf of the Egyptian Sea.[f] He will raise his hand over the Euphrates, and with the might of his wind, he will split it into seven streams[g] that can be easily crossed in sandals. [16]Then there will be a highway leading out of Assyria for his remnant people to return, just as there was for Israel when they were set free from Egypt.

Song of Praise for the Redeemed

12 In that day you will sing,[h]
"I praise you, Lord Yahweh,
for even though you were angry with me,
your anger turned away,
and now you tenderly comfort me.[i]
[2]Behold—God is my salvation![j]
I am confident, unafraid, and I will trust *in you*."
Yes! The Lord Yah is my might and my melody;
he has become my salvation![k]
[3]With *triumphant* joy you will drink deeply
from the wells[l] of salvation.[m]

---

a 11:12 Or "He will gather the dispersed of Judah."
b 11:13 This is the healing of the divided kingdom. See Jer. 3:18; Ezek. 37:22.
c 11:14 Or "on the shoulder of Philistia." The shoulder becomes a metaphor for the hills.
d 11:14 The Ammonites lived in modern-day Jordan.
e 11:15 Or "divide" or "destroy."
f 11:15 Or "tongue of the Red Sea."
g 11:15 Or "wadis."
h 12:1 Isaiah contains nine songs: the Song of Zion (Isa. 1–4), the Song of the Beloved and his vineyard (Isa. 5), the Song of Praise for the Redeemed (Isa. 12), the Song of the Strong City (Isa. 26:1–4), the Joyful Song of the Redeemed (Isa. 35:1–10), the New Song of the Lord (Isa. 42:10), the Song of Joy in Creation (Isa. 44:23), the Song of Salvation (Isa. 52:7–12), and the Song of the Suffering Savior (Isa. 53).
i 12:1 Or, as a jussive (expression of desire), "May your anger be turned away and may you comfort me" (Masoretic Text).
j 12:2 Or "the God who gives me triumph." The Hebrew word for "salvation," *yĕshuw'ah*, is found in Isaiah twenty-eight times and is very similar to the Hebrew name of Jesus: Yeshua. Redemption is God's last word, not judgment. To know Jesus is to know the God of salvation.
k 12:2 See Ex. 15:2; Ps. 118:14.
l 12:3 Or "fountains," "wells," "springs," or "streams" (LXX). The streams of salvation represent Jesus' life in us. See Isa. 41:17–18; Jer. 2:13; 17:13; John 4:13–14; 7:37–39; Rev. 7:17. Through Christ, God's sons and daughters are living wells of salvation, containers bringing the water of life to others.
m 12:3 Or "the savior (*yĕshuw'ah*)."

[4]In that *glorious* day, you will say to one another,
  "Give thanks to the Lord and ask him for more![a]
  Tell the world about all that he does!
  Let them know how magnificent he is!"[b]
[5]Sing praises to the Lord, for he has done marvelous wonders,
  and let his fame be known throughout the earth!
[6]Give out a shout of cheer;
  sing for joy,[c] O people of Zion,
  for great and mighty is the Holy One of Israel
  who lives among you!

Pronouncement of Judgment on Babylon

13 This is the prophecy against Babylon[d] that God revealed to Isaiah, son of Amoz:

[2]"Raise high a signal flag on a barren hilltop! Shout out!
  Beckon my *armies* to invade the gates of the nobles,
[3]for I have given orders to my consecrated ones.
  I have summoned my mighty heroes,
  those who rejoice in my triumph,
  that they may execute my anger."[e]

[4]*Listen!* A thunderous noise is heard on the mountain,
  like that of a massive multitude.
  Listen! Kingdoms are in an uproar;
  nations are assembling together.
  The almighty Lord Yahweh is mustering an army for war.
[5]They are coming from a faraway land,
  from the end of the heavens.[f]
  Here comes Yahweh with his instruments of judgment,
  ready to ravage the entire land.[g]

---

a 12:4 Or "call upon his name"; that is, invoke his name for help.

b 12:4 Or "proclaim that his name is exalted."

c 12:6 See Ps. 47:1; Pss. 148–150.

d 13:1 This begins a new section of Isaiah (13–23) that contains ten prophecies against ten nations. Babylon (related to Babel) means "confusion" and points to the political and religious confusion and disorder among the nations. This prophecy against Babylon was spoken by Isaiah at least 174 years before Babylon fell in 536 BC. The Greek historian Herodotus described the city of Babylon as fifteen miles wide on each side with walls that were more than eighty-five feet thick and 350 feet high. It had one hundred gates to the city and was the commercial center of the East. In the book of Revelation, Babylon becomes a metaphor for the world's political and religious system. See Isa. 46–47; Rev. 18.

e 13:3 These are God's armies consecrated by him to carry out his judgment on Babylon. God is mustering his army from among the Medes to invade Babylon (v. 17; 21:2).

f 13:5 Or possibly "horizon." See Joel 2:1–10; 2 Thess. 1:7–10; Jude 14–15. The heavenly sons and daughters of God are also consecrated, mighty ones, and warriors who rejoice in his triumph.

g 13:5 Or "all the earth."

⁶Wail, for the day of the Lord Yahweh is near!
  It will come with the destructive power of Shaddai.
⁷For this reason, every hand will go limp
  and every heart will melt.
⁸All *the Babylonians* will be seized with panic and pain.
  Anguish will grip them like a woman in labor.
  They will look at one another with astonishment,
  and their faces will be flames of fire!
⁹Behold! The day of the Lord is coming
  with pitiless fury and fierce anger.
  The land will be made desolate,
  destroying the sinners who inhabit it.
¹⁰For the stars of the heavens and their constellations*ᵃ*
  will not give their light.
  The rising sun will be obscured, and the moon won't shine.

¹¹"I will bring punishment to the world for its evil
  and the wicked for their sins.
  I will shatter the arrogance of the proud,
  and will humble the pride of the high and mighty.*ᵇ*
¹²I will make a person scarcer than fine gold
  and people rarer than a wedge of gold from Ophir.*ᶜ*
¹³Therefore, I will make the heavens shudder
  and the earth shake from its foundation
  because of the wrath of the Lord, Commander of Angel Armies,
  in the day of his fierce anger."
¹⁴Like a hunted gazelle, each will return to his own people,
  and like sheep with no one to gather them,
  each will flee to his native land.
¹⁵Captured ones will be slain,
  and those who are caught will die by the sword.
¹⁶Their infants will be dashed to pieces
  before their very eyes.*ᵈ*
  Their houses will be looted and their wives raped.*ᵉ*
¹⁷Behold! I am stirring up the Medes*ᶠ* against them,
  who neither value silver nor delight in gold.

---

a 13:10 Or "Orion." See Amos 5:8; Joel 2:31; Matt. 24:29; Acts 2:20; Heb. 12:26–29. Stars may also be a metaphor for ministries (Jude 13) and constellations a metaphor for fellowships (networks, denominations).

b 13:11 Or "tyrants."

c 13:12 A region of the southern coast of Arabia.

d 13:16 See Ps. 137:9.

e 13:16 See Zech. 14:2.

f 13:17 The Medes were people who lived on the Zagros Mountains, in present-day central Iran.

[18]They will slaughter the young men,[a]
and show no pity on infants nor compassion on children."

[19]God will overthrow Babylon, the jewel of kingdoms,
the splendor and pride of the Babylonians,
exactly as he did to Sodom and Gomorrah.
[20]Babylon will never rise again,
nor will it be inhabited for many generations.
Bedouins will not even pitch their tents there,
and shepherds will refuse to rest their flocks there.
[21]Wild animals will roam there,
and their vacant houses will be overrun by eerie creatures[b]—
nothing but owls[c] and goat-shaped demons[d] dancing!
[22]Hyenas will howl in her houses,
and jackals will make their dens in her palaces.
Babylon's time is up, and her days are numbered!

Restoration of Judah

14 The Lord Yahweh will most certainly
show tender mercy to the Israelites.[e]
He will choose them again and settle them in their own land.[f]
Even foreigners will accompany them
and join with the Jewish people.[g]
[2]Nations will take them back to their own place,[h]
and the Jews[i] will own their enemies[j] as their inheritance
in the land Yahweh gave them.
They will take their captors captive[k]
and rule over those who once oppressed them.[l]

---

a 13:18 Or "With their bows they will strike down the young (men)."

b 13:21 Or "wild dogs" or "hyenas."

c 13:21 Or "ostriches" or "skunks."

d 13:21 Or "satyrs." See Koehler and Baumgartner's *Lexicon in Veteris Testamenti Libros*, Leiden, 1958, 926, and *A Hebrew and English Lexicon of the Old Testament* by Brown, Driver, and Briggs, 1980, 972.

e 14:1 Or "to Jacob." See Rom. 9–11.

f 14:1 See 1 Kings 8:56; Isa. 32:18.

g 14:1 Or "house of Jacob." "Foreigners" (gentiles) and Jews make up "the one new race of humanity." See Eph. 2:11–22.

h 14:2 See Isa. 49:22; 60:9; 66:20. They will bring them to their own place; that is, into the body of Christ (John 14:1–3; 1 Cor. 12:18; Eph. 4:16).

i 14:2 Or "house of Israel."

j 14:2 Or "possess them as menservants and maidservants."

k 14:2 See Ps. 126.

l 14:2 See Isa. 60:14. The oppressors today are Satan (Rom. 16:20) and the mind of man (2 Cor. 10:3–5).

Downfall of the King of Babylon

[3]In that day, when the Lord Yahweh has given you rest from your pain, trouble, and cruel bondage,[a] [4]you will jeer at the king of Babylon and recite this proverb:[b]

"Your oppressor has been stilled and your onslaught is over![c]
[5]The Lord Yahweh has shattered the staff of the wicked,
the brutal rod[d] of the rulers.
[6]With their unceasing blows they used it cruelly
to strike down nations.
They subdued nations in anger with unrelenting persecution.
[7]But now the whole earth rests and is at peace.
It bursts out with singing;[e]
[8]even the cypresses and cedars[f] of Lebanon join in,
rejoicing over your demise, saying,
'Now that you were laid low,
no woodsman comes to cut us down.'"

The Underworld

[9]The underworld[g] is all astir in preparation,
ready to meet you when you show up.
It rouses the spirits of the dead to greet you!
All the former tyrants[h] and despots[i]
rise from their thrones!
[10]One and all will say to you:
"*Look at you!* You've become as weak as we are.
Now you're just like us!
[11]Your pompous pride brought you down to the underworld
with the hum of harps.[j]

---

a 14:3 See Matt. 11:28–30; Rom. 6:1–14; Heb. 3–4.

b 14:4 "Proverb" is the Hebrew word *mashal*, a homonym for both "proverb" (Prov.1:1) and "to rule (as king)," "to triumph," or "to take dominion." The life and power of "Babylon" (confusion) is conquered by the indwelling life of Christ.

c 14:4 Or "The golden city has ceased."

d 14:5 A "brutal rod," a metonymy, represents the authority of wicked rulers.

e 14:7 With the oppressive tyranny of the systems of Babylon destroyed, the prophet now sees the people break out with rejoicing and singing. See Isa. 44:23; 49:13; 52:9; 54:1; 55:12.

f 14:8 In the Christian tradition, the cypress is a symbol of death, life, and resurrection. The cypress supplied boards and timber for doors (1 Kings 6:15–23) and beams for roofing the temple (2 Chron. 3:5). The towering cedars of Lebanon speak of God's anointed servants standing tall and upright, bringing favor to the world (Ps. 92:12).

g 14:9 Or "Sheol," which represents both the underworld and the personification of the evil it represents.

h 14:9 Or "great goats," a likely symbol of tyrants, or "It roused all the giants that ruled the earth" (LXX).

i 14:9 Or "kings." These former rulers are depicted in the underworld (Sheol) as sitting on thrones of darkness.

j 14:11 Or "the sound of your harps." The Hebrew word for "harp" can also be translated "jars" and "pitchers," with an implication of the noise of clashing jars being broken.

But you will lie on a bed of maggots,
and a blanket of worms will cover you!

The Son of the Dawn

[12]"Look how you have fallen from your heavenly place,
O shining one,[a] son of the dawn!
You have been cut down to the ground,
you who conquered nations.[b]
[13]You said in your heart,
'I will ascend into heaven
and exalt my throne above the stars of God.[c]
I will rule on the mountain of the congregation,
on the highest place of the sacred mountain.[d]
[14]I will rise past the tops of the clouds
and rival the Most High God!'
[15]Yet down to the underworld you go—
into the depths of the pit![e]
[16]Everyone will stare at you and ponder your fate,[f] saying,
'Is this the man who shook the earth
and made the kingdoms tremble?
[17]Is this the man who made the world a desert
and overthrew its cities and refused to free his prisoners
and let them return home?'
[18]Every king at death lies in state,
each in his crypt of splendor,
[19]but you are an unburied, trampled corpse,
thrown out of your grave like a rotten stick
and wrapped in the bloody clothing
of those slain by the sword.
[20]You will not have a burial like them,
because you destroyed both your land and your people.
May your wicked descendants never be mentioned again!
[21]Prepare to execute his sons because of the sins of their father.[g]
May they never rise to conquer the earth
and cover the world with their cities."

---

a 14:12 Or "daystar" or "morning star." Many scholars and expositors view this passage (vv. 12–21) as not only the fall of Babylon under Nebuchadnezzar but also the fall of Satan from heaven (Luke 10:18). Lucifer, a name for Satan, is the Latin word for the morning star or Venus. Some view this passage as referring to Adam and the sin of man (2 Thess. 2:3–8).

b 14:12 Or "laid low the people."

c 14:13 This is the Hebrew word *El* ("God, Mighty One"). It is possible that the "stars of El" is a reference to angels (Rev. 1:20).

d 14:13 Or "the summit of Zaphon" or "the far reaches of the north" (Ps. 48:1–2).

e 14:15 Or "cistern," a metaphor for the underworld.

f 14:16 Or "peer at you closely."

g 14:21 As translated from the Syriac and LXX. Hebrew is "fathers (ancestors)." See also Ezek. 18:20.

Utter Extermination of Babylon

[22]"I will rise up against them,"
declares the Lord Yahweh, Commander of Angel Armies.
"I will blot out the name Babylon and her survivors,
her offspring and descendants," declares the Lord Yahweh.
[23]"I will turn it into a swampland and a place for wild animals.[a]
Like dirt on the floor I will sweep it away
with the broom of destruction,"
declares the Lord Yahweh, Commander of Angel Armies.

The Lord's Plan for Assyria

[24]The Lord Yahweh, Commander of Angel Armies,
makes this solemn decree:
"Be sure of this: Just as I have planned,[b] so it will be.
Every purpose of my heart will surely come to pass.
[25]I will crush the Assyrians who invade my land.
I will trample them on my mountains.
Their yoke of slavery will be removed from my people
and their heavy burden from their shoulders.
[26]This is the plan that I have determined for the entire world.
I will accomplish it by the demonstration of my mighty power[c]
throughout the earth!"
[27]For the Lord Yahweh, the Commander of Angel Armies,
has an amazing strategy, and who can thwart him?
When he moves in power,[d] who can stop him?

God's Judgment of the Philistines

[28]This prophecy came to Isaiah in the year King Ahaz died:[e]

Don't rejoice too soon, you Philistines,[f]
just because the rod[g] that beat you is broken!
[29]A snake[h] will sprout from the root of that serpent,

---

a 14:23 The meaning of the Hebrew word *qippod* is uncertain. Some translate it as "hedgehog,"
"porcupine," or "owl."

b 14:24 Or "imagined it."

c 14:26 Or "the hand stretched out," a metaphor for God accomplishing by his power.

d 14:27 Or "When his hand is stretched out, who will turn it back?"

e 14:28 This prophecy was one of three that are dated in the book. See Isa. 6; 20:1–2.

f 14:28 The Hebrew meaning of *Philistines* is "those who roll in the dust." This becomes a picture of believers who are walking in the flesh (Gal. 5:16) and not living by the dynamic power of the Holy Spirit (Rom. 8:4).

g 14:28 The rod is a likely figure of speech for Ahaz, although some see it as a reference to Uzziah, the demise of the Davidic monarchy, or an Assyrian king.

h 14:29 The snake is possibly Ahaz's son, Hezekiah, who would be like a snake to the Philistines, ready to strike them.

and his descendant[a] will be like a flying, fiery burning one.[b]
[30]And through him the poorest of the poor will find pasture[c]
and the needy will lie down in peace.
The Lord will starve the root of the Philistines with a famine
that will annihilate your survivors.
[31]Wail, O gate! Cry out, O city! Melt with fear, Philistia!
For a cloud of smoke[d] comes out of the north,
and there is no straggler among them.[e]
[32]And what will be the answer of the messengers of the nations?
That the Lord has laid the foundation of Zion,[f]
and in her his needy ones will find shelter.[g]

The Lord's Judgment of Moab

15 Here is a prophecy concerning Moab:[h]

The *city of* Ar[i] was devastated, destroyed in the night.
The *city of* Kir[j] was devastated, destroyed in the night.
[2]The people of Dibon[k] went to their temple to weep;
they went up to their high places to lament.
Moab wails with sorrow over what happened
to Mount Nebo[l] and Mount Medeba.[m]
Humiliated, every head is shaved bald and every beard cut off.
[3]They *pour into the streets* wearing sackcloth.
In public and in private,[n] they fall down sobbing.

---

a 14:29 Or "firstfruit." The oldest commentaries and the Jewish Targums interpreted this last clause as a prophecy of the Messiah, who would be "like a fiery, burning one." The Targum states, "For from the sons of the son of Jesse shall the Messiah come forth and his deeds shall be among you as a deadly serpent" (Stenning, pp. 50–51). He will be more dangerous to the Philistines (a metaphor for the flesh) than any other king.

b 14:29 Or "seraph (burning one)." Some see the seraph as a type of fiery serpent, but the meaning of the Hebrew word *seraph* is clearly "a burning one." See Isa. 6:6.

c 14:30 Or "The firstborn (or firstfruits) of the poor will graze (in my pastures)." The "firstborn of the poor" is likely a figure of speech for "the poorest of the poor."

d 14:31 The Syriac is "a stout (brave, valiant) one."

e 14:31 The meaning of this Hebrew clause is uncertain. This seems to be a picture of an invading army; however, the Septuagint is "And there is nothing more they need to live."

f 14:32 See Ps. 118:22; Isa. 28:16; Matt. 21:42; Eph. 2:20; 1 Peter 2:6–7.

g 14:32 Or "Through him the humble will be saved" (LXX).

h 15:1 Moab ("seed of the father") was a descendant of Lot, conceived out of incest with his daughter (Gen. 19:31–37). The Moabites settled in a region east of the Dead Sea. This chapter shows the heart of the prophet Isaiah as he is painfully grieved over the sorrows coming to Moab. Ruth, a Moabite, had a role in forming the house of David, for she was his great-grandmother (Ruth 4:17–21).

i 15:1 See Num. 21:28.

j 15:1 Present-day Al-Kerak Jordan.

k 15:2 *Dibon*, present-day Dhiban Jordan, means "wasting."

l 15:2 *Nebo* means "prophet" or "scribe (interpreter)."

m 15:2 *Medeba* means "waters of peace (gently flowing)" and is present-day Madaba Jordan.

n 15:3 Or "on their roofs and in their town squares."

[4]The cities of Heshbon[a] and Elealah[b] cry out;
  their voices are heard as far away as Jahaz;[c]
  even the bravest warriors[d] of Moab are shaken to the core.
[5]My heart cries out for the people of Moab,
  for her fugitives who flee to Zoar[e] and to Eglath-shelishiyah.[f]
  Weeping, they climb the upward road to Luhith.[g]
  Their loud cries of anguish are heard
  all along the way to Horonaim.[h]
[6]The River Nimrim[i] has dried up; the grass has withered;
  new growth has failed, and vegetation has vanished.
[7]Therefore, the refugees take with them
  over the Wadi of the Willows
  their possessions and the wealth they have acquired.
[8]From one end of the land to the other, Moab is weeping;
  her wailing reaches to Eglaim[j] and Beer-Elim.[k]
[9]For the waters of Dimon[l] are full of blood,
  but I have something even worse in store for them:
  lions[m] for the fugitives of Moab
  and upon the remnant of the land![n]

A Plea for Mercy

16 Send a *flock of* lambs from the rock[o] of the desert
  as a gift to the leaders in Jerusalem,[p]
to the mountain of the Daughter of Zion.
[2]At the banks of the River Arnon, the women of Moab
  are like newly hatched, fluttering birds.
[3]They say, "Make a decision!
  Give us shelter.[q] Hide the fugitives. Don't betray them!

---

a 15:4 *Heshbon* means "intelligence" or "human reasoning."

b 15:4 *Elealeh* means "ascent of God" or "God has ascended."

c 15:4 *Jahaz* means "trampled on."

d 15:4 Or "prepared ones."

e 15:5 *Zoar* means "small" or "reduced." See Gen. 19:23.

f 15:5 *Eglath-shelishiyah* means "a three-year-old heifer."

g 15:5 *Luhith* means "polished" or "made of planks."

h 15:5 *Horonaim* means "double caves" or "two hollows."

i 15:6 *Nimrim* means "clear waters." Possibly present-day Wadi Numeira.

j 15:8 *Eglaim* means "double reservoir."

k 15:8 *Beer-Elim* means the "well of God" or "the well of the mighty ones."

l 15:9 Some manuscripts have "Dibon." *Dimon* means "consumed."

m 15:9 Or "Arabians" (LXX).

n 15:9 Or "the remnant of Admah" (LXX).

o 16:1 Or possibly a place in Edom (2 Kings 14:7) called *Sela*, which means "rock or cliff."

p 16:1 Or "Send a lamb of the lord of the land." This would have been a gift of tribute sent to secure Judah's protection.

q 16:3 Or "Make your shade like night at noon."

4Allow the Moabite fugitives to stay with you.
  Be a shelter for them from the destroyer!"
  One day the oppressor will be no more.
  The destroyer*a* will come to an end,
  and the tyrant will vanish from the land.
5Then a government of unfailing love*b* will be established,
  with a faithful king in the tabernacle of David,
  passionate for justice and swift to do what is right.

Moab's Demise

6We have heard about Moab's pride.
  How haughty he is—filled with arrogance and insolence,
  with nothing more than empty boasts!
7So now Moab will wail;
  everyone will wail over the ruin of their country.
  Lament and grieve for the foundations of Kir-Hareseth.*c*
8All the *lush* fields of Heshbon are dried up.
  The vineyards of Sibmah have struck down*d* the lords of nations,
  whose vines reached *northward* to Jazer*e*
  and spread to the desert.
  Their shoots spread out and extend across the *Dead* Sea.*f*
9So I weep along with Jazer over the vines of Sibmah.
  I drench you with my tears, O Heshbon and Elealeh,*g*
  for the shouts of joy over the harvest
  of fruit and grain have ceased.
10Joyful celebrations are stilled in the orchards;
  in the vineyards, no one sings or shouts,
  and no one treads out wine in the presses.
  I have silenced your gleeful shouts.
11Like harp strings, my heartstrings throb for Moab,*h*
  and my inner being sighs for your *broken* walls, Kir-Hareseth.*i*
12When Moab comes to their high places
  to plead with all their might
  and enter their temples to pray, it will have no effect.

---

a 16:4 Or "destruction."

b 16:5 Or "a throne," a metonymy for a king or government being established.

c 16:7 Or "over the raisin cakes (delicacies) of Kir-Hareseth (wall of earthen potsherds)" or "You shall care for those who dwell in Seth" (LXX).

d 16:8 "The lords of the nations have broken down its vines."

e 16:8 Modern Sumia, a suburb of Heshbon.

f 16:8 Moab's spreading, creeping vines of Heshbon ("stronghold") become a metaphor for the tentacles of pride that spread throughout the heart of man.

g 16:9 Elealeh is a city and means "a mighty one (God) ascends." See Num. 32:37.

h 16:11 Even for pride-filled Moab, God's heart was moved with compassion.

i 16:11 Or "for Kir-Hareseth (walls of earthen potsherds)."

[13]This was the word the Lord Yahweh spoke in the past about Moab, [14]but now the Lord Yahweh says, "In exactly three years,[a] the splendor of Moab and its huge population will shrink to nothing; only a small and feeble remnant will remain."

A Prophecy about Damascus

17 This is God's message for Damascus:

"Behold, Damascus is gone!
It is no longer a city, only a heap of rubble.
[2]Her ruins[b] will be abandoned—
left for flocks to lie down in with nothing to fear.
[3]Damascus will lose the power of its fortress,
and the strongholds of the northern kingdom[c] will disappear.
The remnant of Syria[d] will be like Israel—*stripped of its* glory,"
says the Lord Yahweh, Commander of Angel Armies.
[4]"On that day, the beautiful splendor of Jacob's *northern tribes*
will be brought low, and they will become like skin and bones.
[5]It will be as when a farmer harvests the standing grain
and gathers armloads of grain,
and as one gathers ears of grain in the Valley of Giants.[e]
[6]Yet some gleanings will remain,
as when an olive tree is shaken,[f]
leaving two or three olives in the highest branches[g]
and four or five on its fruitful branches,"[h]
declares Lord Yahweh, the God of Israel.

[7]In that day, people will gaze toward their Creator,[i]
and their eyes will look *in faith* toward the Holy One of Israel.
[8]They will not be infatuated with the religious altars
their own hands crafted,

---

a 16:14 Or "in three years as the years (counted by) of a hireling."

b 17:2 Or "the towns of Aroer." *Aroer* means "ruins."

c 17:3 Or "Ephraim."

d 17:3 Or "Aram."

e 17:5 Or "mighty men (Heb. *rephaim*)." Jesus' life within us will soon reap a harvest of glory (James 3:18). Armloads (sons and daughters of power) of grain (spiritual harvest) will be seen in coming days through mighty men and women.

f 17:6 Olives were harvested by shaking (Heb. "beating") the tree. See Heb. 12:26.

g 17:6 The Torah required farmers to leave some fruit behind for the poor and the stranger to glean. See Lev. 19:9–10. "Two or three" are sufficient for any need when they gather in agreement with Jesus. See Matt. 18:19–20. The uppermost branches point us to our heavenly life in the heavenly realm, "our glorious resurrection life" (Col. 3:1–5).

h 17:6 Or "on her boughs, the many-branched one." This points to the fruitful branches of Christ as he branches out through us and brings his fruit to the earth through yielded ones. See John 15:1–8. God appoints some to the "four or five" grace ministries appointed to "nurture and prepare all the holy believers" (Eph. 4:11–12).

i 17:7 Or "At that time, the Adam (James 1:22–25) will look toward the Creator."

nor by what their own fingers have made,[a]
nor with their sacred groves[b] or altars of incense.
[9]On that day their bustling cities will become deserted
like those conquered by the Israelites—
abandoned to thickets and undergrowth,
it will all become desolate.
[10]For you have ignored and forgotten the God who saves you
and have not remembered your Rock of Safety.[c]
So what do you do?
You cultivate your beautiful gardens and plant imported vines.
[11]Even if on the day you plant them they begin to grow,
and even if immediately you see them bud,
your harvest will wither away in a day of grief and agony.

The Uproar of the Nations

[12]Ah, the thunder of many people joining together![d]
They roar like the roar of the sea.
Woe to the uproar of the many nations!
They thunder like the crashing of ocean waves.
[13]The nations are roaring like the roar of a massive waterfall,
but when God rebukes them they disperse
like chaff on the mountains,
like a *tumbleweed* whirling in the wind.
[14]In the evening—behold, sudden terror!
Before the morning comes, they vanish!
Such is the fate of those who plunder and try to rob us.[e]

A Prophecy regarding Cush

18 Ah, the land of whirring wings,[f]
that is beyond the rivers of Cush,[g]
[2]sending their messengers by the way of the Nile
in papyrus vessels gliding on the water!
Go, you swift messengers,
to a tall, smooth-skinned people[h] feared far and wide,
to a mighty conquering nation whose land the rivers divide.[i]

---

a 17:8 See Acts 17:18–34.
b 17:8 Or "poles" or "goddesses (Heb. *asherim*)." Asherim (plural) have a specific pagan context of the Canaanite religions stretching back into Israel's history. See Ex. 34:13–14.
c 17:10 See Deut. 32:15.
d 17:12 That is, the armies of Assyria. See Ps. 2:1–3.
e 17:14 See John 10:10.
f 18:1 Or "locusts."
g 18:1 The Hebrew word *kuwsh* (Ethiopia, or modern-day Sudan) means "burned" or "darkened."
h 18:2 The meaning of this Hebrew clause is uncertain.
i 18:2 That is, the Upper Nile region. The land is divided by the White Nile and the Blue Nile rivers.

³Everyone everywhere, all who dwell on the earth,
  when a signal flag is raised on the mountain, take notice!
  When the shofar is blown, listen!
⁴Here is what the Lord Yahweh said to me:
  "I will rest calm and confident*ᵃ* as I look from my dwelling place,*ᵇ*
  serene as on a pleasant summer day*ᶜ*
  or a cool, refreshing cloud*ᵈ* in the heat of harvest."
⁵Before the harvest, when the bud is ripening
  and the flower finishes, he will take his pruning hooks
  and cut off the shoots and remove them.
⁶They will all be left for the birds of prey on the mountains
  and for the wild animals *to devour.*
  Birds will eat them throughout the summer,
  and the animals will *gnaw on the bones of the fallen* all winter.*ᵉ*
⁷At that time, a tall, smooth-skinned people will bring gifts of tribute*ᶠ*
  to the Lord Yahweh, Commander of Angel Armies.
  They are a people feared far and wide,
  a mighty conquering nation whose land the rivers divide.
  They will bring their gifts to Mount Zion,
  the place of the name of the Lord Yahweh,
  Commander of Angel Armies.

A Prophecy concerning Egypt

19 A prophecy concerning Egypt:*ᵍ*

Behold! The Lord Yahweh is riding on a swift-soaring cloud!*ʰ*
He is on his way to Egypt!
The god-idols of Egypt will tremble at his presence,*ⁱ*
and the hearts of the Egyptians will melt within them!

²"I will stir up *civil strife*
  and cause the Egyptians to fight against one another—
  one against the other, neighbor against neighbor,
  city against city, kingdom against kingdom.
³The spirit of the Egyptians will be in panic,
  and I will confuse*ʲ* their strategies.

---

a 18:4 See Isa. 57:20; 62:1; Heb. 3–4.
b 14:4 The body of Christ is now his dwelling place (Eph. 2:19–22).
c 18:4 The meaning of this Hebrew clause is uncertain.
d 18:4 See Isa. 19:1; 25:5; 44:22; 60:8.
e 18:6 Scripture often mention birds of prey and wild animals as symbols of demonic powers.
f 18:7 See Ps. 68:28–29; 76:11; Matt. 2:11.
g 19:1 Egypt is a recognized symbol of the world and its temptations and snares.
h 19:1 See Deut. 33:26; Ps. 18:9–11; 68:34; 104:3; Isa. 60:8. Clouds can be a metaphor for God's sons and daughters in glory.
i 19:1 See Heb. 12:26–29.
j 19:3 Or "swallow." The Hebrew homonym can mean either "confuse" or "swallow."

They will seek guidance from their idols
and by the spirits of the dead
and consult with mediums and wizards.
⁴I will give over the Egyptians into the hands of a cruel master;*ᵃ*
a brutal king will rule over them," says the sovereign God,
the Lord Yahweh, Commander of Angel Armies.

⁵The Nile delta*ᵇ* will dry up
and the riverbed will become parched and dry.
⁶Its canals will become stagnant and stink with rotting reeds,
and the streams of Egypt will dry up, from a trickle to nothing.
⁷All that is planted by the mouth of the river will dry up,*ᶜ*
and the fields along the brooks will wither
and turn to dust blown away by the wind.*ᵈ*
⁸Fishermen*ᵉ* will mourn. All who cast a fishhook into the river
and those who cast their nets will catch nothing.
⁹Those who make clothing from combed flax will despair,*ᶠ*
and the weavers of linen will be distressed.*ᵍ*
¹⁰The pillars of Egypt's foundations will be shattered
and every worker grieved.*ʰ*

The Wisdom of Egypt Is Foolishness to God
¹¹The elite of Zoan*ⁱ* are nothing but fools,
and the wisest of Pharaoh's counselors gives foolish advice.
How in the world can you say to Pharaoh,
"I am a brilliant sage and a descendant of the ancient kings"?*ʲ*
¹²Where, oh where, are all your sages?*ᵏ*
If they're so wise, let them discover and tell you
what the Lord Yahweh, Commander of Angel Armies,
has planned for Egypt.

---

a 19:4 Or "lords of severity"; that is, the king of Assyria.

b 19:5 Or "the waters of the sea." Waters could be viewed as an emblem of life-giving ministries.

c 19:7 "All that is planted" could point to the teaching of the Word, sown as seeds into hearts. See Matt. 13:19–23.

d 19:7 See Ps. 1:4.

e 19:8 Fishermen can be seen as evangelists. See Matt. 4:18–19.

f 19:9 Flax was arduously combed to produce linen.

g 19:9 Or "become (white) pale." See Isa. 38:12.

h 19:10 The foundations of worldliness (Egypt) will be broken off of our lives. See Ps. 11:3.

i 19:11 That is, her leaders. Zoan, one of the oldest cities in the world, is in lower Egypt, known by the Greeks as Tunis. *Zoan* means "the place of departure" or "depressed, low region." (See also v. 13.) In the fields of Zoan Moses worked miracles to prove to Pharaoh that God had sent him to demand the release of the Hebrews from their slavery.

j 19:11 Or "I am a son of a wise man and a descendent of the (wise) Kedemite kings."

k 19:12 See 1 Cor. 1:18–31.

¹³Zoan's elite have become utter fools;
  the nobles of Memphis are utterly deceived,
  and Egypt has been led astray by her tribal chiefs.ᵃ
¹⁴The Lord Yahweh has mixed up their minds
  and poured into them a distorted spirit
  that will make Egypt dizzy and act like a drunk
  who staggers around in his own vomit.
¹⁵There is nothing anyone in Egypt can do—
  neither head nor tail,ᵇ nor anyone of high or low position.ᶜ

¹⁶In that day, the Egyptians will become like women who tremble in fearᵈ because the Lord Yahweh, Commander of Angel Armies, shakes his fistᵉ at them. ¹⁷The land of Judah will become the dread of the Egyptians. They will quake whenever anybody even mentions it to them, because of what the Lord Yahweh, Commander of Angel Armies, has in store for them!

Divine Grace for Egypt

¹⁸In that day, there will be fiveᶠ Egyptian cities that speak the language of Canaanᵍ and swear their allegiance to the Lord Yahweh, Commander of Angel Armies, and oneʰ will be called the City of the Sun.ⁱ

  ¹⁹In that day, there will be an altar to the Lord Yahweh in the middle of Egypt and a sacred monument to honor him on its border.ʲ ²⁰It will be a sign and a visible reminder in the land of Egypt of the Lord Yahweh, Commander of Angel

---

a 19:13 Or "cornerstones," a metaphor for Egypt's rulers. Egypt was known for its wisdom, but the wisdom of this world (Egypt) has been found empty and vain. Christ is our wisdom (1 Cor. 1:30).

b 19:15 The head represents leaders; the tail, lying prophets. See Isa. 9:14–15.

c 19:15 Or "palm branch or reed," a metaphor for the "strong or the weak, high or low."

d 19:16 See Heb. 12:26–29.

e 19:16 Or "hand." The hand with its five fingers can be a metaphor for the five-fold ministry (Eph. 4:11).

f 19:18 Possibly a figurative number (i.e., the five senses).

g 19:18 That is, they will speak the language (Heb. "lip") of the people of God—a language of hope, not despair; of love, not hatred; a spiritual language of all that is sacred and holy. See Isa. 50:4; Zeph. 3:9. The Hebrew word for Canaan means "to be humbled" or "to bend the knee." The language of Canaan would be the language of humility.

h 19:18 Or "each one."

i 19:18 Most Hebrew manuscripts have "the City of Destruction," but the Dead Sea scroll 1QIsaᵃ and a few medieval Hebrew manuscripts, along with the Targum and Vulgate, have "the City of the Sun (Hierapolis)." The other four Egyptian cities could be Leontopolis, Daphne, Migdol, and Memphis.

j 19:19 There has been conjecture that this pillar (memorial) may be the great pyramid in Egypt and might have been built by Job (Egyptian name Cheops). Job was a grandson of Jacob and a nephew of Joseph, who went into Egypt with the Israelites. He is mentioned in Gen. 46:13 and 1 Chron. 7:1 as Jashub or, in the Masoretic text, Job. Others view this as a future monument built to glorify God.

Armies. And they will cry out to him when they are oppressed, he will send a mighty deliverer*a* and champion to their rescue!*b*

²¹The Lord Yahweh will reveal to them who he really is, and the Egyptians will know him *intimately*. They will worship him with sacrifices and burnt offerings. They will make vows to the Lord Yahweh, and they will keep them.*c*

²²The Lord Yahweh will wound the Egyptians, but *when they turn back to him*, he will heal them. *Yes*, the Lord Yahweh will listen to their hearts' cry, and he will heal and restore them.

²³In that day there will be a highway all the way from Egypt to Assyria.*d* *Like long-lost brothers*, the Egyptians and the Assyrians will be joined together and they will worship and serve the Lord Yahweh! And in that day, Israel will become the third partner with Egypt and Assyria as a blessing to all the earth. For the Lord Yahweh, Commander of Angel Armies, will bless them, saying, "Blessed be Egypt, my people! Blessed be Assyria, my handiwork! And blessed be Israel, my inheritance!"

A Prophecy concerning Egypt and Cush

20 In the year that the Assyrian king Sargon*e* sent his supreme commander to attack Ashdod, he came and captured it.*f* ²At that time the Lord Yahweh said to Isaiah, the son of Amoz, "Take off your clothes*g* and sandals." Isaiah did as he was told and walked about naked and barefoot.*h*

³Then the Lord Yahweh said, "Just as my servant Isaiah has walked naked and barefoot for three years*i* as a prophetic sign and a wonder as a warning of what is coming to Egypt and Cush, ⁴so will the king of Assyria lead away the captives of Egypt and Cush, both young and old. They will be stripped and barefoot, with buttocks bared, to publicly humiliate Egypt. ⁵And those who put their hope in 'glorious Cush' and 'mighty Egypt,' will be shattered and totally ashamed."

⁶When that day comes, those who live on the coastal region *of Philistia* will say, "Oh no! If this is what happened to those we hoped would come and rescue us from the Assyrian king, what chance do we have of escape?"

---

a 19:20 Or "savior."

b 19:20 If God responds to the prayers of the "Egyptians" (worldly people), how much more will he rescue his own people? See James 4:10; 2 Chron. 6:32–33.

c 19:21 In response to the plagues (Ex. 7–10), Pharaoh promised to let the children of Israel go but then took back that promise. Isaiah proclaims that this spirit of broken promises will be broken off Egypt.

d 19:23 The ancient Assyrian empire would include parts of northern Iraq, northwestern Iran, and southeastern Turkey.

e 20:1 *Sargon* means "sun prince." He was the father of Sennacherib.

f 20:1 *Ashdod* means "stronghold, fortress," or "oppressor."

g 20:2 Or "sackcloth," a coarse, durable fabric used mainly to make sacks for carrying goods on the backs of animals but sometimes worn during fasts or by prophets.

h 20:2 This is the only symbolic action recorded about Isaiah. He became a walking parable. Scholars are divided over whether Isaiah was completely or partially nude. See 2 Sam. 6:20; Mic. 1:8.

i 20:3 Isaiah's three-year ministry of walking about in loincloth is a type of the ministry of Jesus, who did as he was told by his Father (John 5:19).

A Prophecy concerning Babylon

21 Here is a prophecy concerning *Babylon*, the Desert by the Sea:[a]

As whirlwinds rushing in from the southland,
an invader[b] comes in from the desert, from a land to be feared.
[2]A terrifying revelation has been given to me:
The betrayer betrays; the destroyer destroys.
Arise, you Elamites![c] Lay siege you Medes![d]
I will put an end
to all the grief she brought *to the nations.*
[3]There's a churning deep inside me,
like labor pains of a woman about to give birth.
I'm too anguished by what I hear
and too frightened by what I see.[e]
[4]My mind is reeling; I'm filled with panic.
I longed for twilight, but now I tremble through the night.[f]
[5]*I see them* prepare the table and spread their rugs,
then they eat and they drink.[g]
Get up, you military officers! Anoint your shields[h] for battle!

[6]For this is what the Lord said to me:

"Go post a sentry and have him report what he sees.
[7]When he sees them come with chariots
and advancing warriors riding on horses, donkeys, and camels,
let him be alert—extremely alert!"
[8]Then the sentry cries out,[i]
"I continually stand on this watchtower day after day
for you, O Lord.
I'm stationed at my post throughout the night.[j]

---

a 21:1 That is, by the Persian Gulf.

b 21:1 Or "disaster."

c 21:2 Elam ("hidden, concealed") is the modern-day coastal area of Iran. Media ("middle-land") is the north-central region of Iran. Both regions made up a major portion of the Persian empire, which destroyed Babylon in 539.

d 21:2 It is as though God is commanding Babylon's enemies to betray and destroy her. This prophecy was given to Isaiah two hundred years before it took place.

e 21:3 Or "too anguished to hear, too frightened to see."

f 21:4 The wording of vv. 3–4 seems to indicate that Isaiah is brought into a state of prophetic ecstasy as he shook under the intensity of the weight of the prophetic utterance. See Scott, *Vestus Testamentum 2*, 1952, 278–282.

g 21:5 It's as though Isaiah sees prophetically into the room where Belshazzar is feasting, and Belshazzar has no clue his fall is imminent (Dan. 5).

h 21:5 Or "Oil your shields."

i 21:8 Or "He cried out, 'A lion!'" See Rev. 5:5.

j 21:8 The New Testament ministry of a "watchman" is an intercessor. It is important that every church and every city has intercessors *to stand on this watchtower day after day.*

⁹Look! Someone's coming!
It's a man in a chariot with a team of horses.
He shouts out, 'Fallen, fallen, Babylon has fallen!
All the idols of their gods lie shattered on the ground!'"

¹⁰My people, lying crushed on the threshing floor,
I declare to you what I have heard from the God of Israel,
Yahweh, the Commander of Angel Armies.

A Prophecy concerning Dumah (Edom)
¹¹Here is a prophecy about Dumah:*a*

Someone keeps calling me from the land of Edom,*b* saying,
"Watchman, how much longer is the night?
Watchman, how much longer is the night?"
¹²The watchman answers,
"Morning comes, but *a dark* night endures.*c*
If you want to ask again,*d* then come back and ask."

A Prophecy Concerning Arabia
¹³A prophecy concerning Arabia:

You caravans from Dedan,
you will camp among the thickets in the desert land of Arabia.*e*
¹⁴People of Tema,*f* come and bring water to the thirsty
and bread for the fugitives.
¹⁵For they have fled from the battle, from the drawn swords,
from the bent bows, and from the weight of warfare.
¹⁶This is what the Sovereign God said to me:
"Within exactly one year,*g*
all the splendor of Kedar*h* will end.

---

a 21:11 Dumah is a location in northern Arabia and is a poetic term for Edom, an ancient kingdom situated south of the Dead Sea. *Dumah* means "stillness (of death)" and was the land of Esau's descendants. See also Gen. 32:3; Num. 24:18. The Hebrew root word for Edom is "Adam."

b 21:11 Or "Seir," a mountain in Edom. This is another name for the land inhabited by the Edomites. *Seir* means "hairy goat, faun, satyr" and is found thirty-nine times in the Old Testament.

c 21:12 Or "Morning (a new day) is coming, but so is night (judgment)."

d 21:12 Or "Turn (repent), then come back and ask again."

e 21:13 That is, they will be forced off the beaten path to hide from the invading Assyrians. The Dedanites were merchants who shipped their goods to Tyre (Phoenicia). *Arabia*, or "the land of Arabs," means "sterility, darkened, intermixed, stranger, barren, or wild." Arabia is mentioned six times in the Old Testament. See also Gal. 1:17.

f 21:14 Tema was a descendant of Abraham (1 Chron. 1:28–30). Tema (modern-day Tayma) is also a city in northern Saudi Arabia. *Tema* means "sunny, good fortune, prosperity."

g 21:16 Or "Within one year according to the years of a hired worker."

h 21:16 *Kedar*, a son of Ishmael, means "dark skinned." Kedar's descendants settled in the Arabian desert. Kedar is likely a metonymy for northern Arabia.

[17]And all the weapons left of Kedar's warriors will be few,
for the Lord Yahweh, the God of Israel, has spoken."

A Prophecy concerning Jerusalem

22 A prophecy concerning "The Valley of Vision":[a]

What's happening with you?
Why have you all gone up to the rooftops?
[2]The whole city is in an uproar.
What's happened to the once happy, bustling city?[b]
The bodies of the slain *litter your streets.*
They were not slain by the sword on the battlefield
but executed.
[3]All your leaders have fled far away,
and those who were found were taken captive—
before they even shot a single arrow.[c]
[4]That is why I said,
"Leave me alone to weep my bitter tears.
Don't even try to comfort me
concerning my beloved people[d] being destroyed."

[5]The Lord Yahweh, Commander of Angel Armies,
has a day in store—a day of tumult, trampling,
and terror in the "Valley of Vision."[e]
It is a day when they breach the walls[f]
and the people cry out to the mountain *of holiness.*[g]
[6]*The soldiers of* Elam attacked with chariots and cavalry,
armed with bows and arrows.
The troops of Kir advanced with shields ready.
[7]Your lush valleys were full of chariots,
and the horsemen took their stand at your gates.
[8]He removed his protection from Judah.[h]
In that day, you looked for additional weapons
from the storehouse of the Forest *of Lebanon.*[i]

---

a 22:1 Although Isaiah frequently refers to Jerusalem as a mountain (Mount Zion), he now sees it as a valley, from which nothing can be seen. See Jer. 7:31–34; 21:13. Jerusalem is both on a hill and surrounded by hills. The valley of vision is where Yahweh imparts revelation.

b 22:2 See Ps. 48:1–2.

c 22:3 Or "They were taken without their bows" or "The mighty ones among you fled away" (LXX).

d 22:4 Or "the young women (daughter) of my people," a metaphor to show how Isaiah loved the people of Jerusalem.

e 22:5 Or "the valley of Zion" (LXX).

f 22:5 The Hebrew of this clause is uncertain. It can also be translated "The people shout."

g 22:5 The word *hill* is singular and refers to the Temple Mount, the hill of holiness.

h 22:8 Or "He (the invading army) has taken away Judah's covering."

i 22:8 Or "the House of the Forest," likely a royal armory mentioned in 1 Kings 10:17. A forest is often a metaphor for humanity. See Song. 2:3; Isa. 55:12.

⁹You discovered the many breaches in the City of David,
  and you collected water in the lower pool.ᵃ
¹⁰You inspected the houses in Jerusalem
  and tore some down to fortify the wall.
¹¹You built a reservoirᵇ between the two walls in the city
  to conserve water flowing down from the old pool,
  but you gave no thought to the one who made it.
  You did not trust in the one who formed it long ago!

¹²In that day, the Lord Yahweh, Commander of Angel Armies,
  called you to *repent* with weeping and mourning
  and to *show your remorse* by shaving your heads
  and wearing sackcloth.
¹³But instead, you celebrated with joy and festivity,
  slaughtering the sheep and the fatted ox, saying,
  "We will feast on meat and drink much wine.
  Eat and drink, for tomorrow we die."ᶜ
¹⁴Revealed in my ears are the words of the Lord Yahweh,
  Commander of Angel Armies:
  "Until your dying day, certainly I will not forgive this sin."ᵈ

Denunciation of Self-serving Officials

¹⁵This is what the Lord Yahweh, the Commander of Angel Armies, has to say:

"Go to Shebna, the treasurerᵉ of the palace, and say to him, ¹⁶"What right do you have to be here, and who gave you permission? And why do you chisel out a tomb for yourself here, carving out your *royal* burial place, a dwelling place in the rock?ᶠ ¹⁷Watch out, O strong man, for the Lord is about to seize you and hurl you down. ¹⁸He will sling you around and aroundᵍ and throw you like a ball into a distant, barren land. There you will die, and all your splendid chariots will lie

---

a 22:9 Possibly the Pool of Siloam.

b 22:11 Or "mikveh," a pool for an immersion ritual offering repentance and consecration. *Mikveh* can also be translated "ditch," perhaps suggesting Hezekiah's tunnel.

c 22:13 See 1 Cor.15:32.

d 22:14 See 2 Kings 24:3–4.

e 22:15 The meaning of the Hebrew word *sōḵēn* (a hapax legomenon) is uncertain, although most scholars view it as a word for a high government official in Hezekiah's court, like a comptroller or perhaps a treasurer. In 2 Kings 18:18 Shebna is mentioned as the king's scribe or secretary. The name Shebna means "one who rests himself" or "one who is captive." Shebna becomes a picture of the Adam-life (the spirit of anti-Christ) that seeks self-promotion. But God will replace our "Shebna" with Eliakim (the Christ-life within us). This principle of replacement is found throughout the Scriptures (Isaac for Ishmael, David for Saul, Esther for Vashti, Samuel for Eli, Matthias for Judas, etc.).

f 22:16 This elevated cliff may have been on the other side of the Kidron Valley, where the village of Silwan is now situated. Many rock-cut tombs have been discovered there. It appears that Shebna hewing out his tomb on a cliff was a gross display of self-promotion.

g 22:18 Or "I will wind you up over and over like a headdress (turban)."

there *in the dust*. You are a disgrace to your master's house! ¹⁹I will kick you out of office and pull you down from your high position!'

²⁰"On that day, I will appoint my servant Eliakim,ᵃ son of Hilkiah,ᵇ *to take your place*. ²¹I will *honor him* by clothing him with your robe and binding your priestly sash upon him. I will transfer your authority into his hands, and he will be a fatherᶜ to those living in Jerusalem and to the people of Judah. ²²I will place upon his shoulders the key *to the treasures* of David's palace. He will open doors that no one can shut, and he will shut doors that no one can open.ᵈ ²³I will strike a blow to him as a nailᵉ in a secureᶠ place, and he will be a glorious throne of honor for his father's house.ᵍ ²⁴All the glory of his father's house they will fasten to him, including offspring and branches *that will trust in him*.ʰ Every vessel, jar, and bowl, both small and great, will be fastened to him.

²⁵"And in that day," declares the Lord Yahweh, Commander of Angel Armies, "the nail fastened in a secure place will give way and be cut off and fall. And all the load hanging on it will fall off." The Lord Yahweh has spoken.ⁱ

A Prophecy concerning Tyre and Sidon

23 A prophecy for Tyre and *Sidon*:

Wail, you cargo ships of Tarshish!ʲ
For *Tyre*,ᵏ *your port city*, has fallen without a house or a harbor!
Word has come to them from the land of Cyprus.

---

a 22:20 *Eliakim* means "raised up by God," and he becomes a picture of the Lord Jesus, who was raised up by the power of God to rule over God's house. It is possible that Eliakim was the high priest. The Hebrew text uses priestly terms for his clothing and sash. See Rev. 1:13.

b 22:20 There was a high priest named Hilkiah who could be the Hilkiah mentioned here as father of Eliakim. *Hilkiah* means "my portion is Yahweh." See 2 Kings 22:4.

c 22:21 As a father, Eliakim (Jesus) cares for, provides for, and loves his people. See Isa. 9:6–7.

d 22:22 See Rev. 3:7. Eliakim (a picture of Jesus) is to have unlimited control. The doors he opens (looses) are doors of revelation, treasures, favor, and opportunity. When he closes (binds) those doors, no amount of human striving can open them.

e 22:23 The Hebrew word *yathed* can be translated as either peg or nail.

f 22:23 The Hebrew word *'aman* is most frequently translated "believe." It is also a form of our word *amen*. God fastened Jesus on the cross, the sinner's place of security, so that we would believe in him.

g 22:23 We are now seated with Christ as part of his Father's house (sons and daughters). See Eph. 2:6; Rev. 3:21.

h 22:24 Or "leaves" or "everyone small or great" (LXX). The Hebrew is uncertain.

i 22:25 That is, the Lord has decreed that even Eliakim's authority and prominence will one day be cut off. Human authority is always temporary.

j 23:1 Tarshish refers most likely to the city of Tartessus, Spain, on the Guadalquivir River. Archaeological evidence suggests it may have been near present-day Sevilla.

k 23:1 *Tyre* means "rock, compressed, pressed together." Tyre, a Phoenician port on the Mediterranean, was once a symbol of power on the sea and a world capital of commerce. It was known as wealthy, influential, and evil. Now it is a small village known as Sur. Isaiah used it as a metaphor for commerce and trafficking.

²Be silent, you inhabitants of the coast
  and you merchants of Sidon,ᵃ once thronged by seafarers.
³On the great waters your revenue
  was the grain from the Nile basin.ᵇ
  The harvest of the Nile was your revenue.
  You were merchants who traded with the nations.
⁴Sidon, be ashamed,
  for the sea, the stronghold of the sea, declares,
  "I have never gone into labor to give birth to children,
  nor have I raised up sons or daughters."ᶜ
⁵When the Egyptians hear it, they will be stunned
  over the destruction of Tyre.
⁶Cross over to Tarshish.
  Wail, you inhabitants of the coast.
⁷Is this your once boisterous city, founded so long ago?
  Is this the city that once sent settlers over the sea?

⁸Who has planned this for imperial Tyre, who once wore her crown?
  Your merchants were nobles,
  and your traders were honored by the world.
⁹Yahweh, the Commander of Angel Armies, has planned it!
  His plan is to eliminateᵈ the pride of your *presumed* splendor
  and to humiliate the honored of the world.
¹⁰Daughter Tarshish, cross overᵉ your land
  as one crosses the Nile,
  for there is no more harbor marketplace.ᶠ
¹¹Yahweh has stretched out his hand over the sea *of humanity*
  and has shaken the kingdoms of this world.
  He has given his command to destroy Phoenicia'sᵍ fortresses.
¹²He said, "Fair Sidon, the oppressed one,
  your celebrating is over.
  Rise and cross over to Cyprus;
  even there you will find no rest."

¹³Behold the land of the Babylonians.
  They are a people who have lost their identity.

---

a 23:2 *Sidon*, a coastal town in Lebanon, means "one who lies in wait, to hunt, to trap."

b 23:3 Or "Sihor," a tributary of the Nile, which means "to wipe out, uproot."

c 23:4 In this cryptic verse, it appears that Tyre is given the name "sea, the stronghold of the sea." With poetic impact, the sea is personified and speaks of being childless. There are churches today that are "childless" (without evangelism outreach) and don't "raise up sons and daughters" (training and equipping them for ministry).

d 23:9 Or "pollute, defile."

e 23:10 Or "farm your land."

f 23:10 Or "waistband." The Hebrew of this verse is uncertain.

g 23:11 Or "He has given his command to Canaan to destroy its fortresses."

The Assyrians have made it a home for wild animals.
They erected siege towers against it,
demolished her palaces,
and made it a heap of ruins.
[14]Wail, you merchant ships of Tarshish,
for your fortress is destroyed.

[15]In that day, Tyre will remain forgotten for seventy years, equal to the life span of a king. After seventy years, it will happen to Tyre as in the song about the prostitute:

[16]Take a harp and go about the city,
you prostitute long forgotten.
Make your sweet melody and sing many songs
so that you will be remembered again.

[17]At the end of seventy years, the Lord Yahweh will restore Tyre, but she will return to her trade. She will prostitute herself again with every kingdom of the world. [18]But her merchandise and earnings will be set apart as holy to the Lord Yahweh. They will neither be stored nor hoarded, but they will supply abundant[a] food and splendid garments for those who live in the presence of the Lord Yahweh![b]

Isaiah's Apocalypse[c]

24 Behold! The Lord Yahweh is about to devastate the earth
and make it desolate.
He will mar its surface and scatter the inhabitants.
[2]Everyone will experience the same fate—
priests and people, masters and slaves,
their maids and mistresses, buyers and sellers,
lenders and borrowers, rich and poor.[d]
[3]The earth will be utterly devastated and ruined,
for the Lord Yahweh has spoken this word!

[4]The ground itself mourns[e] and withers;
the soil languishes over the sins of its people,
and the wealthy elite wither and languish.
[5]The people have polluted the earth beneath their feet
by disobeying laws, violating truth,[f]

---

a 23:18 See John 10:10; 3 John 2.

b 23.18 Or "for those on whom Yahweh's face shines." Or "for those who live before Yahweh's face."

c Isaiah 24–27 is known as Isaiah's Apocalypse because it contains eschatological prophecies that are also found in the book of Revelation.

d 24:2 Or "debtor and creditor." See Rev. 6:15.

e 24:4 The Hebrew homonym can mean the ground "mourns (over the sin of its inhabitants)" or "dries up (with drought)." This is a powerful play on words in the Hebrew.

f 24:5 Or "moved past statutes." See Mal. 2:5–7.

and breaking the ancient, everlasting covenant.*a*
[6]Therefore a curse devours the earth;
 its people suffer under their guilt,
 causing earth's inhabitants to dwindle,*b*
 and their number is reduced to so few.
[7]The new wine dries up, the vine withers,
 and all the party-goers groan *with disappointment.*
[8]The joyful mirth of the tambourines is stilled,
 the jubilant noise of the revelers is ended,
 and the happy sound of the harp falls silent.
[9]No more wine and song!
 Hard liquor has become bitter to those who drink it.
[10]The city lies in chaos, and no one can enter.
[11]Riots break out because there is no wine.
 The sun has set on their gladness and joy;
 celebrations have disappeared from the earth.
[12]The city is left desolate with its gates battered down.
[13]As an olive tree is shaken clean of its olives
 and a grapevine picked clean of its grapes,
 so will be the fate of the nations.

The Song of the Remnant
[14]*The remnant*c lifts up its voice with a joyful shout.
 From the west they praise the majesty of the Lord Yahweh,
[15]and in the east*d* they give glory to the Lord God!
 The coastlands magnify the name of Yahweh,
 the Lord God of Israel!
[16]From all over the world we hear their songs of praise—
 songs of glory and beauty to the Righteous One!
 But I said, "I *feel I'm* wasting away.
 I'm doomed; I'm wasting away."
 With deception, deceivers deceive!
 With treachery, the treacherous betray!*e*
[17]Terror, pit, and trap are waiting for you, inhabitants of the earth.
[18]The one who flees from the report of terror will fall into the pit.
 And whoever crawls out of the pit will be caught by the trap.
 Heaven's floodgates opened and earth's foundations tremble.

---

a 24:5 See Rom. 1.

b 24:6 Or "were burned up." The Hebrew homonym *kharah* can mean "to diminish" or "to burn."

c 24:14 Or "they." Vv. 14–16 are some of the more difficult verses to translate in Isaiah due to a number of textual variants.

d 24:15 Or "in the lights (fires)," a possible metaphor for the sunrise (the east).

e 24:16 These lines contain a notable wordplay, using five Hebrew words with the identical triliteral root, *bgd.*

[19] The earth is breaking, breaking!
  The earth is crumbling, crumbling!
  The earth is tottering, tottering!
[20] The earth staggers like a drunkard,
  as a hut sways *in a storm.*
  Its sin lies heavy upon it; it falls to rise no more.

The Lord Almighty Will Reign

[21] In that day, the Lord Yahweh will punish heaven's host[a]
  and the kings of the earth.
[22] They will be gathered together
  and locked up in a prison like prisoners in a pit,
  and after many days, they will be punished.[b]
[23] Then the sun and moon will hang their heads in shame,
  for Yahweh, Commander of Angel Armies, will reign![c]
  He will manifest his glory on Mount Zion in Jerusalem,
  before all her elders!

Song of God's Faithfulness

25 Lord Yahweh, you are my *glorious* God!
  I will exalt you and praise your name forever,
  for you have done so many wonderful things.
  Well-thought-out plans you formed in ages past;
  you've been faithful and true to fulfill them all!
[2] The city that was once mighty[d]
  you've turned into a heap of rubble;
  the fortified city now lies in ruins.
  The foreigner's fortress is no more and will never be rebuilt.
[3] Therefore, superpower nations will glorify you
  and the cities of terrorist nations will revere you.
[4] You have been a fortress-protector for the poor,
  a mighty stronghold for the needy in their distress,
  a shelter from the sudden storm,
  and a shade from the shimmering heat of the day.
  For the fury of tyrants
  was like a winter windstorm battering against the wall,
[5] and like the heat of a drought in a desert land;
  but you subdued the heat under the shade of clouds.
  You alone silence the song of tyrants.

---

a 24:21 In this context, heaven's host becomes a figure of speech for dark powers that operate in rebellion to God. See Eph. 6:10–14; Col. 2:14–15.

b 24:22 Or "They will be remembered."

c 24:23 When God is unveiled in his glory-light, the sun and moon are nothing compared to him.

d 25:2 That is, Babylon. See Jer. 50–52; Rev. 17–18.

The Rich Feast of the Lord

⁶The Lord Yahweh, Commander of Angel Armies,
 will host a rich feast on this mountain[a] for all peoples—
 a feast with plenty of meat and well-aged wine,
 with an abundance of food and the finest of wine.
⁷And on this mountain, he will destroy the shroud[b]
 wrapped around all the people, the veil spread over all nations.
⁸It is *the gloom of* death![c]
He will swallow it up in victory forever![d]
And God, Lord Yahweh, will wipe away
 every tear from every face.[e]
He will remove every trace of disgrace
 that his people have suffered throughout the world,
 for the Lord Yahweh has promised it!
⁹In that day they will say,
 "Behold! This is our God!
We've waited[f] for him, and he saved us!
This one, the Lord Yahweh—he is worth the wait![g]
We will keep shouting with joy
 as we find our bliss in his salvation-kiss!"

¹⁰The *mighty, gracious* hand of the Lord Yahweh
 will rest upon this mountain,
 but the Moabites will be trampled under his feet
 as straw gets trampled into the manure.[h]
¹¹They will stretch out their arms in it
 like a swimmer stretches out his arms to swim,

---

a 25:6 That is, the Zion-realm, the higher realm of glory that is offered to the church. We have already come to the top of this mountain! This feast is the love-feast and the fellowship with Christ that we experience in the family of God. See Ps. 36:8; 63:5; Isa. 55:1–2; Heb. 12:2–24. The seven significant mountains in the Bible are Moriah, Sinai, Gerizim, Nebo, Carmel, Calvary, and Zion.

b 25:7 Or "the face of the shroud."

c 25:8 The gloom of death is like a shroud over every life. The curse of death is defeated in Christ so that all may come to the rich, joyous feast of the Lord. See 1 Cor. 15:54–56.

d 25:8 The Hebrew word *netsach* can mean "victory" or "forever." The translation includes both concepts. *Netsach* comes from a root word that means "to glitter from afar, to excel." Jesus' death, burial, resurrection, and ascension have brought an endless victory, endless life, and the conquest of every enemy. Now he waits for his sons and daughters to arise and become the second witness to his eternal victory. See Rom. 8:19–21; 2 Cor. 13:1; Heb. 2:6–13.

e 25:8 See Rev. 21:4.

f 25:9 The Hebrew word *qavah* (the root word for "rope") means "to wait, to entwine." Waiting on God means binding and connecting our hearts to who God is and to his promise. The Hebrew concept of waiting on the Lord is never a passive thing but active, full of expectation.

g 25:9 Or "We waited for him!"

h 25:10 Or "as straw is trampled down at Madmenah (a village outside Jerusalem)." Madmenah can also be translated "dung heap." See Isa. 10:31.

yet God will bring down their pride,
and they will thrash and sink despite their struggle.[a]
[12]He will tear down the high walls of Moab's fortresses
and flatten them into the dust.

Song of Judah's Triumph

26 A day is coming when this song will be sung in the land of Judah:

"The city is a stronghold for us!
The Lord's salvation,[b] like inner and outer walls,
makes it secure.
[2]Open the gates and let a righteous,
faith-filled people enter in.
[3]Perfect, absolute peace surrounds[c] those
whose imaginations[d] are consumed with you;
they confidently trust in you.
[4]Yes, trust in the Lord Yahweh forever and ever!
For Yah, the Lord God, is your Rock of Ages![e]
[5]He knocks down the high and mighty,
and the lofty city he humbles and levels down to the dust,
[6]to be trampled down by the feet of the poor and exploited."

[7]The path of the righteous is smooth and level;
God, the Just One, you make a clear path for them.
[8]Yes, we will follow your ways, Lord Yahweh,
and entwine our hearts with yours,[f]
for the fame of your name is all that we desire.
[9]At night I yearn for you with all my heart;
in the morning my spirit reaches out to you.

---

a 25:11 The Hebrew of this clause is uncertain.

b 26:1 The Lord's salvation is the Hebrew word yâshuw'ah, almost identical to Yeshua. Jesus is our salvation that saves us and delivers us inside and out.

c 26:3 Or "watches over."

d 26:3 Or "steadfast mind." The Hebrew is yêtser. According to the Brown-Driver-Briggs Hebrew Lexicon, the Hebrew word yêtser means "imagination" that forms and frames up. Imagination frames up one's reality. It is unfortunate that many today have rejected the God-created imagination that each of us possesses. Our imagination must be set apart for God and continually made holy. The imagination, both good and evil, is a frequent concept in the Bible. The Hebrew word yêtser is found nine times in the Old Testament (Gen. 6:5; 8:21; Deut. 31:21; 1 Chron. 28:9; 29:18; Ps. 103:14; Isa. 26:3; 29:16; Hab. 2:18).

e 26:4 The concept of God being our Rock speaks of the enduring protection, safety, and security we have in him. We plant our feet on the Rock and find boldness and confidence. Throughout every age and season of our lives, God remains our faithful Rock of all Ages.

f 26:8 The Hebrew word qavah (the root word for "rope") means "to wait, to entwine." Waiting on God means binding and connecting our hearts to who God is and to his promise. The Hebrew concept of waiting on the Lord is never a passive thing but active, full of hope and expectation.

When you display your judgments on the earth,
people learn *the ways of* righteousness.
¹⁰But when mercy is shown to scoundrels,
they still aren't able to learn righteousness.
Even in a land of integrity, they still do wrong,
for they ignore the great majesty of the Lord Yahweh.
¹¹Lord Yahweh, you lift your mighty hand,
but they do not see it.
Let them witness how much you love your people
and be ashamed.
Let the fire reserved for your enemies consume them.
¹²Lord Yahweh, you will establish peace and prosperity for us,
for all we have accomplished is the result
of what you work through us.
¹³Lord Yahweh, our God, other lords have ruled over us,
but we praise your name alone.
¹⁴Their dead don't come back to life; their ghosts do not rise.
For you have punished and destroyed them,
wiping out even the memory of them.
¹⁵You have made our nation grow!
Lord Yahweh, you have made our nation grow;
you have revealed your glory,
and you have extended all the borders of the land.
¹⁶Lord Yahweh, in their distress, they reached out to you.
When you chastened them, they poured out prayer to you.
¹⁷Lord Yahweh,
we were like a pregnant woman going into labor pains—
writhing, screaming, and ready to deliver, all because of you.
¹⁸We were full term.
We pushed and strained, but we gave birth only to wind!
We accomplished nothing
and have not brought deliverance*ᵃ* into the world,*ᵇ*
nor its inhabitants new life.*ᶜ*
¹⁹But your dead will live again!
Their bodies will rise from the dead!
It's time to awaken and sing for joy, you dwellers in the dust!
As the glistening, radiant dew refreshes the earth,*ᵈ*
so the Lord will awaken those dwelling among the dead.
²⁰Go, my people, into your inner chambers
and close the doors behind you.

---

a 26:18 Or "salvation" or "victory."
b 26:18 See Rom. 8:19–21.
c 26:18 "its inhabitants have not fallen out," an idiom for birthing or bringing to life.
d 26:19 See Ps. 110:3.

Hide for a little while, until his indignation[a] is over.
²¹For the Lord is coming out from his *heavenly* place
to punish people for their sins.
The earth itself will expose the blood spilled upon it,
and the ground will no longer hide its slain.

Israel's Redemption

27 In that day, the Lord Yahweh
will mercilessly wield his massive, mighty sword
and punish Leviathan, the swift, slithering serpent.
He will slay the dragon of the sea—[b]
Leviathan, the twisting serpent.[c]
²In that day, they will sing the song "The Vineyard of Delight."

³"I, the Lord, watch over my vineyard of delight.
Moment by moment, I water it *in love*
and protect it day and night.
⁴There is no anger in me,
for if I found briars and thorns
I would burn them up and march to battle against them.
⁵So let the branches cling to my protection[d]
when they make true peace with me.
Yes, let them make me their friend."[e]

Cleansing, Not Destruction

⁶The coming ones[f] of Jacob's tribes will take root.
Israel's branches will bud and blossom,
and her beautiful fruit will cover the face of the earth.
⁷Has Yahweh struck Israel
as other nations have struck her?[g]
Has Israel been killed like her enemies have been killed?

---

a 26:20 Or "curse."

b 27:1 See Job 41:1–10; Ps. 74:13–14; Isa. 51:9; Ezek. 29:3.

c 27:1 Or "the crooked serpent" or "the serpent of confusion." Satan always attempts to twist and distort the words of God to deceive humanity (2 Cor. 11:3). The sword of the Lord is merciless to the enemies of Christ (Rev. 19:15). The massive, mighty sword of the Lord is the message of the cross (1 Cor. 1:18–25). It is mighty to save and will thwart every principality and power (Col 2:14–15; Heb. 2:14–15). *Leviathan* means "coiled" or "contorted."

d 27:5 See John 15:5.

e 27:5 Or "make true peace with me."

f 27:6 Although most translations read "In days to come," the literal Hebrew is "Those to come."

g 27:7 Commentators and linguists agree that this is one of the more difficult verses to translate in Isaiah (as is the section to follow). A literal rendering is "Like the striking down of the one striking him down, does he strike him down?" A possible meaning of this verse could be "Israel has not been punished by the Lord as he has punished Israel's enemies."

⁸No, but with measured justice
  he exiled them and contended with them.*ᵃ*
  He removed them *from the land* with his severe blast
  on the day his searing east wind blew.
⁹By *the mercy of Yahweh* the guilt of Jacob will be forgiven.*ᵇ*
  Yet the full proof of their forgiveness will be
  when they crush all the altars to false gods
  and make them into chalkstones, crushed to pieces,
  with neither cultic poles nor incense altars still standing.
¹⁰The fortified city lies in ruins,
  forsaken and deserted like a wilderness.
  Cattle graze there and lie down,
  chewing on twigs and branches.
¹¹The trees are withered and stripped bare,
  and their women gather dead branches for firewood,
  because they are a people of no understanding.
  That is why their Maker will show them no compassion,
  and he who formed them will show them no favor.

¹²In that day, from the Egyptian border to the Euphrates, the Lord Yahweh will gather one by one the people of Israel, as one sifts wheat from the chaff. ¹³When that day comes, a great trumpet will sound, and those lost in the land of Assyria and Egypt—*all the exiles*—will come and bow down before the Lord Yahweh in Jerusalem and worship him on the holy mountain!

Ephraim's False Hope

28 Woe to the pride of Israel's*ᶜ* drunkards,
  worn like a garland on their heads!
  Their glory is but wilted flowers,
  worn like a crown on the heads of those
  bloated with rich food and overcome by wine.
²Behold! The Lord has one who is strong and mighty,
  and he will come like a hailstorm and like a destroying wind!
  With a storm of massive, flooding waters,
  his mighty power will knock it to the ground.*ᵈ*

---

a 27:8 The meaning of this line is uncertain.

b 27:9 Or "atoned for."

c 28:1 Or "Ephraim," a likely metonymy for the northern kingdom of Israel (Samaria). Read through this chapter to see the vivid contrast between the fading glory of mankind and the greater glory of God.

d 28:2 There are three fulfillments to this prophecy: (1) The immediate fulfillment of this was the Assyrian army coming to invade the northern kingdom of Israel in 740 BC. (2) The distant fulfillment was the advent of Jesus, the Mighty One, whom the Father sent with the sword of truth to demolish the lies and pride of man. (3) The future fulfillment will be the appearing of the overcomers (Rev. 2–3) who follow the Lamb as dread champions and who overturn the tables of religion and the arrogance of man.

³That proud crown of the drunkards of Ephraim
  will be trampled underfoot,
⁴and the glory of these proud leaders will fade and disappear
  like the first figs of the season, which are picked and eaten
  as soon they are ripe.
⁵In that day, Lord Yahweh, Commander of Angel Armies,
  will be a crown of glory*a* and a diadem of beauty
  for the remnant of his people.
⁶He will be a Spirit of justice
  for judges to render right decisions.
  And he will be strength *and bravery*
  for those who turn back the battle at the gate.

Judah's Drunken Prophets

⁷Moreover, the prophets and priests are drunk.
  They stagger because of wine
  and stumble around because of strong drink.
  They are confused*b* with wine,
  stumbling because of strong drink.
  They're too drunk to understand their prophetic visions.
  They're too drunk to render right decisions in judgment.
⁸All of their *banqueting* tables are covered with filthy vomit;
  vomit is everywhere!
⁹They say,
  "Who does this prophet*c* think he is to try to teach us?
  Who really cares about his message?
  It's only good for babies just learning to talk.*d*
¹⁰Do, do this, and do, do that,
  a rule about this and a rule about that,
  here a little, there a little."*e*

¹¹Since they won't listen to me,
  God*f* will use another *mouthpiece* to speak to them.
  With stammering lips
  and in a foreign language,*g* he will speak to this people.

---

a 28:5 God himself is to be our "crown," not human pride. See Heb. 2:9.

b 28:7 This is a play on words, for the word *bala'* is a homophone for "confused" and "to swallow
   (wine)." It could be translated "The wine they swallow swallows them."

c 28:9 Or "he."

d 28:9 Or "babies just weaned."

e 28:10 The meaning of the Hebrew text of this verse is uncertain. The Septuagint reads "You
   expect trouble upon trouble, hope upon hope; yet a little and yet a little."

f 28:11 Or "he."

g 28:11 That is, the foreign language of the Assyrians, which was Aramaic. See also Deut. 28:49;
   1 Cor. 14:21–22.

¹²For he has said to them,
"This is your rest, so let the weary rest;ᵃ
this is your comfort"—but they would not listen.
¹³Therefore, the word of Yahweh will be to them
"Do, do this, and do, do that,
a rule about this and a rule about that,
here a little, there a little,"ᵇ
in order that they will stumble backwards
and be broken and captured.

A False Covenant with Death

¹⁴Therefore, listen to the word of Yahweh,
you scornful jesters—rulers of Jerusalem.ᶜ
¹⁵For you have said,
"We have made a covenant with death
and a pact with the underworld,ᵈ
so when the overwhelming scourge sweeps over us,
it will not harm us.
For we have made lies our refugeᵉ
and find our shelter in falsehood."ᶠ

Zion's Foundation Stone

¹⁶Here's what the Lord God says:
"Behold, I set in place in Zion a Foundation Stone,ᵍ
fully tested and proven to be faithful and secure.ʰ

---

a 28:12 See Matt. 11:28–30; Heb. 4:9.

b 28:13 The meaning of the Hebrew text of this verse is uncertain. The Septuagint reads "You expect trouble upon trouble, hope upon hope; yet a little and yet a little." The Tanakh is "Mutter upon mutter; murmur upon murmur. Now here, now there."

c 28:14 Starting with 28:14 and going through 31:9, Isaiah speaks warnings to Judah and Jerusalem.

d 28:15 Or "Sheol." Some scholars conclude that death and the underworld are metaphors for an alliance with Egypt and its false gods. However, it is more likely that they had made an actual pact with evil spirits, such as Death (*Mot*) and the Underworld (*Resheph*), to protect them from the plague. Christ has broken the covenant with death, for we are crucified to death in him (Gal. 2:20). Now death "belongs" to the believer, for we have been given a life that triumphs over man's covenant with death (Rom. 8:38–39; 1 Cor. 3:21–22).

e 28:15 Many today still hide behind lies, refusing to come to the truth in Christ.

f 28:15 Or "false gods."

g 28:16 The Foundation Stone is Christ, set in place in the councils of eternity. The Hebrew word for "stone" is taken from the root word for "son" (*ben*). God's Foundation Stone is his Son, Jesus Christ. See Rom. 9:33. Now the Son/Stone has become many (1 Peter 2:5–7). From these stones/sons, the Father is building us into his holy temple.

h 28:16 The promised one, Jesus Christ, is the Chief Cornerstone on which we rest our faith, because we are those who dwell in Zion's realm (Heb. 12:22). Believers throughout all time have proven that he is faithful. See Ps. 118:22; Acts 4:11; Eph. 2:20; Rev. 21:19–20.

And written upon this precious cornerstone is this:
'Those who trust *in him* will not act in haste.'[a]
[17]I will set justice as the true measurement
and integrity its plumb line.
My hailstorm[b] will sweep away your refuge of lies,
and *my* floodwaters will overwhelm your hiding place.
[18]Then your covenant with death will be annulled
and your pact with the underworld will not stand.
And when the overwhelming scourge sweeps over you,
it will sweep you away![c]
[19]As often as *disaster* passes by, it will carry you away;
morning by morning, day after day, it will sweep you away!"

When you fully understand this message,
it will bring nothing but terror to you!
[20]Your bed is too short to stretch yourself out on,
and your covering is too narrow to wrap yourself in.[d]
[21]The Lord Yahweh will suddenly arise
as on Mount Perazim[e] and in the valley of Gibeon.[f]
He arises to accomplish his strange work—peculiar as it is—
his strange work *of judgment.*[g]
[22]So do not mock, or your bonds will grow tighter.
For I have heard the decree from my Lord Yahweh,
Commander of Angel Armies.
He spoke a decree of destruction against the whole land.

The Wonderful Ways of God
[23]Hear my voice, listen to my words,
and pay close attention to my parable.[h]

---

a 28:16 Or "will never run away (in fear)." Faith, firmly set upon Christ, is patient and never rushes, for faith leaves the timing of all things in God's hands. Peter quotes this verse, saying, "Whoever believes in him will certainly not be disappointed" (1 Peter 2:6).

b 28:17 Hail is a biblical metaphor for divine judgment. See v. 2; Ex. 9–10; Josh. 10:11; Ps. 18:12–13; 148:8; Isa. 32:19; Rev. 8:7; 11:19; 16:21.

c 28:18 Or "It will trample you down."

d 28:20 The bed is a metaphor for their confidence in lies—resting in illusions, not the truth. Those who trust in lies will not be comfortable. The covering being too narrow means their nakedness (like hiding behind fig leaves) will still be exposed. They will be too cramped and too cold. Every resting place and shelter will fail them.

e 28:21 This mountain is also called Baal-Perazim ("lord of the breakthrough"), the place where the Lord broke through, enabling David to conquer the Philistines. See 2 Sam. 5:20.

f 28:21 In this valley, Yahweh rained down hailstones on the Amorites. See Josh. 10:8–14.

g 28:21 The prophet describes God's work of judgment as strange or foreign to what he delights in doing. God is love and longs to pour out his love upon his people, those he has chosen and established as his own. Yet God is holy, and although in mercy he may delay judgment, he will judge his people. To see God's work of judgment as strange (alien) is to understand that heaven's default is always mercy. See also James 2:13.

h 28:23 Or "to my speech." Isaiah uses the parable of a farmer preparing his field to sow seed

²⁴Does a farmer plow continually at planting time
and never plant a crop?ᵃ
Does he continually break open the clods of the groundᵇ
and never sow his seed?
²⁵Once he has leveled its surface, does he not sow dill and cumin,
planting his wheat in rows, his barley in its proper place,
and his rye in a patch?
²⁶Yes, his God has instructed him
and taught him the right way *of farming the land.*
²⁷Dill, a small seed, is not threshed with a threshing sledge,
nor is a wagon wheel rolled over cumin.ᶜ
Dill is beaten with a rod and cumin with a stick.
²⁸Grain is crushedᵈ and milled for bread,
but it is not threshed endlessly.
One drives the wagon's wheels over it,
but his horses' hooves do not pulverize it.
²⁹This counsel also comes from Lord Yahweh,
Commander of Angel Armies.
For his guidance is unfathomable,
and the *heavenly* wisdom he imparts is magnificent.ᵉ

The Siege of David's City

29 "Woe to Arielᶠ—Ariel, the town where David encamped!ᵍ
Go ahead—keep your annual feasts,
and year after year celebrate your annual festivals.
²I will bring distress to Ariel and there will be great mourning.
Jerusalem will be to me like *what the name Ariel means—a burning* altar
hearth.
³I will lay siege to you on all sides,ʰ encircling you with towers
and raising up my siege works against you.

---

as a description of God's ways within us. He begins by essentially saying, "If your ears are
opened by my Spirit, then hear what I have to say."

a 28:24 The sharp teeth and cutting edge of God's Word as it plows on the soil of our hearts
will result in planting the life and glory of Jesus within us. God knows how the purpose of his
painful plowing in our hearts is to prepare us for the beautiful Jesus to come forth from within.
The outward shell, the hardened clods of soil, must be broken open so that Christ may be our
true life. See Hos. 10:12.

b 28:24 The clods of the ground are an apt metaphor for human nature, for we have been taken
from the dust of the ground.

c 28:27 God knows how fragile we are as "seeds of the kingdom." He will thresh us, but only
according to what is needed to lay bare our hearts and cause the seed to grow. See 1 Cor. 10:13.

d 28:28 God does not crush the grain but only frees it from the chaff.

e 28:29 Or "He makes counsel wonderful; he makes wisdom great." See also Rom. 11:33.

f 29:1 Ariel is a name for the altar in the temple (Ezek. 43). It is used as a metonymy for the
entire city of Jerusalem. The meaning of *Ariel* is "lion of God" or "altar hearth."

g 29:1 Or "the town David besieged."

h 29:3 Or "Like David I will encamp against you" (LXX).

⁴Brought low, you will speak from the dust of the earth.
  Your voice will be heard speaking from the ground,
  and like the voice of a ghost, you will whisper out of the dust.ᵃ
⁵Then suddenly, in an instant, your ruthless enemies
  will become nothing more than dust in the wind
  and your vile tyrants like wind-driven chaff!
⁶She will be visited by the Lord Yahweh,
  Commander of Angel Armies,
  with thunder, earthquake, and deafening noise,
  with whirlwind, tempest, and the blaze of a consuming fire!
⁷As quickly as a fading dream or as fleeting as a vision of the night,
  so will all the vast hordes of all the nations fade away
  and all who war against Arielᵇ and her fortress disappear.
⁸Just as a hungry man dreams that he is eating
  but wakes up still hungry,ᶜ
  or as a thirsty man dreams that he is drinking
  but wakes up weak and still longing for water,ᵈ
  so it will be for the vast hordes of all the nations
  that fight against Mount Zion."

Insensitive to God

⁹Be totally shocked and amazed by what I am about to say to you:

  "Blind yourselves—and be totally blind!
  (They are drunk but not from wine.
  They stagger but not from hard liquor.)
¹⁰For Yahweh has poured out over you
  the spirit of a deep, deep sleep—ᵉ
  putting the covers over your slumbering seersᶠ
  and *rocking* all your prophets to sleep."

¹¹This entire prophetic revelation will become to you like the words of a sealed book. If it's given to one who can read it with the command "Read this," he responds, "I can't because it is sealed." ¹²Or if it's given to one who is illiterate with the command "Read this," he responds, "I can't because I cannot read."

¹³This is what the Lord says about these people:

  "They come near to me with hollow words
  and honor me superficially with their lips;

---

a 29:4 Isaiah is using a series of metaphors to describe Israel's defeated condition, as though Israel is speaking out of the dust of defeat.
b 29:7 Or "Attack her and besiege her."
c 29:8 Or "Empty is his soul."
d 29:8 Or "His soul is craving."
e 29:10 See Rom. 11:8.
f 29:10 Or "He has covered the heads of the seers."

all the while their hearts run far away from me!
Their worship is nothing more than man-made rules.
¹⁴So therefore, I will again jolt this people awake
with astonishing wonders upon wonders!
And the wisdom of their wise ones will fail,
and the intelligent know-it-alls will have no explanations.ᵃ
¹⁵Woe to you who think you can hide
your plan from the Lord Yahweh.
Ha! Do you actually think your secret schemes are so hidden
that you say, 'Who sees us doing this?
No one knows what we're doing!'
¹⁶Oh, how great is your perversion!
Who is more intelligent—the potter or the clay?
Should a created thing say to its creator,
'You didn't makeᵇ me'?
Should a clay pot say to the potter, 'You don't understand'?"

Our Future Hope

¹⁷Before you know it, Lebanon will be transformed
into a fruitful field, and the fruitful field will seem like a forest.ᶜ
¹⁸In that day the deaf will begin to hear
the words that have been written,ᵈ
and out of the darkness and gloom,
the eyes of the blind will be opened to see.
¹⁹The meek will overflow with fresh joy in the Lord Yahweh,
and the poor will shout their praises
to the Holy One of Israel!
²⁰For the terrible oneᵉ will be no more,
the scornful jester will not be found,
and all the lovers of evilᶠ will be cut off.
²¹Those who make the innocent appear guilty,
those who ensnare others with deceitful tactics,
and those who lie to keep the innocent from getting justice
will likewise be destroyed.

---

a 29:14 Or "The discernment of the discerning ones will be kept hidden." See 1 Cor. 1:18–31.

b 29:16 Or "imagine" (Heb. *yêtser*). The root word of *yêtser* is *yâtsar* and has the primary meaning of "to form, fashion, frame, make, especially as a potter." Before you can form or frame something, it has to be imagined. The first use of *yâtsar* in the Bible is Yahweh forming man from the dust of the ground (Gen. 2:7).

c 29:17 Isaiah frequently used Lebanon as a metaphor for mighty ones and those with great influence (2:13; 10:34; 35:2). This phrase refers to a restoration of God's people who have experienced humiliation.

d 29:18 That is, their hearts are now open and tender to God.

e 29:20 See 2 Thess. 2:3–8.

f 29:20 Or "all the watchers of wrong (those diligent to do evil)." This would include those who use their political power or influence to harm others.

[22]So now, listen to what Yahweh, the God of Israel, who redeemed Abraham, has to say to Jacob's tribes:

"My people[a] will no longer be disgraced,
and your shame-face will disappear.
[23]For when they see *the miracle of* the many children
that I give them, they will see me as holy and honor me.[b]
Yes, they will honor the Holy One of Jacob
and stand in awe of the God of Israel.
[24]Those who are in spiritual error
will come to understanding,
and those who are always complaining
will be glad to accept instruction."

Woe to the Rebellious

30 This is what Yahweh says:

"Woe to the rebellious children,
who carry out their own plans but not mine,
and who sign treaties without consulting my Spirit,
piling one sin upon another.
[2]You travel down to Egypt *to find help*
without being guided by the words of my mouth.
Instead you put your trust in Pharaoh's protection,
seeking shelter in the shadow of Egypt.
[3]Therefore, Pharaoh's protection will become your shame,
and the shelter of Egypt's shadow will end in disaster!
[4]Though *your* officials arrive at Zoan
and *your* ambassadors reach as far away as Hanes,
[5]all will be put to shame because of such unreliable people.
They can offer you no help, only shame and disgrace!"

[6]This is a prophecy of the desert animals:

The burden of the caravan is to
traverse a desert land[c] of distress and trouble,
a land of the lion and lioness, the snake and the fiery flying one![d]
They carry their riches on the donkey's back

---

a 29:22 Or "Jacob," a metonymy for God's people, Israel.
b 29:23 Or "They will sanctify my name."
c 30:6 Or possibly a title: "A burden (oracle) of the animals of the Negev." The caravan, with its beasts of burden, was likely carrying the resources to pay for Egypt's aid. God had once led them through that desert, bringing them into the promised land. Now they trek the other direction in the desert, looking for help but not from Father God. See Deut. 8:15; Jer. 2:6.
d 30:6 Or "seraph."

and their treasures on the camel's hump
  to a nation that will give them nothing in return!
[7]Egypt's help is utterly worthless;
  that's why I nicknamed her
  Rahab, the Do-Nothing Dragon.[a]

A Message to God's Stubborn Children

[8]*God told me* to write down in a book
  words meant for the coming generation as an eternal witness.
[9]For they are stubborn rebels, children always telling lies,
  who refuse to listen to Yahweh's instruction.
[10]They say to the seers:
  "Stop seeing your visions."
  They say to the prophets:[b]
  "Stop prophesying to us about what is right.
  Prophesy only pleasant things to us, even if they're illusions!
[11]Leave this narrow way; turn aside from this *harsh* path.
  Don't confront us anymore with the Holy One of Israel!"

[12]Therefore, this is what the Holy One of Israel has to say:
  "Because you have despised this message,
  and trust in your own clever abilities to deceive,
  and rely upon oppression,
[13]your own sin will become like a high, bulging wall
  that is cracked and about to collapse.
  In an instant, it will all fall down.
[14]It will break into pieces like shattered pottery,
  smashed so ruthlessly that not even a fragment
  big enough to pick up a hot coal
  or to scoop water from a cistern will be found!"

[15]Lord Yahweh, the Holy One of Israel, says:
  "Come back to me! By returning and resting in me you will be saved.
  In quietness and trust you will be made strong.
  But you refused.
[16]And though you boast, 'No! We will flee on horses,'
  you will indeed flee for your lives!
  You say, 'We will ride on swift horses,'
  but your pursuers will be swift to chase you!
[17]A thousand will flee at the threat of one,[c]
  and all will flee at the threat of five,

---

a 30:7 Rahab is used as a poetic term both for a mythical sea monster and for Egypt. See Ps. 87:4; 89:10; Isa. 51:9.

b 30:10 Or "the beholders."

c 30:17 See Deut. 28:25.

until nothing will be left of you—
like a lonely flagstaff on the top of a hill,
or like a signpost on a barren mountain!"

God's Promise to His People

[18]For this reason the Lord is still waiting to show his favor to you
so he can show you his marvelous love.
He waits to be gracious to you.
He sits on his throne ready to show mercy to you.[a]
For Yahweh is the Lord of justice,
faithful to keep his promises.
Overwhelmed with bliss are all
who will entwine their hearts in him,
waiting for him *to help them.*
[19]Yes, the people of Zion who live in Jerusalem
will weep no more.
How compassionate he will be
when he hears your cries for help!
He will answer you when he hears your voice!
[20]Even though the Lord may allow you
to go through a season of hardship and difficulty,[b]
he himself will be there with you.
He will not hide himself from you,
for your eyes will constantly see him as your Teacher.[c]
[21]When you turn to the right or turn to the left,
you will hear his voice behind you *to guide you,* saying,
"This is the right path; follow it."[d]

[22]Then you will see your idols as they are—unclean!
Your silver-overlaid idols and gold-plated images are defiled.
You will discard them like a filthy menstrual cloth,
saying to them, "Good riddance!"
[23]Then God will supply you with abundant rain
for the seeds you sow.

---

a 30:18 See Jer. 29:11–13; Heb. 4:16.

b 30:20 Or "though the Lord gives you the bread of adversity and the water of affliction."

c 30:20 The Hebrew word for "teacher" (*mowreh*) is a homonym for "rain." The gift of a teacher
is to water our hearts with the rain of the Spirit and the rain of Truth. When God teaches our
hearts, it is like spring rain falling, refreshing and renewing our spirits. See 1 Cor. 3:6.

d 30:21 This verse and the preceding verse teach us that (1) God will be with us in our troubles.
(2) God will not hide himself from us when we pass through hard times. (3) God himself will
teach us lessons in our trials. (4) We can set our eyes on him no matter what is happening
around us. (5) His voice will lead us into making good decisions. (6) We have his promise of
constant guidance as we listen to his voice. The voice of the Lord and the Word of God are our
faithful guides throughout our lives.

He will bless you with an incredible, plentiful harvest.[a]
And in that day he will give you lush, broad pastures for your cattle.
24Even your oxen and donkeys that work the soil
will feed on good grain, separated from its chaff.[b]
25On the day of great slaughter,
when all their towers tumble,
God will bless you with sparkling streams and bubbling brooks
flowing down every high hill and every lofty mountain.
26Moonlight will shine as bright as sunlight,
and the sun's glare will become seven times brighter,
like the light of seven days rolled into one.
That will be the day when the Lord Yahweh
heals the bruises and wounds that he has inflicted.

God Will Judge the Nations
27Look! Here comes Yahweh with his mighty power and glory![c]
He comes in his awesome splendor with thick clouds!
Consumed with anger, his lips are filled with fury,
and his words[d] are a devouring fire!
28His breath is as overwhelming as a flooding river
reaching up to the neck.
He sifts the nations in his sieve of destruction
and places a bridle in their jaws that causes them to wander.

29But you will have a joyous song throughout the night,
as one celebrating a holy, consecrated feast.
You will have gladness of heart,
as one celebrating to the sound of a flute
and dancing up the mountain of Yahweh,
the Rock who shelters Israel!
30And Yahweh will cause everyone
to hear his awe-inspiring, majestic voice.[e]
He will open their eyes to see his mighty power[f]
coming down with raging anger and consuming fire!
His power will descend in cloudburst, thunderstorm, and hail.
31And when his rod strikes the Assyrians,
they will be terror-stricken by the mighty voice of Lord Yahweh.

---

a 30:23 Or "bread and the produce of the ground will be rich and plentiful."
b 30:24 Or "The oxen and donkey that till the ground will feed on silage that has been winnowed with pitchfork and shovel."
c 30:27 Or "The name of Yahweh comes from far away."
d 30:27 Or "his tongue."
e 30:30 See Ps. 29.
f 30:30 Or "arm," a metaphor for his power.

³²Every stroke of Yahweh's punishing rod*
will be to the sound of cymbals and strumming harps.
God himself fights them in battle with dancing!*
³³From long ago, the king's fiery burial place has been prepared,
stacked high with plenty of firewood to fuel the flame.*
Yahweh's breath, like a stream of sulfur, kindles it.

Trust the Holy One of Israel

31 Woe to those who run down to Egypt for help,
trusting in the might of their multitude
of cavalry, chariots, and riders.
Their confident trust is not in the Holy One of Israel,
nor do they consult with Yahweh.
²Yet he is wiser than them all!
He can call down calamity *upon evildoers*
and never needs to retract his words.
He will stand up against the wicked and those who protect them.
³The Egyptians are not gods;* they're only human!*
Their horses are not supernatural; they're only flesh!
When Yahweh demonstrates his power,*
the helper will stumble and the helped will fall—
both will perish together!

The Lord Will Fight for His People

⁴This is what Yahweh said to me:

"When a lion,* the great beast, growls* over his prey,
and when the shepherds band together against him,
the lion is neither terrified by their shouts
nor disturbed by all the noise they make.
So will Yahweh, the Commander of Angel Armies,
come down to fight *for you* on Mount Zion and on Zion's hill!

---

a 30:32 Or "established (destined for punishment) rod."
b 30:32 As translated by some scholars. The Hebrew word *uvémilkhamot* ("with battles of") is emended by some to read *uvimkholot* ("with dancing"). The majority view of the Hebrew text is "battles of brandishing (uplifted weapons/arms)." This "punishing rod" will fall on the spiritual forces of darkness as we celebrate and dance in the victory of the risen Christ.
c 30:33 Although the Hebrew of this verse is uncertain, the implication is that the king of Assyria will be thrown into fire. There is also the hint of our eternal foe, Satan, the king of darkness, being cast into the lake of fire. See Rev. 20:10.
d 31:3 Or "mighty ones."
e 31:3 "Human" is the Hebrew word *adam*.
f 31:3 Or "stretches out his hand" (Eph. 4:11).
g 31:4 See Rev. 5.
h 31:4 The Hebrew word for "growl" *(hagah)* is more commonly translated "meditates."

⁵Just as a bird hovers over its nest to protect its young,
  so will Yahweh, Commander of Angel Armies, shield Jerusalem.
  He will protect her, deliver her, spare her, and rescue her!"

Repent and Return

⁶"People of Israel! Repent and turn back to God,
  whom you have deeply betrayed.
⁷For a time is coming
  when all people will throw away
  their sinful idols of silver and gold
  and forsake all that their own hands have made.ᵃ
⁸Assyria will fall by the sword but not the sword of man.
  It will not be man's sword that will slaughter them *but God's*!
  They will run from battle,
  and their young men will be made slaves.
⁹Fear will cause them to surrender their high fortress,ᵇ
  and they will panic at the sight of princes,
  and desert their battle flag,"
  says the Lord God of the fire that burns in Zion
  and whose furnace burns in Jerusalem!

A King and His Princes

32 Look—a new era begins!
  A king will reign with righteousness,
  and his princesᶜ according to justice!
²Each will be a hiding place from the stormy wind
  and a secret shelter from the tempest.ᵈ
  Life will flow from each one, like streams of waterᵉ in the desert,
  like the refreshing shade of a massive rock
  in a weary, thirsty land.
³Then at last, eyes that are ready to see
  will finally be opened!ᶠ
  Ears that are ready to hear
  will finally be opened!ᵍ
⁴The hearts of those who were once hasty *to form opinions*
  will finally understand and know.

---

a 31:7 See Acts 17:29; Rev. 13:13–18.

b 31:9 Or "rock cliff" (Heb. *sela*).

c 32:1 Although some scholars believe Hezekiah is the king mentioned here, we see Jesus. He
  is the King of Righteousness, and his princes are the sons and daughters who make up his
  kingdom. See Rom. 8:14, 29; Heb. 2:6–13.

d 32:2 Spiritual leaders, like our Lord Jesus, are to be a source of protection and refreshing for
  God's people. See John 10:10–11.

e 32:2 See Ezek. 47:1–12; John 7:37–39.

f 32:3 See John 3:1-8; Eph. 1:18.

g 32:3 See Rev. 3:13, 20–22.

And those with stammering tongues[a]
will speak dazzling truths!
[5]The fool[b] will no longer be called Your Honor,
nor the scoundrel[c] highly respected,
[6]for the fool is recognized by his foolish words.
Their minds plot treachery, they excel in ungodliness,
and they say misleading things about Yahweh.
They refuse to feed the hungry or give drink to the thirsty.
[7]The deceiver's schemes[d] and plans are evil.
He schemes of cheating the poor,
even when their plea is just.
[8]But a person of honor has honorable plans,
and his integrity[e] gives him security.

A Warning of Disaster

[9]You careless women,
it is time to get up and hear my voice.
You complacent daughters, pay attention to what I say.
[10]Although you are carefree now,
you will tremble for many days and years,[f]
for your grape harvest will fail
and your fruit harvest will not come!
[11]Tremble, you careless ones.
Take off your *fine* garments and expose yourselves.
Shake with fear and put on sackcloth.[g]
[12]Beat your breasts *in sorrow*
for your pleasant fields and fruitful vines.
[13]Mourn for the soil of my people,
for it will grow nothing but thorns and briars.[h]
Yes, mourn for all the houses of joy in the joyous city,
[14]for the bustling city with its mansions will be deserted.
The high ground and watchtower will be empty,
becoming the joy of wild donkeys and a grazing ground for flocks.

---

a 32:4 See 1 Cor. 14:2.
b 32:5 The Hebrew word for "fool," *nabal*, is one of the strongest negative terms used in the Old Testament to describe a person who is "worthless" or "godless." See 1 Sam. 25:25.
c 32:5 Or "miserly (one who withholds, stingy, covetous)."
d 32:7 Or "weapons."
e 32:8 The Hebrew word *nadiyb* is used three times in this verse and can be translated "honor, noble, integrity, willing, princely."
f 32:10 Or "days upon a year." This phrase is obscure and not easy to define. It could be a figure of speech for "days and years (of trouble)" or "in a year or more."
g 32:11 The five imperative Hebrew verbs, though seemingly addressed to women, are all in the masculine form.
h 32:13 See Matt. 13:3–9, 18–23.

The Outpouring

[15]The desolation will not end
until[a] the Spirit is poured out[b] upon us from heaven![c]
Then the wilderness will blossom into a fruitful orchard
and the trees of the orchard will grow into a forest!
[16]Then justice will reside in the wilderness
and righteousness will dwell in the fruitful orchard.
[17]The work of righteousness is peace,[d]
and the result of righteousness
is quietness and confidence forever.
[18]My people will live free from worry
in secure, quiet homes of peace.
[19]No matter if hail destroys the forest and the city is leveled,
[20]you will be happy and blessed
as you sow your seed beside every stream
and loose your ox and donkey to graze freely.

Zion Restored

33 Woe to you, destroyer, you who have not been destroyed.
Woe to you, traitor, you who have not been betrayed.
When you have finished your work of destroying,
you will be destroyed,
and when you have completed your betrayal,
you will be betrayed.[e]
[2]Yahweh, be gracious to us,
for we wait for you.[f]
Be our strength[g] every morning
and rescue us when troubles come.
[3]The nations retreat at the sound of *your* roaring voice.
The nations scatter as you arise in your majesty.
[4]Their[h] spoil will be harvested,
carried away like locusts *that strip a field bare.*
And like leaping locusts, men will leap upon the spoils.
[5]Yahweh is high and lifted up; he dwells[i] on high!

---

a 32:15 See Acts 3:19–21; Eph. 4:13.

b 32:15 Or "emptied out." See Ezek. 36:25–27; Joel 2:28.

c 32:15 Or "from on high."

d 32:17 That is, peace comes from righteousness, not simply the works of man. See Isa. 26:12; Matt. 5:9.

e 33:1 This refers to Sennacherib, the king of Assyria. When Assyria is finished destroying Jerusalem, God will destroy Assyria. See 2 Kings 19:35–37.

f 33:2 The Hebrew concept of waiting is not passive but includes joining our hearts to God and looking to him alone to help us.

g 33:2 Or "arm," a metaphor for strength.

h 33:4 Or "your."

i 33:5 The Hebrew uses the word *shakan*, a word from which we get "shekinah (glory)." You could say, "Yahweh is shekinah'd on high."

He lavished his justice and righteousness on Zion!
[6]He will be your constant source of stability in changing times,
and out of his abundant *love* he gives you
the riches of salvation, wisdom, and knowledge.
Yes, the fear of the Lord is the key to this treasure!

[7]Listen! The valiant ones[a] cry in the streets
and envoys of peace weep bitterly.
[8]The highways are deserted
and the travelers have disappeared.
Covenants are broken and witnesses[b] rejected,
and no one is respected.
[9]The land mourns and languishes.
Lebanon is disgraced and withered.
The fields of Sharon are like a desert.
The lands of Bashan and Carmel are stripped bare.

[10]"Now I will arise," says the Lord.
"Now I will exalt myself; now I will unveil my majesty!
[11]*Assyria*, your plans are worthless, as useless as chaff.[c]
My breath[d] will be a fire that consumes you.
[12]As a thorn bush is cut down and thrown into the fire,
your nation will be burned to ashes of lime.

The Righteous King

[13]"You who are far away, listen to what I have done,
and you who draw near to me,
acknowledge my power and strength!
[14]Sinners in Zion are afraid,
and the godless are gripped with panic,
saying, 'Who can dwell with such an all-consuming fire?
Who can live in the presence of the never-ending flame?'
[15]Only those who walk with integrity and speak what is true,[e]
who despise even the thought of cheating the poor,
and do not accept a bribe, nor plot violence,
nor contemplate doing evil—[f]
[16]they will live safely on the heights
and make their safe place the mountain strongholds,
with bread in steady supply and water assured."[g]

---

a 33:7 Or "the Arielites (lions of God)." Others translate it "priests."
b 33:8 As translated from Dead Sea scroll 1QIsaᵃ. Some manuscripts have "cities."
c 33:11 Or "You conceive straw and are pregnant with chaff."
d 33:11 Or "your breath."
e 33:15 See Ps. 15.
f 33:15 Or "(who) shut their eyes from seeing evil (harming others)."
g 33:16 This verse refers to those who are enthroned with Christ and seated with him in the

¹⁷*In this high place,* your eyes will see
the king*ᵃ* in his *stunning* beauty
and gaze upon his broad domain.*ᵇ*
¹⁸You will look back on the fears of your past and say,
"Now, where is the scholar?*ᶜ* Where is the advisor?*ᵈ*
Where is the one who numbers those who are maturing?"*ᵉ*
¹⁹You will no longer see the defiant foreigner
who speaks a strange, incomprehensible language.
²⁰Set your gaze on Zion,
the city where we gather for Yahweh's feasts.*ᶠ*
Your eyes will see Jerusalem as a quiet, pleasant place.
It is a secure dwelling, permanent and unmovable,
not like a tabernacle that must be taken down,
pegs pulled up, and transported.
²¹Glorious Yahweh will be there for us
in a land with broad rivers and *life-giving* streams,*ᵍ*
where the hostile, majestic ships will not sail.*ʰ*
²²The Lord Yahweh is our Judge, our Lawgiver, and our King;*ⁱ*
he will save us *completely!*ʲ*

²³Your ropes hang loose,
your mast is not secure, and your sail is not unfurled.*ᵏ*

Then there will be a great plunder,
such an abundant treasure divided*ˡ*
that even the lame will seize their rich share.*ᵐ*

---

heavenly realm (Rev. 3:21; Eph. 2:6). They receive a supernatural supply of revelation-bread and living water. Their eyes are fixed on their beautiful King, not on themselves or their ministries.

a 33:17 This is the King of Glory, the King of Kings. No earthly king is in view here. See Song. 2:10–13; Eph. 1:3; 2:6; 2 Peter 1:3–4.

b 33:17 Or "land of distances."

c 33:18 As translated from the Septuagint. The Hebrew is "Where is the counter?"

d 33:18 As translated from the Septuagint. The Hebrew is "Where is the one who weighs the money (tribute)?"

e 33:18 As translated from the Septuagint. The Hebrew is "Where is the one who counts the towers?"

f 33:20 See Lev. 23; Deut. 16.

g 33:21 This points to a restoration of Eden's paradise. See Gen. 2:10; Ezek. 47:1–12; Acts 3:21.

h 33:21 The Hebrew of this clause is uncertain.

i 33:22 Isaiah refers to the three forms of Israel's governmental history: the laws of Moses, the judges, and the kings.

j 33:22 See 1 Thess. 5:23.

k 33:23 Their "cords (of faith)" were not tightly fastened to Yahweh, their "mast" (human strength) was not secure, and their "sail" (to move forward by the Spirit-wind of God) was not unfurled, yet God would be faithful to them.

l 33:23 These are the spoils of the great victory of Christ, won for us through his death, resurrection, and ascension. See Matt. 12:30–33; Eph. 1:3, 4:8; Col. 2:13–15.

m 33:23 The "lame (feeble)" are those who worship with a limp (Gen. 32:24–32).

²⁴No one living in *Zion* will say, "I am sick,"
for all who live there will have their sin forgiven.

God Judges His Enemies

34 Come close to me, you nations, and listen!
Pay attention to me, you peoples!
Let all the world hear me,
the earth and all that springs from it.
²For Yahweh has turned his anger toward the nations
and his fury against all their armies.
He has doomed them to destruction
and will annihilate them all.
³Their slain will be cast out,
the stench of their corpses will rise,
and the mountains will stream with their blood.
⁴The heavenly powers[a] will fade away to nothing,[b]
and the heavens will be rolled up like a scroll.
All their mighty host will wither
as leaves fall from a withered vine
or fruit from a withering fig tree.[c]

⁵*The Lord says:*
"Indeed, my judgment-sword has appeared in the heavens,[d]
and when it has drunk its fill,
you will see it descend on the people of Edom,
those whom I have doomed to judgment."
⁶Lord Yahweh has a judgment-sword dripping with blood.
It is smeared with fat,
dripping with the blood of lambs and goats,
and covered with the fat of ram's kidneys.
Lord Yahweh has a sacrifice in Bozrah[e]
and a great slaughter in the land of Edom.
⁷Cattle and young bulls will also be slain;[f]
their land will be drenched[g] with blood
and the dust soaked with fat.

---

a 34:4 Or "The host of heaven," which can refer to demonic powers. See 2 Kings 17:16; 21:3, 5; 23:4–5; Eph. 6:10–18.

b 34:4 The Dead Sea scroll 1QIsaᵃ adds "And the valleys will be split open."

c 34:4 See Matt. 24:29; Rev. 6:13–14.

d 34:5 As translated from the Dead Sea scroll 1QIsaᵃ. The Hebrew is "My sword is drenched in the heavens."

e 34:6 Bozrah (modern Busaira) was the capital of Edom. See Isa. 63:1–6; Jer. 49:13; Amos 1:12. *Bozrah* means "sheepfold." The sacrifice the Lord offered in the sheepfold can point to the supreme sacrifice of Jesus, the Lamb of God.

f 34:7 This is likely aurochs, an extinct species of wild cattle.

g 34:7 Or "drunk."

8For Lord Yahweh has a day of vengeance,
 a year of vindication for Zion's cause.
9Edom's streams will be turned to pitch and its soil to sulfur;
 her land will become blazing pitch.
10Night and day it will never be extinguished;
 its smoke will go up forever and ever.
 Through the endless ages it will lie desolate;
 no one will pass through it forever.
11Nothing but desert hawks and wild animals*a* will live there;
 owls and ravens will find a home there.
 The Lord will stretch out over it a measuring line of chaos
 and the plumb line of emptiness.
12It will be named No Kingdom There,
 and all its rulers and princes will come to nothing.*b*
13Its palaces will be overgrown with thorns,
 its fortresses*c* with thistles and briars.
 It will become a haunt for demons*d* and an abode for owls.*e*
14Wild beasts will mingle with wolves
 and goat-demons*f* will howl to one another.
 There too the night-demon*g* will settle in and find her rest.
15There the arrow-snake will build her nest, lay her eggs,
 and hatch her brood in the shadows.
 There too the vultures will gather*h* to breed.

16Seek for Yahweh's book and read it carefully.
 You will learn that none of these *prophecies* will fail;
 none will lack a *fulfillment as its* companion.
 For the Lord has issued his decree.
 It is his Spirit that has gathered them.
17He is the one who apportioned it to them by lot,
 whose hand measured the share of each.*i*
 They will possess it for all time
 and dwell there throughout the ages.

---

a 34:11 The exact meaning of the animals listed here is uncertain. Some translations include hedgehogs, pelicans, porcupines, hawks, and several types of owls.

b 34:12 See 1 Cor. 2:8; Eph. 6:12.

c 34:13 See 2 Cor. 10:3–6.

d 34:13 Or "dragons," or "jackals."

e 34:13 The Hebrew word for "owls" is uncertain.

f 34:14 Or "satyrs."

g 34:14 Or "Lilith," a female goddess known as the sexually perverse "night-demon." The Dead Sea scroll 4Q510-511 lists Lilith among a list of demonic monsters.

h 34:15 See Matt. 24:28.

i 34:17 See Eph. 4:7, 11.

The Redeemed Return to Zion[a]

35 The wilderness and dry land will be joyously glad!
The desert will blossom like a rose and rejoice!
[2]Every dry and barren place will burst forth with abundant blossoms,[b]
dancing and spinning with delight![c]
Lebanon's lush splendor covers it,
the magnificent beauty of Carmel[d] and Sharon.[e]
My people[f] will see the awesome glory of Yahweh,
the beautiful grandeur of our God.
[3]Strengthen those who are discouraged.[g]
Energize those who feel defeated.[h]
[4]Say to the anxious and fearful,
"Be strong and never afraid.
Look, here comes your God!
He is breaking through to give you victory!
He comes to avenge your enemies.
With divine retribution he comes to save you!"[i]
[5]Then blind eyes will open and deaf ears will hear.
[6]Then the lame will leap[j] like *playful* deer
and the tongue-tied will sing songs of triumph.
Gushing water will spring up in the wilderness
and streams will flow through the desert.[k]
[7]The burning sand will become a *refreshing* oasis,
the parched ground bubbling springs,

---

a 35 This chapter is recognized as a Hebrew poem of rare and superb beauty, one of the most glorious chapters in the Bible. It is a picture of the last-days church rising up out of the wilderness to shine in all the radiance of its glory. It is a picture of Eden restored as the kingdom-realm of God brings hope to the weak and struggling. "The Sacred Way" is the way of life in Christ as we live in heaven's power and virtue.

b 35:2 Or "Blossoming it will blossom." The Hebrew word (*parach*) implies breaking forth and blooming. It can also mean to "spread (the wings) and fly." This is what will happen to God's people in the last days. Once confined in the wilderness, they will break forth and blossom with beauty and glory as saints of the Most High.

c 35:2 The Hebrew word *giyl* implies spinning with delight and dancing. See Ps. 149:3; Jer. 31:13; Zeph. 3:17.

d 35:2 Carmel, a mountain range near Israel's Mediterranean coast, means "fruitful, plentiful, orchard, garden, vineyard, or any fruitful field." See Song. 4:11–15; 7:5.

e 35:2 Sharon, a coastal plain in Israel, means "an open, sweeping plain, straight, upright, pleasant, prosperous."

f 35:2 As translated from the Septuagint. The Hebrew is "they."

g 35:3 Or "strengthen the weak hands." See Heb. 12:12–13.

h 35:3 Or "Make firm those with feeble knees."

i 35:4 See Ps. 149:4, 7.

j 35:6 See Acts 3:7–8.

k 35:6 See Ps. 110:7; Judg. 15:18–19.

and the dragon's[a] lair a meadow
with grass, reeds, and papyrus.
[8]There will be a highway of holiness called the Sacred Way.
The impure will not be permitted on this road,
but it will be accessible to God's people.[b]
And not even fools will lose their way.[c]
[9]The lion[d] will not be found there;
no wild beast will travel on it—
they will not be found there.
But the redeemed will find a pathway on it.
[10]Yahweh's ransomed ones will return with glee to Zion.
They will enter with a song of rejoicing
and be crowned with everlasting joy.
Ecstatic joy will overwhelm them;
weariness and grief will disappear!

Two Kings[e]

36 In the fourteenth year of King Hezekiah's reign,[f] Sennacherib,[g] king of Assyria, attacked all the fortified cities of Judah and conquered them. [2]*After defeating Lachish,* Sennacherib sent his chief commander[h] with his massive army from there to King Hezekiah in Jerusalem. He took up a position on the road to the Washerman's Field,[i] at the end of the aqueduct where it empties into

---

a 35:7 Or "serpent, monster, jackal."

b 35:8 Or "It is for those who walk the walk."

c 35:8 Or "Fools will not trespass on it."

d 35:9 The lion is a frequent metaphor for Satan. See 1 Peter 5:8.

e 36 Chs. 36–39 form the conclusion of the first part of the book of Isaiah. They contain the accounts of three historical events, each surrounding the influence of the prophet Isaiah during the reign of Israel's King Hezekiah. This section of Isaiah is frequently called "the Volume of Hezekiah" since he is mentioned thirty-five times in these four chapters. Chs. 36–37 detail the unsuccessful efforts of Sennacherib, king of Assyria, to take possession of Jerusalem by threats and intimidation. Ch. 38 details Hezekiah's sickness and miracle of divine healing. Ch. 39 gives us the account of Hezekiah's sin of pride in showing all his wealth to the Babylonian emissaries.

f 36:1 This would be approximately 701 BC. *Hezekiah* means "strengthened of Yah, captured by Yah, Yah has made firm, power of Yah." The prophets who lived during his reign included Isaiah, Micah, and Nahum. He ascended Judah's throne at the age of twenty-five and reigned a total of twenty-nine years. He was considered to be a godly king and released the greatest period of restoration in Israel's history. He repaired the doors of the temple, cleansed it, and made atonement for the altar. He consecrated the priesthood, ordered the observance of the Feast of Passover, and removed idolatry from the land. He supported the priesthood through tithes and offerings, and the nation prospered. He was buried with great honor in the sepulchers of the sons of David. See 2 Kings 18–20; 2 Chron. 29–32.

g 36:1 Sennacherib means "the thorn laid waste."

h 36:2 Or "Rabshakeh," a possible title of a military official.

i 36:2 Or "Fuller's Field," where cloth was washed and bleached. In Mark 9:3, the Greek text uses the phrase "whiter than any fuller can make them." See also Isa. 7:3; Mal. 3:1–3.

the upper pool.[a] [3]And coming out to meet him were *three officials of the king:* Eliakim, son of Hilkiah, the palace administrator; Shebna, the scribe; and Joah, son of Asaph, the secretary.

[4]Sennacherib's commander said to them, "Tell Hezekiah, this is what the exalted king, the king of Assyria, says: 'What makes you so confident? [5]You think you have a strategy and defensive might, but mere words are no match *for my army!* In whom are you trusting for help that you rebel against me? [6]I know—you are relying on Egypt, that broken staff full of splinters. If anyone leans on it, it will pierce his hand. Pharaoh himself, king of Egypt, is like that splintered staff to those who put their trust in him! But you tell me that you are trusting in Yahweh, your God. For Hezekiah went around destroying every sacred altar from the land. Didn't he insist that Judah and Jerusalem had to worship only at this altar *in your temple?* [8]Now it's time to make a deal with my master, the king of Assyria. I will give you two thousand horses if you're able to come up with as many men to ride them. [9]You're no match against even one officer of the least of my master's officials! Why put your confidence in Egypt's chariots and horsemen? [10]What's more, do you really think I've marched against this land to destroy it on my own without Yahweh's approval?'"

[11]Then Eliakim, Shebna, and Joah replied, "Please speak to us, your servants, in Aramaic, for we understand it. Don't speak to us in Hebrew, for the people on the wall are listening to us, and they will overhear our conversation."

[12]But the commander answered them, "Do you think I came to deliver this message from my master only to you and your king? It is also meant for the men sitting there on the wall to hear! They are the ones who will eat their own excrement and drink their own urine!"

[13]So the commander stood and shouted out in a loud voice in Hebrew *to the men listening on the wall,* "Hear the words of the great King *Sennacherib,* the king of Assyria, [14]for he has sent me with these words: 'Don't let Hezekiah mislead you, for there is nothing he can do to save you. [15]Don't be deceived when he tries to persuade you to trust in Yahweh, saying to you, "Yahweh will come to our rescue and our city will not be handed over to the king of Assyria." [16]Don't listen to Hezekiah, for the king of Assyria says to you, "Make your peace with me and surrender so that you may continue to eat from your own grapes and figs and drink the water from your own cisterns [17]until I come and take you away to a land like your own. It is a good land of grain and wine, bread and vineyards." [18]Don't be deceived by Hezekiah's empty words when he says to you, "Yahweh will save us." Has any god ever saved a nation from the *mighty* hand of the king of Assyria? [19]Where were the gods of Hamath[b] and Arphad?[c] Where were the gods of Sepharvaim? Did any god save *your northern kingdom of* Samaria from me? [20]Where is there a god that could save its people from my mighty hand?'"

[21]But they were silent, and no one answered him a word, for King Hezekiah had ordered them, "Do not answer him."

---

a 36:2 This was possibly Hezekiah's "tunnel."

b 36:19 This is modern Hama, a city of west central Syria.

c 36:19 Or "Arpad," an ancient city of northwestern Syria.

[22]So the three officials of Hezekiah—Eliakim, son of Hilkiah, the palace administrator; Shebna, the scribe; and Joah, son of Asaph the secretary—came to Hezekiah with their clothes torn as a sign of despair and reported what the Assyrian commander had said.

Hezekiah Seeks God's Help

37 When Hezekiah heard what the commander had said, he tore his robe, put on sackcloth, and went to the temple of Yahweh. [2]And he sent Eliakim, the palace administrator; Shebna, the royal scribe; and the leading priests—all clothed in sackcloth—to the prophet Isaiah, son of Amoz. [3]They told him, "Here is Hezekiah's message: 'This is a day of great anguish, rebuke, and humiliation. *We are desperate,* as in the day a woman is in heavy labor but has no strength left to give birth.[a] [4]Perhaps Lord Yahweh, your God, will take note of all the *blasphemous* words of the Assyrian commander who was sent by his master, the king of Assyria, to ridicule the living God. And may Lord Yahweh, your God, rebuke him for the words he heard him speak. So therefore, we come to ask you to pray for us, the remnant that still survives.'"

[5-6]Isaiah answered the king's delegation, saying, "Tell your master these words: 'Here is what Lord Yahweh says about this matter: "Don't fear or be frightened by the blasphemous words of the servants of the king of Assyria. [7]I will put in him a mind-set[b] that will cause him, when he hears a certain rumor, to flee back to his own country. And when he returns I will cause him to fall by the sword in his own land."'"

[8]Meanwhile, the Assyrian commander returned to the king, for he had heard that the king had left Lachish to lay siege against the city of Libnah.[c] [9]Now, King Sennacherib had heard a report that the king of Ethiopia, Tirhakah, *had allied with Hezekiah and* was coming to fight against him. So when he heard it he sent messengers to Hezekiah with this message:

[10]"Don't let this God in whom you trust mislead you into thinking that Jerusalem will not fall and be delivered into the hand of the *mighty* king of Assyria. [11]Certainly you have heard what the kings of Assyria have done to all the lands, destroying them all. Do you really think you'll be delivered? [12]Did any of their gods come to their rescue? *Where were the gods* of Gozan, Haran, Rezeph, and the people of Eden, who were in Tel Azzar when my predecessors destroyed their lands?[d] [13]*Tell me,* where is the king of Hamath, the king of Arphad, the king of the city of Sepharvaim, or of Hena or Ivva?"[e]

Hezekiah's Prayer

[14]When the messengers delivered Sennacherib's message to Hezekiah, he read it and immediately went into the temple of Yahweh and spread it out before the Lord. [15]And he prayed:

---

a 37:3 See Isa. 66:8; Rom. 8:19–21.

b 37:7 Or "I will put a spirit (attitude) in him."

c 37:8 Libnah was one of the thirteen cities allotted to the priests in Israel. See Josh. 21:13-21.

d 37:12 These are cities of northern Mesopotamia located between the Tigris and Euphrates Rivers.

e 37:13 These are cities of Syria.

¹⁶"O Yahweh, Commander of Angel Armies, the God of Israel, you are enthroned between the wings of the cherubim and you reign supreme as God over all the kingdoms of the world, for you alone are Creator of heaven and earth. ¹⁷Please lean down to hear my prayer. Yahweh, open your eyes and see me here calling out to you. Listen carefully to every blasphemous word Sennacherib has sent to ridicule and insult you, the living God.

¹⁸"Lord Yahweh, truly the Assyrian kings have annihilated all these nations and conquered their lands. ¹⁹They *smashed* and burned their gods, for they're not truly gods but mere idols made by human hands shaped from wood and stone. That's why they could be destroyed. ²⁰So now, our loving God, Yahweh, save us from the Assyrians so that the whole world will know that you alone are Yahweh, Lord God Almighty."

Isaiah's Prophecy to Hezekiah
²¹Then Isaiah, son of Amoz, sent this message to Hezekiah:

"Hear the words of Yahweh, the God of Israel: 'Because you prayed to me about the taunts of Sennacherib, king of Assyria, ²²this is what I, Yahweh, decree concerning him:

"The virgin daughter of Zion
despises you and ridicules you.
My daughter, Jerusalem,
tosses her head back and makes fun of you!
²³Who do you think you're mocking and blaspheming?
Against whom do you raise your voice?
And who have you looked down upon in your arrogance?
None other than me, the Holy One of Israel!
²⁴You sent your messengers to mock the Lord.
You boast, 'My vast number of chariots
has taken me up the highest mountains,
to the heights of Lebanon's forests.
I cut down its loftiest cedars, its choicest cypresses.
I ascended its highest peak and claimed its great forests.
²⁵I dug wells and drank foreign water.*ᵃ*
The feet of my armies trampled the Nile delta dry.'

²⁶"Have you not learned that I planned all this long ago?
Yes, from ages past I planned it, and now I fulfill it,
that you would conquer fortified cities
and turn them into piles of stones.
²⁷The inhabitants were frightened and ashamed.
They became *as fragile* as weeds and tender grass,

---

a 37:25 As translated from the Dead Sea scroll 1QIsaᵃ. See also 2 Kings 19:24.

as short-lived as the grass that grows on the rooftop
and is scorched before the east wind.[a]
[28]I know where you live, every movement you make,
all that you do, and your rage against me.
[29]I have heard your arrogant words,
and because you rage against me,
I will put my hook in your nose and my bit in your mouth,
and I will make you return by the way you came.'"

[30]"Hezekiah, this will be a sign for you: This year you will eat only grain that grows of itself. Next year you will eat what comes of that. Then, in the third year, *life will be normal again.* You will sow and reap, plant vineyards and eat their fruit. [31]Judah's remnant will flourish again, sending deep roots into the ground and bearing luscious fruit above, [32]for a remnant will go out from Mount Zion and Jerusalem. The fiery passion of Yahweh, Commander of Angel Armies, will accomplish this!

[33]"Therefore, here is what I, Yahweh, have to say about the king of Assyria: He will neither enter this city, nor shoot even one arrow here, nor raise a warrior's shield, nor build a siege ramp against Jerusalem. [34]I declare that by the way he came, by that same way he will leave. He will not set foot in the city. [35]I promise to defend this city and protect it, for the sake of my own honor and for the sake of David, my loving servant."

God's Miraculous Deliverance
[36]That night the angel of Yahweh came into the Assyrian camp and slaughtered 185,000 soldiers. When morning dawned, there were only dead bodies in the enemy's camp! [37]Sennacherib, the *great* king of Assyria, left, returning *the same way he came,* and retreated to Nineveh, *the Assyrian capital.* [38]Then *one day,* as he was worshiping in the temple of his god, Nisroch, his sons, Adrammelech and Sharezer, entered the temple and killed him with swords. They escaped into the land of Ararat and the king's son Esar-haddon succeeded him.[b]

Hezekiah's Illness
38 Now, Hezekiah became sick and was at the point of death. The prophet Isaiah, son of Amoz, came and prophesied to him, saying, "This is what Yahweh has to say to you: Set your affairs in order, for you will not recover from this illness. You are going to die." [2]Then Hezekiah *broke down and wept,* turned his face to the wall, and prayed, "O please, Yahweh, please. I beg you, *let me live.* [3]Remember how I have walked faithfully before your face. With all my heart, I have sought to do only what is good in your eyes." Bitter tears streamed down his face.

[4]Then Isaiah received another prophetic word for Hezekiah. Yahweh said to him, [5]"Go deliver this message to Hezekiah: 'This is what Yahweh, the God of your ancestor David, has to say to you: I have heard your *heartfelt* prayer and

---

a 37:27 As translated from the Dead Sea scroll 1QIsaᵃ.
b 37:38 See 2 Kings 19:35–37; 2 Chron. 32:21–22.

I have seen you cry tear after bitter tear. I will give you another fifteen years. ⁶I will defend Jerusalem, and I will deliver you and this city from the hand of the king of Assyria. ⁷This will be a sign to you from Yahweh as a confirmation that I will do for you what I have promised. ⁸I will cause the sun's shadow to retreat ten steps on the stairway of Ahaz.'"

Then the sunlight went back up the ten steps it had gone down.ᵃ

Hezekiah's Psalm of Praise

⁹Here is the poem of Hezekiah, king of Judah, which he wrote when he was healed from his illness:

¹⁰I was dying in the prime of life.
  I thought, "Must I leave this world now?
  Must I go through the gates of death
  and miss out on the rest of my years?"
¹¹I thought, "I won't get to seeᵇ Yah again
  in the land of the living.
  No longer will I see my friends or family
  nor enjoy the company of anyone living on earth.
¹²My body is being folded up and taken from me,
  taken down like a shepherd's tent.
  He cuts my life short,
  as a weaver cuts his cloth from the loom and rolls it up.
  From day to night, you bring my life to an end.
¹³I felt as though a lion were crushing all my bones
  as I cried out for help until morning.
  From day to night, you bring my life to an end.
¹⁴I *could only* chirp like a swallow or small bird;
  I could only moan like a dove.
  My eyes are weary from looking up into heaven.
  Yahweh, I am so depressed. Come and be my strength.ᶜ
¹⁵But what can I say?
  For he has spoken to me and told me
  that he is the one who has done this.ᵈ
  I can't sleep a winkᵉ because I'm overwhelmed with grief.ᶠ
¹⁶Lord, it is because of your kindnessᵍ that life is given.
  It is in you that my spirit lives.ʰ

---

a 38:8 It is possible that these steps functioned as some type of a sundial. See *Hebrew and Aramaic Lexicon of the Old Testament,* 614, s.v.

b 38:11 Or "appear before (in the temple)."

c 38:14 Or "stability."

d 38:15 This is almost the same as saying, "It is finished."

e 38:15 Or "All my sleep has fled" or "I walk slowly all my years." The Hebrew is uncertain.

f 38:15 Or "because of the bitterness of my soul."

g 38:16 Or "because of these things (kindness, mercy, acts of love, goodness of God)."

h 38:16 The meaning of this Hebrew sentence is uncertain.

Now restore my health and give me life *again*!
¹⁷Truly, it was for my own good
 that I had this bitter experience.
For you loved my soul out of the pit of oblivion.
You cast all my sins behind your back.
¹⁸The grave and those buried there cannot praise you.
Neither the realm of death nor those who enter it
 can give you thanks or hope for your faithfulness.
¹⁹It's the living who thank you as I do today.
One generation makes your faithfulness known to the next.
²⁰Yahweh is pleased to *heal me and* save me!
We will sing to the music of stringed instruments
 every day of our lives in Yahweh's house."

²¹Now, Isaiah had said to Hezekiah, "Have the *physicians* apply a poultice of cakes of dried figs to your boil, and you will recover."

²²And Hezekiah had said, "What will be the sign from God that I will be healed and go up again to worship in Yahweh's house?"*ᵃ*

Hezekiah's Failure

39 Shortly after *Hezekiah was healed of his illness*, the king of Babylon, Merodach-Baladan,*ᵇ* son of Baladan,*ᶜ* heard that King Hezekiah had been deathly ill and had recovered. So he sent envoys carrying letters and a *lavish* gift. ²*Delighted by the king's gesture, and having a desire to impress them*, Hezekiah welcomed the envoys from Babylon and opened the doors of the king's store-houses of treasures and showed them to the envoys. He let them see all of his gold, silver, spices, and costly fragrant oils, as well as his entire armory. All of the king's royal treasures, all that was in the king's palace, and all the wealth of his whole kingdom was shown to them.

³Then Isaiah the prophet visited the king and said to him, "*What have you done?* What did these men say and where did they come from?"

Hezekiah replied, "They are envoys from distant Babylon."

⁴Then Isaiah asked, "What did they see in your palace?"

"They have seen everything in my palace," responded Hezekiah. "I showed them everything in my royal treasuries."

⁵Isaiah said to Hezekiah, "Here is what Yahweh, Commander of Angel Armies, has to say to you: ⁶'The days are coming when all the treasures in your palace and all the wealth that your ancestors have stored up until this day will be carried off to Babylon; absolutely nothing will be left,' says the Lord. ⁷Some of

---

a 38:22 Because this verse seems so out of place, many contemporary translations place it between v. 6 and v. 7. See also 2 Kings 20:7–8. Hezekiah was not afraid of asking for a sign, not wanting to make the mistake of his father, Ahaz (Isa. 7:11–13).

b 39:1 *Merodach-Baladan* means "god of blood and slaughter, mars, war, murder."

c 39:1 *Baladan* means "Baal is his lord."

your own sons who come after you will be deported, *be castrated,* and become eunuchs in the palace of the king of Babylon.'"

⁸Then Hezekiah said to Isaiah, "The word Yahweh has spoken through you is good and right." *For he thought,* "At least for me, there will be peace and security in my lifetime."*ª*

Comfort My People

40 Your God says to you:
"Comfort, comfort my people*ᵇ with gentle, compassionate words.ᶜ*
²Speak *tenderly* from the heart*ᵈ* to *revive* those in Jerusalem,*ᵉ*
and proclaim that their warfare is over.*ᶠ*
Her debt of sin is paid for, and she will not be treated as guilty.*ᵍ*
Prophesy to her that she has received from the hand of Yahweh
twice as *many blessings as* all her sins."*ʰ*

³A *thunderous* voice cries out in the wilderness:*ⁱ*
"Prepare the way*ʲ for* Yahweh's arrival!

---

a 39:8 Hezekiah, the reformer, went from being a man who was favored by God and divinely healed to one who thought only of himself. See 2 Chron. 32:25.

b 40:1 The Targum reads "You prophets, prophesy comfort, comfort to my people." See Jer. 31:13, 20; Zeph. 3:14–17; 2 Cor. 1:3.

c 40:1 The Hebrew *nacham* contains deep emotion, compassionate words that give relief and tender consolation to people. Beginning in Isaiah 40, the prophet's tone and ministry changes from that of chs. 1–39, much like the New Testament brings us an even sweeter, more glorious message than the Old (2 Cor. 3:9). The New Testament begins with John the Baptizer quoting from Isaiah 40, demonstrating that the time has come for the removal of our sins. Compare Isa. 40:3 and Mark 1:3. Isaiah 1–39 speaks of a worldwide desolation; Isaiah 40–66 speaks of a worldwide restoration. The later chapters of this book are described by some scholars as the "New Testament of Isaiah." The New Testament has twenty-seven books, corresponding to Isaiah's last twenty-seven chapters. An outline of the remainder of the book could be: The Book of Comfort (40–43), The Book of Cyrus (44–48), The Book of Messiah, the Servant of the Lord (49–57), the Book of Judah, the Victory of the Bride (58–66).

d 40:2 Or "Speak to the heart (to revive)."

e 40:2 Scripture often contains multiple meanings and applications. Jerusalem here can also mean the church. The church does not replace Jerusalem (Israel), but can be viewed as a "new" Israel (Gal. 6:16). Believers today find their present reality in the New Jerusalem, where God and man have become one. See Gal. 4:26; Heb. 12:22.

f 40:2 For the overcoming believer, the warfare of Romans 7 has ended as we become victorious overcomers who move into Christ's victory found in Romans 8. Our race begins at the finish line (Rom. 6:5–7).

g 40:2 See John 19:30; Rom. 8:1; Col. 2:13–14; 1 Peter 3:18.

h 40:2 The Hebrew text is somewhat ambiguous. It could mean double punishment or double blessing. That is, they will receive from the hand of God twice what they have lost. Favor and mercy always triumph over judgment. God will excel in grace toward his people and give us back even more than what our sins took from us. See Ex. 22:4, 7, 9; Job 42:10; Isa. 61:7; Zech. 9:12; Rom. 5.

i 40:3 Or "In the wilderness prepare the way for Yahweh's arrival." This was a prophecy of John the Baptizer and his ministry of calling people to repentance in preparation for the appearing of the Lord Jesus. Although John came in the spirit of Elijah, he worked no miracles. His prophecy was not to begin a road project but to prepare people's hearts. Even now the voice of the Spirit is crying out in the wilderness of people's souls, bringing them to repentance and faith in Christ.

j 40:3 See John 14:6.

Make a highway straight through the desert for our God!
⁴Every valley will be raised up,ª every mountain brought low.
　The rugged terrain will become level ground
　and the rough places a plain.
⁵Then Yahweh's radiant glory will be unveiled,
　and all humanityᵇ will experience it together.ᶜ
　Believe it, for Yahweh has spoken his decree!"ᵈ

⁶A voice says, "Cry out!"
　And I ask, "What should I say?"
　"All people are as frail as grass,
　and their elegance is like a wilting wildflower.
⁷The grass withers, the flower fades
　when the breath of Yahweh blows upon it;
　the people are just like grass!
⁸But even though grass withers and the flower fades,
　the word of our God stands strong forever!"ᵉ

Proclaim Good News
⁹Go up on a high mountain, you joyful messengers of Zion,
　and lift up your voices with power.
　You who proclaim joyous news to Jerusalem,
　shout it out and don't be afraid.
　Say to the cities of Judah,
　"Here is your God!"
¹⁰Look! Here comes Lord Yahweh as a victorious warrior;
　he triumphs with his awesome power.ᶠ
　Watch as he brings with him his reward
　and the spoils of victory to give *to his people.*
¹¹*He will care for you* as a shepherd tends his flock,
　gathering the *weak* lambs and taking them in his arms.
　He carries them close to his heart
　and gently leads those that have young.ᵍ

The Infinite God
¹²Who has measured the waters *of the sea*
　in the hollow of his hand

---

a 40:4 See Isa. 54:17.
b 40:5 Or "all flesh" (i.e., Jews and gentiles).
c 40:5 Or "All flesh will see it as one." See Rom. 8:19.
d 40:5 See Luke 3:5–6.
e 40:8 See Ps. 103:15–16; 119:89–90; James 1:9–11; 1 Peter 1:24–25.
f 40:10 Or "His mighty arm rules for him."
g 40:10-11 These verses are somewhat parallel to Eph. 4:11, where we can see the *apostle*, "his mighty arm" (v. 10), the *prophet's* "reward" (v. 10 and Matt. 10:41), the *evangelist* (salvation's) "rewards he gives his people" (v. 10), the *pastor* or "shepherd tending his flock" (v. 11), and the *teacher* who "gently leads" (into truth, v. 11).

and used his hand-width to mark off the heavens?
Who knows the exact weight of all the dust of the earth[a]
and has weighed all the mountains and hills on his scale?
[13]Who fully understands the Spirit of Yahweh[b]
or is wise enough to counsel him?[c]
[14]Whom does he consult to be enlightened?
Who teaches him the ways of justice?[d]
Who imparts knowledge to him
or shows him the true path of wisdom?[e]
[15]Even the nations are to him like a drop[f] in a bucket,
regarded as nothing more than dust on a scale.
He picks up the islands like fine grains of sand.
[16]All of Lebanon's *trees*[g] are not enough firewood *for him,*
nor are all its animals enough for a burnt offering.
[17]The nations are nothing in his eyes; ˙
he regards them as absolutely nothing.[h]

Idols Cannot Be Compared to God
[18]Who even comes close to being compared to God?[i]
How could you ever compare God to an idol?
[19]A craftsman forms[j] an idol-god,
then a goldsmith overlays it with gold
and forges its silver chains.[k]
[20]The one who is poor and cannot afford silver or gold[l]
chooses a tree[m] that will not rot,
then seeks a skilled workman
to make an idol that will not topple.

---

a 40:12 Or "Who has weighed the dust of the earth in a basket (third of an ephah)?" The Creator could never be measured by his creation; he is infinitely greater.

b 40:13 See Eph. 1:17.

c 40:13 See Rom. 11:34; 1 Cor. 2:16.

d 40:14 Or "Who teaches him the right way to do things?" or "Who gives him insight to make right decisions?"

e 40:14 That is, who is capable enough to show God how to skillfully design his plan or give him the wisdom needed to carry it out? He is too wise to make a mistake. These verses show us God's heart of love (v. 11), God's hand of power (v. 12), and God's mind of wisdom (vv. 13–14).

f 40:15 The Hebrew word used for "drop" is not a drop of water but a myrrh drop. Myrrh was harvested by piercing a tree and collecting drops of sap in a bucket. Nations are more than a drop of water but like myrrh dropping into a bucket.

g 40:16 Lebanon was known for its lumber and forests.

h 40:17 Or "from nothing but emptiness (as though they didn't exist)."

i 40:18 This is the Hebrew word *'el,* "the mighty God."

j 40:19 Or "melts (pours out)."

k 40:19 The Hebrew clause is uncertain.

l 40:20 The Hebrew clause is uncertain.

m 40:20 Adam and Eve chose the Tree of Good and Evil. See also Jer. 10:3–4.

Fear Not

²¹Don't you realize that God is the Creator?
Don't you hear *the truth?*ᵃ
Haven't you been told this from the beginning?
Haven't you understood this
since he laid a firm foundation for the earth?ᵇ
²²He sits enthroned high above the circle of the earth;
to him the people of earth are like grasshoppers!
He stretches out the heavens like a curtain,
spreading it open like a tent to live in.ᶜ
²³He reduces rulers to nothing
and makes the elite of the earth as nothing at all.
²⁴They barely get planted and barely take root *in their position of power*
when the Lord blows on them and they wither away,
carried off like straw in the stormy wind.

God Above All Others

²⁵The Holy One asks:
"Can you find anyone or anything to compare to me?
Where is the one equal to me?"

²⁶Lift up your eyes to the sky and see for yourself.
Who do you think created the cosmos?ᵈ
He lit every *shining star* and formed every *glowing galaxy,*
and stationed them all where they belong.
He has numbered, counted, and given everyone a name.
They shine because of God's incredible power
and awesome might; not one fails to appear!
²⁷Why, then, O Jacob's tribes, would you ever complain?
And my chosen Israel, why would you say,
"Yahweh isn't paying attention to my situation.ᵉ
He has lost all interest in what happens to me."ᶠ

²⁸Don't you know? Haven't you been listening?
Yahweh is the *one and only* everlasting God,
the Creator of all you can see and imagine!
He never gets weary or worn out.

---

a 40:21 Or "Do you not know? Do you not hear?" These two questions (imperfect tense) are best
seen as invitations rather than a surprise over their ignorance. See Young, *Book of Isaiah,
vol. 3,* 40–66.

b 40:21 See Ps. 24:2.

c 40:22 See Ex. 25:8.

d 40:26 See Col. 1:15–16; Eph. 3:9.

e 40:27 Or "my way is hidden from Yahweh."

f 40:27 Or "my decisions are passed over."

His intelligence is unlimited;
he is never puzzled over what to do!
²⁹He empowers the feeble
and infuses the powerless with increasing strength.
³⁰Even young people faint and get exhausted;
athletic ones*a* may stumble and fall.
³¹But those who wait for Yahweh's *grace*
will experience *divine* strength.*b*
They will rise up on soaring wings and fly like eagles,
run *their race* without growing weary,
and walk *through life* without giving up.*c*

God Promises to Help Israel

41 "You lands of the sea, stand silent before me!*d*
Let the people renew their strength!
Let them approach me and state their case.
Let's come together to decide who is right.
²Who raised up the conqueror from the east?*e*
Who commissioned him for his righteous purpose?*f*
The Lord hands nations over to him*g*
to trample kings under his feet,*h*
to make them like dust with his sword*i*
and like windblown chaff with his bow.*j*
³Swiftly he pursues them and advances unscathed
as he passes over unfamiliar land.*k*
⁴Who achieved all this and made it happen?
Who guides the destiny of each generation*l*
from the first *until now*?
I am the one! I am Yahweh, the first,
the *unchanging* one who will be there in the end!"

---

a 40:30 Or "young men."

b 40:31 Or "will grow new feathers like eagles" (LXX) or "renew their strength." An eagle has the longest lifespan of any bird. See Ps. 103:5.

c 40:31 Or "without fainting." The outer court is where we walk, the Holy Place is where we run, and we soar like eagles (into the heavenly realm) in the Holy of Holies (Heb. 10:19).

d 41:1 Or "hold a feast to me" (LXX).

e 41:2 See Isa. 46:11.

f 41:2 Or "Righteousness summoned him to his foot." Some see King Cyrus as the conqueror mentioned here; others, Abraham. It can also be viewed as a prophecy of the Lord Jesus. He is the Mighty One who conquers nations with his love.

g 41:2 See Gen. 12:1–3; Ps. 2:8; Rev. 2:26–29.

h 41:2 See Ps. 149:6–9.

i 41:2 See Eph. 6:17–18; Heb. 4:12.

j 41:2 See Rev. 6:1–2.

k 41:3 Or "No shackle is placed on his feet" (Old Aramaic).

l 41:4 Or "calling nations (to be formed) from the beginning."

⁵The islands see it and panic;
  the ends of the earth tremble;
  they approach and draw near.
⁶The *idol-makers* all bolster one another up,
  saying, "Take courage!"
⁷The woodworker encourages the metalsmith;
  the one who flattens with the hammer
  spurs on the one who strikes the anvil,
  saying of the welding, "Looks good!"
  They nail down the idol so it won't topple.
⁸"But you—my servant, Israel,*ᵃ*
  Jacob, whom I've chosen,
  seed of my beloved friend*ᵇ* Abraham—
⁹I drew you to myself from the ends of the earth
  and called you from its farthest corner.
  I say to you:
  'You are my servant; I have chosen you.
  I have not rejected you!
¹⁰Do not yield to fear, for I am always near.
  Never turn your gaze from me,*ᶜ* for I am your *faithful* God.
  I will infuse you with my strength
  and help you in every situation.*ᵈ*
  I will hold you firmly with my victorious right hand.'

¹¹"All who rage against you will be ashamed and disgraced.
  All who contend with you will perish and disappear.
¹²You will look for your enemies in vain;
  those who war against you will vanish without a trace!
¹³I am Yahweh, your mighty God!
  I grip your right hand *and won't let you go*!
  I whisper to you:
  'Don't be afraid; I am here to help you!'

¹⁴"Jacob, *although you feel like* a grub worm,*ᵉ* have no fear!
  O men of Israel, I am here to help you!

---

a 41:8-20 Yahweh sings three poems of comfort in this chapter: to his chosen servant, Israel (vv. 8–13), to his redeemed warrior-bride (vv. 14–16), and to the poor and needy (vv. 17–20).

b 41:8 See James 2:23.

c 41:10 Or "Don't be frightened." The Hebrew root word *shā'ah* means "to gaze, to look around."

d 41:10 See Deut. 31:6–8.

e 41:14 David used this term to prophetically point to Jesus as he was being crucified. See Ps. 22:6. The Hebrew word is *tola*, which is a species of worm found in the Middle East (*Coccus ilicus*) that reproduces itself when the female fastens herself to a tree and lays eggs between her body and the tree. When the eggs hatch, the baby worms feed on her living body. When the eggs emerge, the blood remains on the tree as a crimson stain. When Jesus died on the

I am your Kinsman-Redeemer,[a]
the Holy One of Israel![b]
[15]I am making you into a powerful threshing instrument,[c]
with teeth[d] new and sharp!
You will reduce hills to chaff and crush mountains[e] into dust!
[16]You will winnow them, and the stormy wind will blow them away!
Then you will spin and dance with rejoicing[f] in Yahweh,
boasting with admiration in the Holy One of Israel![g]

[17]"I, Yahweh, will respond to the cry of the poor and needy
when they are thirsty and their tongues are parched with thirst!
When they seek a drink of water but there is none,
I, the God of Israel, will not abandon them.
[18]I will open up refreshing streams[h] on the barren hills
and springing fountains in the valleys.[i]
I will make the desert a pleasant pool[j]
and the dry land springs of water.[k]
[19]I will plant in the *treeless* desert cedars and achaia,[l]
myrtle[m] and olive trees.[n]
I will set in the wilderness evergreens,[o]

---

cross (tree), his blood left a crimson stain and he gave birth to the church. He nourishes us and sustains us with body and blood.

a 41:14 A kinsman-redeemer (*go'el*) is a male relative who was culturally responsible to act on behalf of a relative who was in trouble or danger, needed to be redeemed from slavery, or was in need of rescue. He became like a "savior" or "family protector" for his next of kin. Jesus, our next of kin, is our Kinsman-Redeemer. The Hebrew verb *ga'al* ("to act as redeemer") is found more than one hundred times in the Hebrew Bible. See Ruth 2:20.

b 41:14 Although God is holy, he stoops to tenderly help those who feel unholy.

c 41:15 Or "a threshing sledge," a board with iron studs like teeth that is driven over wheat to grind the chaff off the grain, which is then winnowed.

d 41:15 Or "the owner of two mouths." The Word of God is like a "two-mouthed sword" (Heb. 4:12), for it is spoken from God's mouth and is released in power as it is spoken from our mouths. We will become God's two-mouthed *threshing instrument*!

e 41:15 Mountains are a frequent biblical metaphor for kingdoms and nations.

f 41:16 The Hebrew word for "rejoice" (*giyl*) implies "twirling, spinning, shouting with delight and joy."

g 41:16 Or "You will rejoice among the holy things of Israel."

h 41:18 See John 7:37–39.

i 41:18 See Ps. 84:6.

j 41:18 See Isa. 35:1–10.

k 41:18 See 68:5–6.

l 41:19 Acacia wood was used extensively in the tabernacle and was used to form the ark of the covenant.

m 41:19 "Myrtle" is the Hebrew word *Hadassah*, Esther's Jewish name.

n 41:19 Or "trees of oil" (the Holy Spirit).

o 41:19 Or "fir trees."

together with many elm and cypress.*[a]*
²⁰Everyone will see
and know that I, Yahweh, with my mighty hands have done this.
They will consider and comprehend
that the Holy One of Israel has created it."*[b]*

Pagan Gods Are Nothing
²¹Yahweh says, "Present your case."
"Let's hear your arguments," says the King of Jacob's tribes.
²²"*Come, you idols,* and let's hear your prophecy for the future.
Tell us, tell us about your former *prophecies*
so we can test them and see if they were fulfilled,
or decree some future event for us.
²³Prophesy what the future holds
to prove to us that you are gods.
Do something—anything!*[c]*
Frighten us or put us in awe!
²⁴But you are nothing at all! What have you ever accomplished?
Whoever chooses to worship you is disgusting!

²⁵"I stirred up one from the north,
who comes from the rising of the sun.
He will call on my name.*[d]*
He will trample rulers into the mud as a potter treads clay.
²⁶Which of you foretold this from the start?
Who prophesied it from long ago that we can say, 'He is right'?
None of you prophesied it!
None of you announced it ahead of time!
No one heard you say a thing about it!
²⁷I was the first to decree to Zion, 'Look, this is what's about to happen!'*[e]*
I am bringing a messenger to Jerusalem with good news.
²⁸But when I look, I find no one who is capable to counsel me!
There is no one who can respond to me with the right answer!
Who could I even ask?
²⁹Look, all these *gods* are nothingness!
What have they ever accomplished?
Their metal images are nothing but empty wind and confusion!

---

a 41:19 These seven trees speak of fullness of new creation life. Compare them to the seven branches of the lampstand and the seven Spirits of God.
b 41:20 That is, the Lord created the unity of this forest. God is the one who makes us one.
c 41:23 Or "Do good, do harm."
d 41:25 Or "He is summoned in my name." Some believe that Cyrus fulfilled this prophecy, for he came from the east (Persia) and descended on Israel from the north. Others see the Messiah, who came from the north (Ps. 48:2) and is the Dayspring from the rising of the sun.
e 41:27 Fulfilled prophecy is one of many evidences that God is real and powerful and that he knows all things.

The Lord's Servant

42 "Take a good look at my servant!*a*
I love him dearly,*b* for he is my chosen one.
I have taken hold of him in my strength,*c*
and I have clothed him with my Spirit.*d*
He will cause justice to spring up for the nations.
²He will be gentle and will not quarrel with others in public.
He will not exalt his own voice.
³He would never crush a broken heart*e*
nor disregard the weak and vulnerable.*f*
He will make sure justice comes to those who are wronged.
⁴His *inner being* will not become faint or discouraged,
nor will *his light* grow dim before he establishes justice on the earth.
Even the distant lands beyond the seas
will hunger for his instruction."*g*

⁵Here are the words of the true God, Yahweh,
the one who created the starry heavens and stretched them out.
He is the one who formed the earth and filled it with life.
He gives breath to every person
and spirit to everyone everywhere.
⁶"I, Yahweh, have commissioned you in righteousness *to succeed.*
I will take your hand *in love* and watch over you.
I will give you as a covenant*h* for the people,
a walking-light to the nations.
⁷*Your mission is* to open blind eyes,
to set prisoners free from dark dwellings,

---

a 42:1 Isaiah introduces to us the Lord Jesus, the Messiah, as the chosen servant of the Lord, sustained by Yahweh, sent on a divine mission to bring light and freedom to the hearts of his covenant people. Starting with ch. 42, Isaiah gives us four Servant Songs. (1) This chapter presents him as the Faithful Servant who brings light to the nations. (2) In 49:1–13 he is the Chosen Servant to bring salvation to the nations and to restore Israel. (3) In 50:4–9, we have the song of the Obedient Servant who reveals the Father. (4) In 52:13–53:12 we find the Suffering Servant. See also Matt. 12:18–21.

b 42:1 Or "I find all my delight in him." See Matt. 3:17.

c 42:1 Or "whom I uphold (by my strength)."

d 42:1 Or "placed my Spirit upon him."

e 42:3 "A bruised (bent over) reed." A reed can be seen as a biblical metaphor for the feebleness of humanity. Jesus, God's servant, is extraordinarily gentle. Rather than break weak ones, he restores and heals them. See Matt. 12:20.

f 42:3 Or "nor extinguish a smoldering candle (those whose light and faith is growing dim)."

g 42:4 These first four verses give us the qualifications for ministry: (1) chosen and anointed by God, (2) committed to reach the unreached, (3) gentle and compassionate, and (4) not discouraged but having unfailing courage.

h 42:6 The Hebrew text is clear that this covenant is a person, the servant of the Lord. In him is found all the blessings of the covenant. He is the embodiment of God's covenant promises.

and to open prison doors to those who are held by darkness.[a]
⁸I am Yahweh; that is my name.
 I will not give my glory to another *god*
 nor my renown to idols.
⁹Don't you see that what I have prophesied has come to pass?[b]
 And now I am foretelling the future.
 I declare it to you before it sprouts up."[c]

A New Song for a New Day
¹⁰Sing to Yahweh a brand-new song![d]
 Sing his praise *until it echoes* from the ends of the earth!
 Sailors and sea creatures, praise him!
 Islands and all their inhabitants, sing his praise!
¹¹Let the desert and its villages lift their voices in praise!
 Let the *tent* villages of Kedar[e] shout their praises!
 Let the residents of Sela's cliffs[f] shout with glee,
 with a celebration shout from the mountaintops![g]
¹²Let them give Yahweh the glorious praise he deserves
 and declare his praise in the islands!

Our Hero-God
¹³Yahweh goes out to battle like a hero[h]
 and stirs up his passion and zeal like a mighty warrior.
 Yes, his God-shout is a mighty battle cry;
 he will triumph heroically over *all* his foes.[i]

¹⁴For a long time, I said nothing.[j]
 I restrained myself and kept silent.
 Now I will groan, pant, and gasp like a woman in labor.
¹⁵I will level their hills and mountains[k]
 and dry up all their vegetation.
 I will turn rivers into islands and dry up their lakes.

---

a 42:7 See Isa. 61:1–2; Luke 4:16–21.

b 42:9 Or "The former things (prophecies), behold—they have come!"

c 42:9 A possible metaphor for the resurrection of Jesus.

d 42:10 Every new thing God does requires a new song to declare it. See Rev. 5:9.

e 42:11 Kedar was a son of Ishmael (Gen. 25:13) and his tribe were considered nomads. Kedar can also be seen as a metaphor for the old nature.

f 42:11 *Sela* means "rock" (Song. 2:14) and was once the capitol of Edom.

g 42:11 See Song. 4:8.

h 42:13 As he carried our cross, Jesus went out from Jerusalem as a hero to conquer our foes.

i 42:13 Or "He shows himself superior to his enemies." Every spiritual enemy is conquered by the Son of God—even death.

j 42:14 Or "I have been silent. Should I remain silent forever and hold my peace?" (LXX).

k 42:15 Hills and mountains are frequent metaphors for governments, nations, and kingdoms.

[16]I will walk[a] the blind by an unknown way[b]
and guide them on paths they've never traveled.
I will smooth their difficult road[c]
and make their dark *mysteries* bright with light.[d]
These are things I will do for them,
for I will never abandon *my beloved ones.*[e]
[17]But those who trust in idols,
who say to their metal images,
"You are our gods,"
will be turned aside in total disgrace.[f]

Blind and Deaf to Truth
[18]Hear me, you deaf! Look up, you blind, and see!
[19]Who is as blind as my servant *Israel*
or as deaf as the messenger I send?[g]
Who is as blind as my covenant friend,
as blind as Yahweh's servant?
[20]*Israel*, you have seen so much, but you don't get it!
You have been taught so much,[h] but what did you really hear?[i]

[21]For the sake of his righteousness,
Yahweh was eager to exalt his law and make it glorious.[j]
[22]But this is a people plundered and robbed,
trapped in holes and hidden in houses of bondage.[k]
They are like prey that no one will rescue,
like spoil with no one to say, "Bring them back!"

---

a 42:16 See John 16:13; Rom. 8:14.

b 42:16 See Josh. 3:4; John 14:6; Heb. 10:19–22.

c 42:16 This can be seen as a metaphor for God changing our hearts and removing obstacles for us to walk with him. No obstacle within us will prevent God from accomplishing his plan.

d 42:16 Darkness is a frequent biblical metaphor for ignorance and light for understanding (revelation light).

e 42:16 See Matt. 28:18–20; Heb. 13:5.

f 42:17 Or "In shame you will be ashamed."

g 42:19 Israel is given a divine mission to serve God and his purposes. The nation is to become his messenger. See Rom. 11.

h 42:20 Or "You have ears to hear."

i 42:20 See Prov. 28:9.

j 42:21 Or "It pleased Yahweh to praise his justice and make his law glorious."

k 42:22 Or "prisons." This section (vv. 18–25) deals with God's people in bondage. Judah was held captive in Babylon; the church is held captive to religious systems and to concepts from which Jesus came to set us free (Gal. 4:3, 8). We must always be careful to hear and see with hearts open to God and ready to receive the new thing God is doing on the earth today. Jesus was blind and deaf to doing anything other than the will of his Father. God is still restoring his church and making us like Christ, free and full of new life.

²³Doesn't anyone understand this?
Will any of you pay attention to this in the future?
²⁴Who gave up Jacob to looters and Israel to robbers?
It was Yahweh himself, against whom we sinned
by not walking in holy ways nor heeding holy words.
²⁵So he poured out the heat of his anger
and *they suffered* the fury of war.
His anger enveloped them in flames,
but they still did not understand—
consumed by fire yet they did not take it to heart.

Promise of Restoration

43 Now, this is what Yahweh says:
"*Listen*, Jacob, to the One who created you,
Israel, to the one who shaped who you are.ᵃ
Do not fear,
for I, your Kinsman-Redeemer, will rescue you.
I have called you by name, and you are mine.
²When you pass throughᵇ the *deep, stormy* sea,
you can count on me to be there with you.
When you pass through *raging* rivers,
You will not drown.
When you walk through *persecution like* fiery flames,
you will not be burned;
the flames will not harm you,
³for I am your Savior, Yahweh, your mighty God,
the Holy One of Israel!
I give up Egypt as the price to set you free,
Cush and Seba in exchange to *bring you back*.ᶜ
⁴Since you are *cherished and* preciousᵈ in my eyes,
and because I love you *dearly* and *want* to honorᵉ you,
I willingly give up nations in exchange for you—
a manᶠ to save your life.

---

a 43:1 Jacob was created, but Israel was formed. God forms (transforms) Jacob into Israel. God is seen here as the one who changes the nature of man. See Gen. 32:28.

b 43:2 God's method of deliverance is often not "out of" but "through." His presence as we go *through* difficulties becomes our deliverance. See Ps. 23:4.

c 43:3 Seba was an African nation that bordered Egypt. God is saying that there is no price too high for him to pay to set his people free. In the days of Isaiah, these nations (Egypt, Cush, and Seba) were united as one dynasty. They were given in exchange, as it were, to Persia for Israel's future deliverance through the successors of Cyrus.

d 43:4 Or "dear, costly, of great price."

e 43:4 This is the Hebrew word for "glory" (*kabad*).

f 43:4 Or "people" (Heb. *adam*). God gave up a Man (the last "Adam," 1 Cor. 15:45) for those who are precious to him.

⁵I am with you now, *even close to you*,
  so never yield to fear.
  I will bring your children*ᵃ* from the east;
  from the west I will gather you.
⁶I will say to the north, 'Hand them over!'
  and to the south, 'Don't hold them back!'
  Bring me my sons from far away,
  my daughters from the ends of the earth!
⁷*Bring me* everyone who is called by my name,*ᵇ*
  the ones I created to experience my glory.*ᶜ*
  I myself formed them to be *who they are*
  and made them *for my glory*."*ᵈ*

God's Witness
⁸Lead out those who have eyes but are blind,
  those who have ears but are deaf.
⁹Let all the nations gather together and the people assemble.
  Which of their *gods*ᵉ prophesied this?
  Which of them foretold what is about to happen?
  Let them bring out their witnesses to make their case;
  let them take the stand and testify, "It is true."
¹⁰Yahweh says, "You are my witnesses, my chosen servants.
  I chose you in order that you would know me *intimately*,
  believe me always, and fully understand that I am the only God.
  There was no god before me,
  and there will be no other god after me.
¹¹I, only I, am Yahweh, and there is no Savior-God but me.
¹²I am the only one who revealed this to you.
  I saved you, foretold*ᶠ* the future, *and brought it to pass.*
  It was not some foreign god who did this!
  You are my witnesses that I am God," declares Yahweh.
¹³"From the very beginning, I am the only God!*ᵍ*
  No one can be snatched from my hand.
  When I *choose to* act, who can reverse it?"

---

a 43:5 Or "your seed."

b 43:7 Isaiah is prophesying of Israel's restoration and foretelling of a great worldwide harvest among the nations as a fulfillment of the Feast of Ingathering (Harvest) known as Tabernacles.

c 43:7 Or "for my glory."

d 43:7 We were created both to bring God glory and to experience his glory. See Rom. 8:30; Rev. 4:11.

e 43:9 Or "who of them."

f 43:12 Or "proclaimed," a word often used for proclaiming what is to come (v. 9).

g 43:13 Or "Ever since day was, I am he."

God, Israel's Protector

¹⁴This is what Yahweh,
  your Kinsman-Redeemer, the Holy One of Israel, says:ᵃ
  "For your good, I will send for the Babylonians;
  I will bring them all as fugitives
  and turn the shouting of the Chaldeans into mourning.ᵇ
¹⁵I am Yahweh, your Holy One and your King,
  the Creator of Israel."

God Will Do a New Thing

¹⁶Yahweh is the one who makes a way in the sea,
  a pathway in the mighty waters.ᶜ
¹⁷He destroyedᵈ chariots and horsesᵉ
  and all their mighty warriors.
  They fell, never to rise again—
  gone forever, snuffed out like a wick. This is what he says:
¹⁸"Stop dwelling on the past.
  Don't even remember these former things.
¹⁹I am doing something brand new, *something unheard of.*
  Even now it sprouts and grows and matures.
  Don't you perceive it?ᶠ
  I will make a way in the wilderness
  and open up flowing streamsᵍ in the desert.
²⁰Wild beasts,ʰ jackals, and owls will glorify me.ⁱ
  For I supply streams of water in the desert
  and rivers in the wilderness
  to satisfy the thirst of my people, my chosen ones,
²¹so that you, whom I have shaped and formed for myself,
  will proclaim my praise.ʲ
²²Yet you did not call out to me, O Jacob.
  Are you so wearyᵏ of me, O Israel?

---

a 43:14 It is a beautiful thought that the Holy One, who must punish evil, is also our Kinsman-Redeemer. He loves us so much that he became the sacrifice to return us to God. See Lev. 25:25; Ruth 3:9; 4:14; Isa. 44:24.

b 43:14 Or "in ships their joyful shout." The Hebrew of this clause is uncertain.

c 43:16 Jesus, walking on the water, made a way (or journey) in the sea. See Ps. 77:19.

d 43:17 Or "led out (to destruction)."

e 43:17 Chariots and horses are frequent biblical metaphors for the strength of the flesh.

f 43:19 See Amos 3:7.

g 43:19 Or "paths" (Dead Sea scroll 1QIsaᵃ). See John 7:37–39.

h 43:20 The beast is a common biblical metaphor for human nature. See Ps. 73:22.

i 43:20 The Hebrew word for "jackals" (*tannim*) and can be translated "dragon."

j 43:21 See 1 Peter 2:9–10.

k 43:22 Or "weary yourself (with longing)."

²³You have not brought me your sheep for burnt offerings
or honored me with your sacrifices.
I have not burdened you by requiring *many* grain offerings
or wearied you with demands for frankincense.
²⁴You did not buy me fragrant calamus reeds
or lavish me with the fat of your sacrifices.*ᵃ*
Instead, you have burdened me with your many sins
and wearied me with your evil deeds.
²⁵I, yes I, am the One and Only,*ᵇ*
who completely erases your sins, *never to be seen again.*
I will not remember them again.
Freely I do this because of who I am!*ᶜ*
²⁶Help me remember *the past.* Let's debate!
Bring me your version to prove your innocence.
²⁷Your earliest ancestor*ᵈ* sinned,
and your spokesmen*ᵉ* rebelled against me.
²⁸So I brought disgrace on the holy priests
of the holy sanctuary*ᶠ*
and brought destruction to Jacob,
humiliation and scorn to Israel.

Yahweh, the Only True God

44 ¹⁻²"Now, listen to me, my servant Jacob,
Israel, my chosen one.
I am Yahweh, your Creator, who shaped you in *my* womb.*ᵍ*
Hear what I have to say to you:
'Don't fear. I will help you, O Jacob my servant,
Do not fear, my pleasing one,*ʰ* *Israel.*
³I will pour refreshing water on the thirsty
and streams on the dry ground.*ⁱ*

---

a 43:24 See Heb. 13:15.

b 43:25 This is doubly emphatic in the Hebrew. God refers to himself with fifteen emphatic personal pronouns in this chapter.

c 43:25 Or "for my own sake."

d 43:27 Some believe this to be a reference to Abraham, Jacob, or Adam.

e 43:27 This is most likely the teaching priests.

f 43:28 One ancient manuscript reads "Your rulers (priests) profaned my holy sanctuary."

g 44:1–2 There is no verse in the Bible that speaks of God as our mother, but there are frequent metaphors that imply God gave us birth (and new birth), nurtured us in his love, and even formed us in his womb. The love God has for us is similar to a mother's love. The Hebrew concept of compassion carries this thought, for compassion (*racham*) is the same word as "womb." God has a womb-love for each of us. This thought resurfaces more than once in these later chapters of Isaiah.

h 44:1–2 Or "Jeshurun," a symbolic name for Israel showing her unique, intimate relationship with God. It is taken from the root word *yashar*, "to please." Others translate this endearing term for Israel as "upright one." God will straighten out the crookedness of Jacob. Jeshurun is found only here and in Deuteronomy (Deut. 32:15; 33:5, 26).

i 44:3 See Ps. 68:5–6.

I will pour out my Spirit on your children,[a]
my blessing upon your descendants.
⁴They will spring up like grass blanketing a meadow,[b]
like poplars growing by gushing streams.
⁵One will say, "I belong to Yahweh."
Another will be called Jacob.
Yet another will write on his hand "Property of Yahweh."
Another will adopt the name Israel.'"

⁶The words of Yahweh,
Israel's true King[c] and Kinsman-Redeemer,
Yahweh, Commander of Angel Armies, says:
"I am the Beginning and I am the Ending,[d]
and I am the only God there is.
⁷Who is like me? Go ahead, stand and speak up.
I'll wait for him to announce it and explain it all to me!
Who else has announced from everlasting[e] what is to come?[f]
Let him prophesy what is yet to be.
⁸Do not fear nor be shaken!
Haven't I foretold it, announcing it to you ahead of time?
You are my witnesses, *so tell me,* is there any god besides me?
There is no other Rock *of shelter*; I know not one."

⁹Idol-makers amount to nothing,
and the things they treasure can do no one any good.
They are witnesses with blind eyes who know nothing;
they will be disgraced.
¹⁰What kind of person would form an idol-god
or cast an image with no ability to do any good?
¹¹*No wonder* those who worship them[g] will be put to shame.
Their craftsmen are only human beings.
Let them all come together and take their stand.
They will all be terrified and put to shame!
¹²The blacksmith takes his tongs and heats it over the coals,

---

a 44:3 See Acts 2:12–17.

b 44:4 Or "like a binu-tree" (Dead Sea scroll 1QIsaᵃ).

c 44:6 See Matt. 27:42; Mark 15:32; John 1:49; 12:13.

d 44:6 Or "I am the First, and I am the Last."

e 44:7 "Everlasting" is *'olam*, and there are nine more everlasting things found in Isaiah: (1) Everlasting God (40:28; 63:12), (2) Everlasting Covenant (55:3; 61:8), (3) Everlasting Kindness (54:8), (4) Everlasting Salvation (45:17), (5) Everlasting Majesty on God's people (60:15), (6) Everlasting Joy (51:11), (7) Everlasting Name (56:5), (8) Everlasting Light (60:19–20), and (9) Everlasting Sign (55:13).

f 44:7 The meaning of the Hebrew is uncertain. "from my placing an eternal people and things to come."

g 44:11 Or "those who produce them."

forming it with hammers, forging it with his strong arm.
But when he gets hungry, his strength ebbs away,
and if he doesn't drink water, he quickly grows weary.
[13]The woodworker stretches out a measuring line,
then marks it and fashions his idol-god with his carving tools.
Then he uses a stylus to trace it out on the wood[a]
and shapes it into the figure of a man,
trying to make it look like a beautiful human
to be displayed somewhere in a shrine.
[14]He chooses a cedar or a cypress or an oak,
but first lets it grow strong in the forest.
He plants a pine tree, and it is nourished by the rain.
[15]The wood serves man for fuel;
some he uses to warm himself
and with some he bakes his bread.
But from this same wood he also makes a god to worship
and bows down to the idol he formed.
[16]Half of the wood he burns in the fire to roast his meat.
Then he eats his fill and is satisfied.
Part he uses to warm himself and says,
"Ah, I'm warm and cozy sitting by the fire."
[17]With the rest of it he makes his idol-god,
bows down to it, and worships it!
He prays to it, saying, "Save me, for you are my god!"
[18]They have no clue what they're doing
and don't comprehend *how absurd it is*!
For they shut their eyes so they cannot see.
They close their hearts so they cannot understand.
[19]They have no knowledge, no understanding,
no discernment to say,
"Half of the wood I burned in the fire.
I roasted meat and cooked my dinner.
Now should I take the rest of the wood
and make it into an abomination?
Should I bow down and worship a block of wood?"
[20]He feeds *his spirit* on ashes![b]
His deluded heart leads him astray.
He can't even ask himself,
"Is this thing I'm holding in my right hand a fraud?"

God Never Forgets Israel
[21]"Remember these things, O Jacob's tribes,
and Israel, you are my servant.

---

a 44:13 Or "rounds it with his instruments."
b 44:20 Or "the shepherd of ashes."

I created you to be my servant, and I will never forget you!
[22]I have swept away your sins like a thick cloud.[a]
I have made your guilt to vanish
like mist disappearing into thin air.
Now come back, come back to me,
for I have paid the price for you."[b]

[23]Sing! Starry sky above, break loose with singing,
for Yahweh has finished it!
Shout! Earth deep below, give up your shout!
Mountains high, break out with joyous songs of praise!
Let the forest choirs join in, with every tree singing its notes!
For Yahweh has paid the ransom price for Jacob's tribes,
and he will be glorified in Israel!

God Is in Control
[24]Here is what Yahweh,
your Kinsman-Redeemer, who formed you in *his* womb, has to say:
"I am Yahweh, Creator of all.
I alone stretched out the canvas of the cosmos.
I who shaped the earth needed no one's help.
[25]Now I make fools of fortune-tellers
and frustrate astrologers' predictions.
I confuse the wise, who think they know it all,
and make their 'knowledge' into foolishness.
[26]I confirm the word of my servants
and fulfill the prophecies of my messengers.
I say to Jerusalem, 'Many people will live in you again,'
and to the cities of Judah, 'I will raise up your ruins; you will be rebuilt!'
[27]I say to deep waters, 'Dry up!' and to rivers, 'Become dry!'[c]
[28]I say concerning Cyrus,[d] 'He is my shepherd,
and he will carry out all the purposes I have for him,'
saying to Jerusalem, 'You will be rebuilt *and flourish again!*'
saying to the temple, 'You will be reconstructed!'[e]

---

a 44:22 This "thick cloud" of our sins was a barrier between God and man. Grace has swept it away so that we can freely come before him.

b 44:22 See Gal. 3:13–14.

c 44:27 This actually happened at the taking of Babylon by Cyrus. See Jer. 50:38; 51:31–36.

d 44:28 Cyrus, king of Persia, reigned from 559–529 BC. He permitted the Jews to return from captivity to Jerusalem and issued a decree to authorize the temple to be rebuilt (2 Chron. 36:22–23; Ezra 1:1–4). Even though Isaiah prophesied 150 years before Cyrus became king, he calls him by name. This is one of the greatest proofs of God's omniscience and sovereignty as well as the supernatural aspect of prophecy.

e 44:28 Josephus, the Jewish historian, wrote that "when Cyrus read this (Isaiah's prophecy), and admired the Divine Power, an earnest desire and ambition seized upon him to fulfill what

God's Shepherd, Cyrus

45 "This is what Yahweh says to his anointed one,[a]
Cyrus,[b] whose right hand I have grasped *as my servant*[c]
to conquer nations and dethrone their kings.[d]
For I will open doors before him
and no fortified gate will remain closed.

[2]I will march out in front of you and level every obstacle.[e]
I will shatter to pieces bronze doors
and slice through iron bars.
[3]I will give you hidden treasures from dark, concealed places
and wealth waiting in secret sites
so that you recognize me, for it is I, Yahweh,
the God of Israel, who calls you by your name![f]
[4]For the sake of my servant Jacob, and Israel my chosen,
I call you by your name and give you a title of honor.
But you don't even know me.
[5]I am Yahweh, the only God there is,
and you'll never find another.
I will strengthen you *for victory*,
even though you do not intimately know who I am.
[6]*Yet through you* everyone will know who I really am.
Those from the rising sun in the east to the west,
everyone everywhere will know
that I am Yahweh, the one and only God,

---

was so written." These verses in chs. 44–45 convinced Cyrus to issue the decree to rebuild the temple. See Josephus Ant. XI. 1.2 and Ezra 5:13.

a 45:1 Or "Messiah (Anointed One)." The Septuagint reads "To Cyrus, my Christ." Cyrus becomes an amazing picture of Jesus, the Anointed One (Acts 10:38). Both Cyrus (44:28) and Jesus (Heb. 13:20) are called shepherds who will perform all God's pleasure (John 8:29). God takes the right hand of both Cyrus and Christ (Heb. 10:12–13) and subdues nations before them (Ps. 2; Phil. 3:21). Both Cyrus and Christ have open doors before them (Rev. 3:7–8) and are given the treasures of darkness (Matt. 27:45), the hidden riches of secret places (Mark 1:35; Col. 2:3; Rev. 2:17).

b 45:1 Cyrus, the Persian king, is mentioned twenty-two times in the Bible. His name means "the rays of the sun." God calls him his "shepherd" (44:28) and his "anointed one." On October 12, 539 BC, he conquered Babylon and its king, Nabonidus, and his son Belshazzar (Dan. 5:25–31). It is possible that Daniel, after the fall of Babylon, showed Cyrus the prophecies of Jer. 25:11–12 and 29:10.

c 45:1 That is, God is about to take Cyrus as a partner to accomplish heaven's purpose.

d 45:1 Or "The belts of their kings I will loosen," a Hebrew idiom for disarming or dethroning. Babylon was taken in one night by Cyrus. Belshazzar, the Chaldean king, was killed. See Dan. 5:1–31.

e 45:2 Or "every swelling," a possible metaphor for what looms up in front of you.

f 45:3 The Hebrew wording allows for this possible translation: "I, Yahweh, who calls you by your name, the gods (judges or mighty ones) of Israel." The word for "gods" is *elohim* (plural) and is translated in some verses as "judges." See Ps. 82:1, 6.

and there is no other.[a]
[7]I create light, and I make it dark.
I make bliss,[b] and I create adversity.[c]
I am Yahweh who does all these things.'

[8]"Shower down righteousness, O heavens above.
Let the clouds drip with deliverance!
Let earth's womb open and bear salvation's[d] fruit,
with righteousness rising up beside it![e]
I, Yahweh, have created all of them!
[9]Shame on the one who argues with his Creator,
like one clay pot among other pots arguing with the potter.
Should the clay say to the potter,
'What in the world are you doing with me?
Your hands are clumsy'?[f]
[10]Shame on the one who complains to a father,
'Why in the world did you conceive me?'
Or to a mother, 'Why in the world did you bring me to birth?'"
[11]Listen to what Yahweh,
the Holy One of Israel, the One who shaped him, has to say:
"Why do you question me about the destiny of my children[g]
or tell me what to do with my children and what I have made?
[12]I created the earth and populated it with people.
With my own hands, I spread out the cosmos
and then commanded the starry host *to shine*!
[13]I am the one who raised him[h] up in righteousness!
I will make all his paths straight and level.
He will build my city and release my exiled people,
not because he was bribed or hired to do it,
declares the Almighty Yahweh!"

---

a 45:6 There are four reasons God chose and favored Cyrus, the heathen king: (1) So that Cyrus would acknowledge the greatness of God. (2) To accomplish God's purpose with Judah (Ps. 78:68–72). (3) So the nations would see that Yahweh is the only true God. (4) So Jerusalem would be rebuilt.

b 45:7 This is the Hebrew word *shalom* and can be translated "prosperity, bliss, wholeness, completeness, health, peace, welfare, safety, soundness, tranquility, perfectness, fullness, rest, harmony, the absence of agitation or discord." *Shalom* comes from a root verb meaning "to be complete, perfect, and (paid in) full."

c 45:7 Or "woe, disaster, calamity (judgment), affliction, disturbance, distress, misery, trouble."

d 45:8 The Hebrew word for "salvation," *yesha'*, is nearly identical to the Hebrew name Yeshua (Jesus).

e 45:8 Or "and blossom with mercy" (LXX).

f 45:9 Or "Your work has no hands (or handles)." This is a way of saying, "What you're doing with me shows that you have no skill, like someone who has no hands forming me!"

g 45:11 Or "Ask me about things to come concerning my children."

h 45:13 Although God has raised up Christ and us in righteousness, the context here points to Cyrus.

Yahweh, the Hope of the Nations

[14]This is what Yahweh says *to Cyrus*:

"Egypt's wealth, Cush's[a] treasures, and the tall Sabeans[b]
will all be handed over to you.
In chains they will walk behind you.
They will be brought before you and they will bow down
and address you reverently, saying,
'Truly God is with you. He alone is God, and there is no other.'"

[15]Truly, O God of Israel, the Savior,
you are a God who hides himself."[c]
[16]All the idol-makers will be ashamed and disgraced,
and each one will walk away in confusion.
[17]But Yahweh saves Israel with everlasting salvation!
You will not be put to shame nor disgraced for all eternity!

[18]This is what Yahweh says, heaven's Creator, who alone is God.
He created the earth, shaped it, and established it all by himself.
He made it fit and orderly and beautiful[d] for its inhabitants.
He says:
"I am Yahweh, and there is no other god.
[19]I didn't whisper in secret, in a realm of darkness.
I didn't say to Jacob's tribes,
'Seek me in vain.'
I am Yahweh!
I speak the truth and declare to you what is right!

[20]"Come together! Assemble yourselves!
Draw near, you refugees from among the nations.
Those who parade their *powerless* wooden idols
have no revelation knowledge.
They keep on praying to gods who cannot save them.
[21]Declare what is to be and state your case.
Go ahead and take counsel together.
Who knew all about this and declared it long ago?
Was it not I, Yahweh? There is no god apart from me.
I am a righteous God and a Savior.
There is no one you can compare to me.
[22]So turn your heart to me, face me now,
and be saved wherever you are,

---

a 45:14 Or "Ethiopia."
b 45:14 A people group once living in the southern parts of Arabia (modern-day Yemen).
c 45:15 Or "a God who keeps himself hidden." These words of Isaiah show us that God must be revealed by his Spirit to each heart.
d 45:18 Or "He did not create it a chaos."

even from the ends of the earth,
for I alone am God, and there is no other.
²³I make this solemn oath to you in my own name;
this word sent from my mouth in righteousness
will not return unfulfilled:
'Truly every knee will bow before me
and every tongue will solemnly swear allegiance to me!'
²⁴All will say of me,
'Yes! Only in Yahweh do I find righteousness and strength!'
And all who were angry with me
will come before me and regret it!
²⁵In Yahweh, all of Israel's offspring will triumph[a] and shine!'"

The Overthrow of Babylon

46 *The gods of Babylon*, Bel,[b] and Nebo[c]
are bowed down and lowered to the ground.
They haul away on ox carts their *wobbling* idols.[d]
²They both stoop and bow down,
and they are powerless to rescue their own images.
There they[e] go—carried off into captivity![f]

³"Listen to me, O Jacob's tribes, all the remnant of Israel.
You never had to carry me, but I have carried you from birth.
I supported you from the moment you left the womb.[g]
⁴Even as you grow old and your hair turns gray,
I'll keep carrying you!
I am your Maker and your Caregiver.
I will carry you and be your Savior.
⁵To whom can you compare me, the incomparable God?
Have you found someone else like me?
⁶The wealthy pour out their gold,[h]
weigh out their silver in the scales,
and hire a goldsmith who crafts it into a "god."
Then they bow down before it to worship it.
⁷They lift it up to their shoulders and have to carry it.
They set it on a stand, and there it sits,

---

a 45:25 Or "will be made right again." See Rom. 11:26–27.
b 46:1 Bel means "lord," a title that was associated with the god Enlil, known in Babylon as the chief of the gods. The Greeks called him Zeus and the Romans, Jupiter. Eventually, the title Bel was transferred to Marduk. See Jer. 50:2.
c 46:1 Or Nabu or Celestial Scribe, known as the god of intellectualism (literacy, wisdom). The Greeks called him Hermes; the Romans, Mercury; the Egyptians, Anubis.
d 46:1 Or "Their idols are beasts and cattle."
e 46:2 Or "their souls."
f 46:2 These false gods and their idols are like captives carried off by their conquerors.
g 46:3 See Ex. 19:4; Deut. 1:31; 32:11; Ps. 28:9.
h 46:6 Or "those who pour out gold from their purses."

unable to move from its place.
When someone cries out to it,
it never answers nor saves anyone from trouble.
⁸Keep this in mind and don't forget it!
Take this to heart, you rebels!
⁹Remember *the miracles* of long ago.
Acknowledge that I am God, and there is no other.
I am God, and there is none like me.
¹⁰I declare from the beginning how it will end
and foretell from the start what has not yet happened.
I decree that my purpose will stand,
and I will fulfill my every plan.
¹¹I called that bird of prey*ᵃ* *Cyrus*, swooping in from the east;
from a distant land he came, the man of my purpose.
I have spoken, and yes, I will bring it to pass.
I have formed my plan, and yes, I will do it.

¹²"Listen to me, you stubborn ones
who are far from righteousness.
¹³I am bringing my righteousness closer to you;
it is not far off.
My deliverance will not be delayed,
for I will set my salvation in Zion
for Israel my glory!

An Ode to the Fall of Babylon

47 "Get down *from your throne* and sit in the dust, O Miss Babylon!
Sit on the ground where you belong,
not on a throne, O Miss Chaldea!
For you will never be described again as 'delicate and dainty.'*ᵇ*
²Take off your *pretty* veil;*ᶜ*
take two millstones and grind grain.*ᵈ*
Lift your skirt, bare your legs, and wade through the rivers.
³Your humiliating nakedness will be uncovered,
your shame exposed and seen by all.*ᵉ*
I will take vengeance and let no one intercede for you."*ᶠ*

---

a 46:11 See Isa. 41:2–3; 44:28–45:1.

b 47:1 Or "pampered and spoiled."

c 47:2 Or "your flowing tresses."

d 47:2 Grinding with millstones was considered the lowest of menial work, usually done by slaves. See Ex. 11:5.

e 47:3 It is true that Babylon has fallen historically, but we can understand that the "Babylonian system" in the church is also falling. Old concepts are crumbling and being swept away (2 Cor. 10:3–6) as God exposes our impurity. Yet the Redeemer stands ready to restore and revive those with hungry, passionate hearts for God.

f 47:3 The Hebrew meaning of this clause is uncertain.

⁴We have a Redeemer. Yahweh is his name,
　the Commander of Angel Armies, the Holy One of Israel!

⁵"Sit silently and go away into the darkness, O Miss Chaldea!
　For you will no longer be called the Mistress of Kingdoms.
⁶I became angry with my people,
　so I wounded*ᵃ* my special ones.
　I handed them over to you, *and you took them captive.*
　You showed them no mercy;
　you even made the elderly suffer under your heavy yoke.
⁷You thought,
　'I will be the Mistress *of Kingdoms* forever.'
　But you never considered what you were doing
　or reflected on how all this would end.

⁸So now, listen to this, you pampered lover of pleasure,
　who sits smug and secure and says in her heart,
　'I am, and there is no one like me!
　I will never have to live as a widow
　or suffer the loss of my children.'
⁹Suddenly both of these losses will overtake you in one day,
　for you will lose your husband and your children.
　Despite your many magic spells and your powerful sorceries,
　you will be overwhelmed by these tragedies in full measure!
¹⁰You felt so smug and secure in your wickedness.
　You thought, 'No one sees me.'
　Your idea of 'wisdom' and self-professed 'knowledge'
　has led you astray, saying in your heart,
　'I am! There is none like me!'
¹¹*An avalanche of* evil will come upon you
　that no magic spell will be able to avert.
　Great disaster is about to fall upon you
　that you will not be able to ward off!
　Total devastation will strike you suddenly.
　It will happen so swiftly you won't even see it coming!

¹²So go ahead—keep trusting in your sorceries
　and the witchcraft you've practiced since your youth.
　Perhaps you might succeed!
　Perhaps you'll scare away *your impending doom*!
¹³You must be fatigued with so much counsel!
　Let the stargazers and astrologers take their stand.
　See if they can help you now!

---

a 47:6 Or "defiled," which comes from a root word "to pierce, to wound."

Let them make their monthly predictions.
Maybe they can reveal what
is about to come upon you.
[14]Look at them!
They're nothing but straw for the consuming fire.
They can't even rescue themselves from the power of the flame.
And this is not some cozy fire
that you sit beside to keep yourself warm!
[15]These traders, with whom you have dealt since your youth,
will do nothing but disappoint you.
Each has wandered off to his own way—
there is no one left to rescue you!

Our All-Knowing God

48 "Listen carefully, O Jacob's tribes,
you who are called by the name Israel
and come from the lineage of Judah,
who solemnly swear in the name of Yahweh
and claim to worship the God of Israel.[a]
But there is no truth or righteousness in your confession!
[2]Indeed, you name yourselves after the holy city
and say that you depend upon Israel's God.
Yahweh, the Commander of Angel Armies, is his name.

[3]"Long ago I prophesied things that would happen.
I issued decrees[b] and made them known.
Then suddenly, I acted and made them happen.
[4]I knew you were stubborn.
Your neck is like a rod of iron,
and you're as hard-hearted as brass![c]
[5]Long ago I told you these things.
Long before they happened
I proclaimed them
so you would never be able to say,
'My idols did this;
my wood and metal idols decreed it!'
[6]You have heard what I foretold and have seen it all unfold,
so admit[d] *that it happened* and I was right![e]
From now on I will tell you about new things never seen before,
hidden things, well-guarded secrets you know nothing about.

---

a 48:1 Or "who cause the God of Israel to be remembered."

b 48:3 Or "They came forth from my mouth."

c 48:4 Or "your forehead hard as brass."

d 48:6 Or "declare."

e 48:6 Or "You should tell this to others." The Hebrew of this sentence is uncertain.

⁷They are created now, brand new today, not long ago!
  You've never heard of them before now,
  so you cannot say, 'Oh, I already knew about that.'

⁸You have never heard nor understood;
  your ear had not been opened beforehand.
  Though I knew that you would fight against me
  as a rebel from birth,
⁹yet, for the sake of my great name and for my glory,
  I held back my anger and was patient with you
  so I did not whittle you down *to nothing.*
¹⁰See, I have purified you in the furnace of adversity,
  but not like silver—I have refined you in the fire.*ᵃ*
¹¹For my own sake alone I will do it,
  so my name will not be dishonored.*ᵇ*
  I will not yield my glory to another.

Consider God's Might
¹²"Listen to me, O Jacob,
  Israel, whom I have called:
  I am the One and Only,
  the First and the Last.
¹³With my mighty hand I laid the foundation of the earth;
  with the span of my right hand I spread out the cosmos.
  And when I speak to them, they both stand at attention.
¹⁴Now, all of you gather around and listen.
  Which *of the gods* has foretold these things?
  I, Yahweh, love this man,
  and he*ᶜ* will carry out my purpose against Babylon.
  He will be my "arm of might" against the Babylonians!
¹⁵I am the one; yes, I am the one
  who called him by name *before he was born.*
  I have led him forward on a prosperous, successful path.

Come Together and Walk with Me
¹⁶"Draw near to me and listen:
  From the beginning, I have not spoken in secret.
  From the beginning of time,*ᵈ* I was there."

---

a 48:10 The implication is that if God had left them in the fire to melt down all their dross, they
  would still be there in the fire with nothing left of them. God limits the intensity and the timing of
  our every trial and uses the furnace of adversity to make us more like Christ. See 1 Cor. 10:13.

b 48:11 God promises to deliver, refine, and rescue his people so that his own name and identity
  as the God of gods will not be defamed. Rescue is as sure as God's identity.

c 48:14 Most scholars view this man to be Cyrus.

d 48:16 Or "from the time of its occurring."

And now Lord Yahweh has sent me, *empowered by[a]* his Spirit!
[17]This is what Yahweh, your Kinsman-Redeemer, the Holy One of Israel says:
"I am Yahweh, your God.
I am the One who teaches you how to succeed
and who leads you *step by step* in the way you should go.
[18]If only you had listened to my commands,
then peace[b] would have flowed like a[c] river for you
and success[d] would *wash over* you like waves of the sea.
[19]Your children would have multiplied
to become like the sand *of the seashore[e]*
and your descendants like grains of sand.
There would be no end of them,
and I would not cut them off."

[20]Go! Leave Babylon!
Flee from Chaldea!
Announce it with joyous singing![f]
Let everyone know!
Proclaim it to the ends of the earth!
Say it loud and clear:
"Yahweh has rescued his servant Jacob!"

[21]The people weren't thirsty
when he led them through barren, desolate deserts,
for he broke open the rock for water to flow for them.
The rock was split open, and rivers gushed out![g]

[22]"There is never peace," Yahweh says, "for the wicked."

The Lord's Special Servant

49 Listen to what I have to say, you islands.
Pay attention to me, you who live in distant lands.
Yahweh called me *as his own* before I was born
and named me while I was still in my mother's womb.
[2]He gives me words that pierce and penetrate.[h]
He hid me and protected me in the shadow of his hand.[i]

---

a 48:16 Or "has sent me and his Spirit."

b 48:18 Or "prosperity (*shalom*)."

c 48:18 Or "the river." See John 7:37–39.

d 48:18 Or "righteousness."

e 48:19 See Gen. 22:17; 32:12.

f 48:20 Or "shouting." The key to fleeing from the Babylonish (*Babylon* means "confusion") systems of the world is to go out with a joyous song. See Jer. 33:7–11.

g 48:21 See 1 Cor. 10:1–11; John 19:34.

h 49:2 Or "He makes my mouth a sharp sword." See Heb. 4:12; Rev. 1:16; 2:12, 16; 19:15.

i 49:2 Jesus was "hidden" in Nazareth for thirty years.

He prepared me like a polished arrow
and concealed me in his quiver.
³And he said to me,
"Israel, you are my special servant;
in you I will be glorified."ᵃ
⁴I said, "I've worked and served for nothing.
I have used up all my strength for nothing."ᵇ
Yet my rights I leave in Yahweh's hands,
and my just reward is with my God.
⁵And now, the Lord Yahweh—
who shaped me in the womb to be his servant,
to bring Jacob's tribes back to him
that Israel would be gathered back to himself,
for I am honored in the sight of Yahweh.
I find the source of all my strength in my God—
⁶who says:
"Is it too small a thing for you, my servant,
to restore greatness to Jacob's tribes and the survivors of Israel?
I will make you to be a light to the nations and
to bring *the light of* my salvation to the ends of the earth!"ᶜ

⁷Yahweh, Israel's Kinsman-Redeemer and Holy One,
says to the one who is deeply despised and repulsed by rulers
and a slave to the ruling class:
"Kings will see and stand up in respect;
princes will bow down to honor the faithfulness of Yahweh,
the Holy One of Israel, who has chosen you."

God's Faithfulness
⁸Yahweh says:
"When the time of showing you favor has come,ᵈ
I will answer your heart's cry.
I will help you in the day of salvation,
for I have fixed my eyes on you.
I have made you a covenant people to restore the land
and to resettle *families* on forgotten inheritances.

---

a 49:3 See Gen. 32:28; Deut. 7:6; 26:18, 19; Eph. 1:4–6.

b 49:4 Or "empty breath."

c 49:6 Although Israel is named in this chapter, the future fulfillment is found in Jesus Christ, the true Servant of the Lord. He was called and named from the womb (v. 1 and Matt. 1:20–23). He was equipped and prepared by God (v. 2). He was appointed and commissioned as God's Servant (v. 3). He brings Israel back to God (v. 5). He is highly favored in the sight of God (v. 5). Jesus found all his strength in his Father and did only what pleased him (v. 5 and John 5:19). He is light and salvation to nations (gentiles, v. 6).

d 49:8 This may be a reference to the year of Jubilee (Lev. 25:8–13). Believers today are now living in that season of God's favor. See Luke 4:18–19.

⁹You will declare to prisoners, 'You're free!'
  and to those in darkness, 'Step out into the light!'
  They will be like sheep that graze beside the roads
  and find pasture on the barren hillside.
¹⁰They will never be hungry or thirsty.*
  Neither scorching sun nor desert wind will hurt them,
  for he, the Loving One, will guide them
  and lead them to *restful, renewing* streams of water.*
¹¹I will level all my mountains as a road *for them*
  and raise up my highways.
¹²Look! They will come from faraway lands—
  some from the north, some from the west,
  and some from the land of Sinim."*

¹³Sing for joy, you heavens!
  Shout, you earth, and rejoice with dancing, shouting, and glee!
  Burst into joyous songs, you mountains,
  for Yahweh has comforted his *beloved* people.
  He will show tenderness and compassion*
  to his suffering ones.

God Will Not Forget Zion
¹⁴But Zion has said, "Yahweh has forsaken me.
  My Lord has forgotten me—*I'm all alone.*"

¹⁵*Yahweh responds,* "But how could a loving mother forget her nursing child
  and not deeply love the one she bore?
  Even if a there is a mother who forgets her child,
  I could never, no never, forget you.
¹⁶Can't you see?
  I have carved your name on the palms of my hands!
  Your walls are always my concern.*

---

a 49:10 See Rev. 7:16.
b 49:10 See Ps. 23:1–3.
c 49:12 There is much scholarly debate about the land of Sinim. There are some convincing arguments that link Sinim etymologically and historically to the Qin dynasty, which eventually grew and became modern-day China. The Sinites as a people group are mentioned in Gen. 10:17 and 1 Chron. 1:15. Others see Sinim as a Persian province, a variant name for Phoenicia, or a region in Aswan (Egypt).
d 49:13 The Hebrew word for "compassion" is *racham*, a Hebrew homophone for "womb." The implication is that God has a compassionate love for you, greater than a birth mother has for her child. God's love comes from deep within his innermost being and births living mercy poured out over us. *Racham* can be translated "pity, grace, favor, tender affection, or compassion." The very core of God's being is filled with love and compassion for you.
e 49:16 Although this is an apparent reference to the walls of Jerusalem, there is an application for each of us. Wherever you are today, your limitations, your walls, are before God's eyes. He knows where you are and what you face.

¹⁷Your children, your builders,ᵃ are running back to you
as those who ruined and destroyed you are running away.
¹⁸Lift up your head and look all around you.
See! All your children, your builders, gather to come back to you.
As surely as I live, *I make this promise*," says Yahweh.
"You will wear them all like jewels,
as a *radiant* brideᵇ wears her beautiful jewelry!

¹⁹"See? Your ruins and devastated places
will soon be overcrowded with settlers
while your destroyers stay far away.
²⁰You thought you had lost the children,ᶜ
but you will hear them say,
'This place is too cramped for me.
Make more room for me to live in.'
²¹And you will say to yourself,
'Where in the world did all these children come from?
Who birthed these for me?
I thought I was bereaved and barren.
I thought I was all alone, forgotten in exile—
so how did they all get here?'"

²²This is what Lord Yahweh says:
"Soon I will raise my hand and signal to the nations,
and they will come with your little boys bundled in their armsᵈ
and your little daughters carried on their shoulders.
²³Kings will be their babysitters
and queens their nursing mothers.
With faces bowed to the ground,
they will lick the dust of your feet.
Then you will know that I am Yahweh,
and I will never disappoint those
who entwineᵉ their hearts with mine."

²⁴Who can snatch the prey
from the hands of a mighty warrior
or rescue captives from a conqueror?"ᶠ

---

a 49:17 The Hebrew root word for "children" (*bnyk*) is a homonym for "builders." This translation includes both terms. See also v. 18.
b 49:18 The Hebrew word for "bride" (*kallah*) also means "completed, perfected, or finished."
   A mature bride will arise, wearing her sons and daughters as her jewelry and crown. See
   1 Thess. 2:19.
c 49:20 Or "the children of your bereavement."
d 49:22 Or "lap, bosom."
e 49:23 Or "whoever waits on me."
f 49:24 Or "tyrant" (1QIsaᵃ, Vulgate, Aramaic). The Hebrew reads "a righteous one."

²⁵But Yahweh says:
"The prey will be freed from the mighty warrior
and captives will be rescued from a conqueror!
For I will fight with those who fight with you,ᵃ
and I myself will save your children.
²⁶I will cause the violence of your oppressors
to come back upon them,ᵇ
and your enemies will kill one another in a killing frenzy!ᶜ
Then all the earth will know that I am Yahweh,
your Savior, your Kinsman-Redeemer,
the mighty hero of Jacob's tribes."

The Lord, the Faithful Husband

50 Yahweh asks,
"Have I abandoned you?
Can you show me your mother's divorce papers
that prove I sent her away?
Do you think I sold you into slavery to pay off a debt?
No, you sold *yourselves into slavery* because of your sins,
and because of your rebellion I sent your mother away!ᵈ
²When I came to you, why was no one there?
When I called, why did no one answer?
Am I powerlessᵉ to rescue you or too weak to deliver you?
With only a threat I can evaporate the sea
and dry up the rivers as a desert,
leaving the fish to rot and die of thirst.
³I dress the sky with darkness and shroud it with sackcloth."

The Servant, Our Teacher

⁴The Lord Yahweh has equipped me
with the anointed, skillful tongueᶠ of a teacher—
to know how to speak a timely word to the weary.
Morning by morning, he awakens *my heart*.
He opens my earsᵍ to hear *his voice*, to be trained to teach.ʰ

---

a 49:25 See Gen. 12:1–3.

b 49:26 Or "I will make your oppressors eat their own flesh," a figure of speech for violently turning on one another.

c 49:26 Or "They will get drunk on their own blood as with wine." See Rev. 16:6.

d 50:1 Or "divorced your mother (Israel)."

e 50:2 Or "Is my arm too short?"

f 50:4 See Ps. 45:1.

g 50:4 Or "He arouses for me an ear."

h 50:4 Seven times Jesus stated that he spoke only what the Father gave (taught) him to say. See John 7:16; 8:28, 47; 12:49; 14:10, 24; 17:8.

The Servant's Surrender to the Cross

⁵The Lord Yahweh has opened my ear,[a]
  and I did not resist; I did not rebel.
⁶I offered my back to those who flogged me
  and my cheek to those who tore out my beard.
  I never hid my face from demeaning insults
  or from those who spit on me.
⁷The Lord Yahweh empowers me, so I am not humiliated.
  For that reason, with holy determination,[b]
  I will do his will and not be ashamed.
⁸The One who makes me righteous is close to me.
  Who would dare challenge me now?
  Who would be my opponent?
  Let him stand before me!
  Who is my accuser?
  Let him confront me!
⁹It is the Lord Yahweh who empowers me;
  who would condemn me?[c]
  My accusers will all fade away
  like worn-out, moth-eaten clothes.[d]

The Fear of God

¹⁰Who among you has true fear and reverence of Yahweh?
  Who of you listens to the voice of his servant?
  Are any of you groping in the dark without light?
  Let him trust in the faithful name of Yahweh
  and rely on his God.
¹¹But if you presume to light your own torch,
  you are playing with fire.
  So go ahead, walk in the light of your own fires
  and the sparks you have kindled.
  But I can promise you this:
  it will take you down into torment!

Zion's Restoration

51 "Listen to me, you who chase after righteousness,[e]
  you who *passionately* pursue the Lord.
Look back to *Abraham*, the rock from which you were cut,
  to *Sarah*, the quarry from which you were dug,

---

a 50:5 A pierced ear was the mark of a willing slave. See Deut. 15:12–17; Ps. 40:6.

b 50:7 Or "I have set my face like flint."

c 50:9 See Rom. 8:30–39.

d 50:9 These old clothes represent the old concepts of an old covenant. See Matt. 6:19–21; Heb. 1:11–12.

e 51:1 See Deut. 16:20; Prov. 15:9; 21:21.

and remember what I did for them.
²Yes, look to Abraham your father and to Sarah, who bore you.
  For when I called Abraham, he was but one person,
  but I blessed him *greatly*ᵃ so that one became many."

³Indeed, Yahweh will comfort Zion, *restore her,*
  and comfort all her broken places.
  He will transform her wilderness into *the garden of* Bliss,ᵇ
  her desert into the garden of Yahweh.
  Joy and laughter will fill the airᶜ
  with thanksgiving and joyous melodies.

⁴"Listen to me, my people;
  pay attention to me, my nation.
  For I release my teaching to the nations,
  and I will cause the light of justice to rest on them.ᵈ
⁵My righteousness is coming closer,ᵉ
  and my salvation has gone out.
  My *mighty* arms will govern the people.
  The islands will trust in me
  and put their hope in the unveiling of my might.ᶠ
⁶Lift up your eyes to the heavenly realm
  and look at the earth far below.
  Though the heavens disappear like smoke,
  though the earth wears out like a garment,
  and though all the people die like gnats,
  my salvation will endure forever
  and my righteousness will never end!
⁷So listen to me, you who care for what is right,
  who treasure my teaching in your hearts:
  Do not fear the insults of others;
  do not be troubled when they revile you.
⁸They are nothing for you to fear,
  for the moth will eat them up like a shirt
  and the worm will consume them like wool,
  but my righteousness will last forever
  and my salvation from generation to generation."

---

a 51:2 Part of the Abrahamic blessing is the power to procreate, even when Sarah was barren.
b 51:3 Or "the garden of Eden." See Joel 2:3.
c 51:3 Or "will abide in her."
d 51:4 Or "I will make my justice a light for the nations." See John 8:12.
e 51:5 See Rom. 14:7 with Mark 1:14–15. Isa. 51:5 gives us three pictures of Jesus Christ: God's righteousness, God's salvation, and God's mighty arms.
f 51:5 Or "hope for my arm (of power)."

Cry Out to God

⁹Awake, God, awake!
  Arm of Yahweh, put on your robe of strength!
  Awake *and do the works of power* as in ancient days,
  as in generations past!
  Wasn't it you who smashed the sea monster[a] to pieces,
  who pierced the dragon[b] in generations long ago?
¹⁰Wasn't it you who dried up the *Red* Sea with its deep waters
  and made a path through the sea to rescue[c] your redeemed?
¹¹Do it again!
  Those Yahweh has set free
  will return to Zion and come celebrating with songs of joy!
  They will be crowned with never-ending joy!
  Gladness and joy will overwhelm them;
  despair and depression will disappear!

¹²"I, yes I, am the one who comforts you.
  All the sons of men will be cut down and fade like grass.
  Why then would you be afraid of a mere human being?
¹³You have forgotten that Yahweh, your Maker,
  stretched out the skies and laid earth's firm foundation.
  But you live each day constantly worrying,[d]
  living in fear of your angry oppressor
  who is bent on your destruction.
  But their fury cannot touch you!
¹⁴Those who are suffering will soon be released.
  They will not die in their *dark* dungeon,
  nor will they go hungry.
¹⁵For I am Yahweh, your *faithful* God,
  who split the sea with its roaring waves.[e]
  My name is Lord Yahweh, Commander of Angel Armies!

Hidden in the Hollow of His Hand

¹⁶"I have placed my words in your mouth[f]
  and have hidden you in the hollow[g] of my hand
  to establish the heavens and make the earth rock solid.
  You will say to Zion, 'You are my people!'"

---

a 51:9 This is the Hebrew word *rahav* (Rahab), a likely metaphor for Egypt.

b 51:9 See Ps. 74:13–14; Ezek. 29:3.

c 51:10 Or "to cross over."

d 51:13 Or "trembling."

e 51:15 See Ps. 74:13; Jer. 31:35.

f 51:16 Jesus Christ is the true Prophet who has the words of God in his mouth.

g 51:16 Or "shadow."

Wake Up, Zion

¹⁷Wake up! Wake up!ª Get up, Jerusalem!
    You have drunk enough from the cup Yahweh handed you.
    It was the cup of his anger, and you've drained it dry—
    the intoxicating bowl that makes men stagger!
¹⁸There are none of Zion's children left,
    none to guide *her home*ᵇ and take her by the hand,
    none among all the children she has raised.
¹⁹Twin calamities have come upon you,
    but who will feel sorry for you?
    Disaster and devastation, famine and war,ᶜ
    but who will comfort you?
²⁰Your children have fainted and lie fallen in the streets,
    like a gazelle caught in a net.
    Yahweh's anger,
    the rebuke of your God, has overwhelmed them.

²¹So listen, you who are weak and wounded,
    who are intoxicated not with wine *but with God's anger*.
²²This is what your sovereign ruler,
    Lord Yahweh, your God,
    the Mighty Defender of his people, says:
    "Look! I have removed from your hand
    the intoxicating cup that made you stagger.
    You will no longer drink from the bowl of my anger.
²³Instead, I will put that bowl
    in the hands of your tormentors who said to you,
    'Lie down so we can walk all over you!'
    For your back became like the ground they trample on,
    like a street for them to walk on."

Zion Rejoicing

52 Wake up! Open your eyes!
    Beautiful Zion, put on your majestic strength!
    Jerusalem, the sacred city,
    put on your glory garments!
    Never again will the uncleanᵈ enter your gates!

---

a 51:17 In v. 9, the people are crying out to God to awaken and arise, but here God is telling the
    people they are the ones who must wake up and arise.
b 51:18 The image here is that Zion has been intoxicated by drinking the cup of God's anger
    (Jer. 49:12) and there is no one there to take her home in that condition. In the culture of that
    day, it was the responsibility of children to guide a drunken parent home.
c 51:19 Although there are four listed, this double calamity is seen in two couplets (disaster and
    devastation, famine and war).
d 52:1 Or "uncircumcised." For the believer today, unclean and detestable thoughts should not
    enter our souls nor be in our minds (gates).

²Arise and shake^{*a*} off your dust!^{*b*}
  Sit enthroned, Jerusalem!
  Break off your shackles of bondage from your neck,
  you captive daughter of Zion!
³For this is what Yahweh has to say:
  "You were sold for nothing;
  now you will be redeemed without any payment."
⁴For Yahweh says:
  "Long ago, my people went down to Egypt
  and lived as foreigners there,
  and for no good reason Assyria oppressed them.
⁵And now, what have I here?" says Yahweh.
  "Indeed, my people have been taken into bondage without cause
  while mocking rulers howl; and every day
  my name is continually despised!"^{*c*} says Yahweh.
⁶"Therefore, my people will know *the power of* my name,
  and they will know in that day
  that I am the one who promised them, saying,
  'Behold, I am here!'"^{*d*}

⁷What a beautiful sight to behold—
  the precious feet of the messenger
  coming over the mountains to announce good news!
  He comes to refresh us with wonderful news,^{*e*}
  announcing salvation^{*f*} to Zion and saying,
  "Your Mighty God reigns!"
⁸Listen! The watchmen are shouting in triumph!
  Lifting their voices together, they are singing for joy!
  For right before their eyes, they can see^{*g*}
  Yahweh returning to Zion!
⁹Burst into joyous songs, you rubble of Jerusalem!
  For Yahweh has *graciously* comforted his people;

---

a 52:2 The Hebrew word (*na'ar*) means "shaking out (of a lion's mane)" or "shaking up and down" and is a homophone for "to growl (like a lion's roar)" (Jer. 51:38).

b 52:2 This dust can also include our "dust nature" received from Adam (1 Cor. 15:47–49). We need to crucify it and be clothed with Christ. Part of Satan's curse is that he was to eat dust (Gen. 3:14). Whatever we withhold from God becomes food for the serpent. We shake off (overcome) the "dust" of our old life and rise up in our new life, enthroned with Jesus Christ (Eph. 2:16; Rom. 8:30; Rev. 3:21).

c 52:5 See Rom. 2:4.

d 52:6 Or "Behold, it's me!"

e 52:7 It is a messenger (singular) here, but it becomes a company of messengers in Rom. 10:15. We are told to proclaim the wonderful news—not the bad news that brings despair and fear but the good news of our God, who reigns in the midst of his people.

f 52:7 This Hebrew word is remarkably similar to Yeshua, the name of Jesus.

g 52:8 Or "They see face-to-face."

he has become the Kinsman-Redeemer of Jerusalem!
¹⁰Yahweh has unveiled his holy arm*a*
before the eyes of all the nations.
To the ends of the earth, everyone everywhere
will see the salvation of our God!

¹¹Go! Go, and leave *Babylon* behind!
Touch nothing unclean as you depart.
Keep your life pure as you leave,
you who carry the vessels*b* of Yahweh!
¹²You will neither have to leave in haste,
nor will you make a frantic escape,
for your God, Yahweh, will go before you.
He will lead you each step and be your rear guard.

The Despised Servant

¹³"Look! My servant*c* will prosper and succeed!*d*
He will be highly honored, raised up, and greatly exalted!*e*
¹⁴Just as many were appalled at the sight of him
(for so marred was his appearance, *like an object of horror;*
he no longer looked like a man),
¹⁵so now he will startle*f* many nations.
Kings*g* will be shocked speechless before him.
For they will now see a sight unheard of,
and things never considered before now fill their thoughts."*h*

---

a 52:10 This is a metaphor for displaying his righteous power. There is a sense in which Jesus Christ can be seen as God's holy arm, which God has unveiled to the nations. The miracles of Jesus, his sacrificial death on the cross, and his mighty resurrection were God flexing his muscles, his holy arm. See John 12:37–38; Rom. 10:16.

b 52:11 Or "armor-bearers." These vessels can also be translated "armor" or "(temple) vessels."

c 52:13 This section of Isaiah is perhaps the greatest description of the life, crucifixion, and resurrection of our Lord Jesus Christ, apart from the four Gospels. Up to this point in Isaiah's writings, the "Servant" has been described as the true Prophet, Teacher, and victorious Redeemer, with no hint whatsoever that his activity would be interrupted by death. But in this section we find him as the unparalleled Suffering Servant and Sin-Bearer who died for us. The prophecy found here is the most remarkable in all of the Old Testament of the sufferings of Jesus Christ and the glory that followed (1 Peter 1:11). Isa. 52:13 through Isa. 53 is quoted in all four Gospels, Acts, Romans, and 1 Peter. It is the epicenter of the gospel.

d 52:13 Or "act wisely," or "prosper" a likely metonymy for "succeed."

e 52:13 This is an obvious reference to God's Servant-Savior, Jesus, who was raised from the dead and highly exalted at the right hand of God. See Phil. 2:5–11.

f 52:15 Or "sprinkle many nations" or "Many nations will marvel at him" (LXX). The words *startle* and *sprinkle* share a homonymic root. The idea is that Jesus would sprinkle to cleanse many with his redeeming blood and also that he would startle the nations with his resurrection power and endless life.

g 52:15 These kings could refer to both human and demonic.

h 52:15 See Rom. 15:21. Vv. 13–15 present Christ as an exalted King, a High Priest who cleanses, and a Prophet who reveals the secrets of God to men.

53
Who has truly believed our revelation?
To whom will Yahweh reveal his mighty arm?[a]

²He sprouted up like a tender plant before the Lord,[b]
like a root[c] in parched soil.
He possessed no distinguishing beauty
or outward splendor to catch our attention—
nothing special in his appearance to make us desire him.
³He was despised and rejected by men,
a man of *deep* sorrows
who was no stranger to suffering and grief.[d]
We hid our faces from him in disgust
and considered him a nobody, not worthy of respect.

The Sin-Bearer Servant
⁴Yet he was the one who carried our sicknesses[e]
and endured the torment of our sufferings.
We viewed him as one who was being punished[f]
for something he himself had done,
as one who was struck down by God and brought low.
⁵But it was because of our rebellious deeds that he was pierced[g]
and because of our sins that he was crushed.
He endured the punishment that made us completely whole,[h]
and in[i] his wounding[j] we found our healing.

---

a 53:1 God's *arm* is a metaphor for his triumphant power. It is said that almost every verse in this chapter is alluded to in the New Testament in reference to Jesus.

b 53:2 Or "before him."

c 53:2 Jesus is the Root of David and the Sprouting of the Lord (Isa. 11:1). The parched soil can represent both the barrenness of humanity before God and the barren season of Israel's history when Jesus appeared. A root cannot live in dry ground, yet we see a hint here that the Messiah would be miraculously born. A root in dry ground is an allusion to the virgin birth of Jesus, who was conceived without a human father.

d 53:3 Yet Jesus was the most emotionally whole and healed man to ever walk the earth. He did not absorb the insults and rejections of even his own neighbors (Luke 4:14–30).

e 53:4 This was fulfilled in two ways. First, when the Lamb of God carried away diseases as he walked the earth (Matt. 8:16–17). And second, by paying the sin price of all humanity on the cross with his sacred blood.

f 53:4 Or "stricken," a word used for one who is struck with leprosy. Because of this, the Jewish Talmud gives many opinions about this verse, then offers an authoritative ruling of the sages. "The rabbis say: 'His name is The Leper . . . as it is said [in Isaiah 53:4], "Surely our sicknesses he himself bore and our sorrows he carried, yet we ourselves esteemed him stricken, smitten of God, and afflicted"'" (b. Sanhedrin 98b). Their conclusion was that the Messiah will be called "the Leper of the House of Rabbi." They understood that he would not be an actual "leper" but that he would carry the "spiritual leprosy" of the people, as a leper carries his affliction.

g 53:5 See Zech. 12:10; John 19:31–37; Rev. 1:7.

h 53:5 This is the Hebrew word *shalom*, meaning "peace, prosperity, wholeness, success, well-being." All of these have come to us through Christ's sufferings.

i 53:5 The Hebrew word could be translated "among his wounds (bruises)" or "in his wounds (bruises)." See the split-open rock of Song. 2:14.

j 53:5 The Hebrew word for *wounding* ("scourging") is *chaburah* and means "blueness of the wounds." But *chaburah* is taken from the root word *chabar*, which means "to join together, to

⁶Like wayward sheep, we have all wandered*a* astray.
Each of us has turned from God's paths and chosen our own way;
even so, Yahweh laid*b* the guilt of our every sin upon him.*c*

The Surrendered Servant

⁷He was oppressed and harshly mistreated;
still he humbly submitted, refusing to defend himself.
He was brought like a *gentle* lamb*d* to be slaughtered.
Like a silent sheep before his shearers,
he didn't even open his mouth.*e*
⁸By coercion and with a perversion of justice
he was taken away.
And who could have imagined his future?*f*
He was cut down in the prime of life;*g*
for the rebellion of his*h* own people,
he was struck down *in their place.*
⁹They gave him a grave among criminals,*i*
but he ended up instead in a rich man's tomb,*j*
although he had done no violence nor spoken deceitfully.

The Servant's Reward

¹⁰Even though it pleased Yahweh
to crush him with grief,*k*

---

unite, to have fellowship, to become a couple." A nuanced translation of Isaiah 53:5 could be "In the fellowship of being one with him is our healing."

a 53:6 The Hebrew verb *wander* has an implication of self-deception. See 1 Peter 2:25.

b 53:6 The Hebrew verb *laid* can also mean "to make intercession." This would mean that the Lord interceded within himself (the Godhead) to orchestrate our salvation.

c 53:6 This entire chapter provides such detail of the last hours of Jesus Christ that one would almost imagine Isaiah was standing at the foot of the cross writing this chapter. Isaiah's prophecy, written more than seven hundred years before the cross, is all stated in the past tense, as though it had already happened. There is no other person in human history who could possibly fulfill all of Isaiah's prophecy. It is believed that Isaiah 53 is referred to eighty-five times in the New Testament. A few of these references include Matt. 8:17; 27:11–13, 26–31, 41–43, 57–60; Mark 15:28; Luke 22:37; John 12:38; Acts 8:32–35; Rom. 5:6–9, 18–19; 10:16; Phil. 2:5–11; 1 Peter 2:21–24.

d 53:7 See Gen. 22:7-8; John 1:29; 1 Cor. 5:7; 1 Peter 1:18–19; Rev. 5:12.

e 53:7 This was the silence of submission to his Father's will. See Matt. 26:63; Luke 23:9; 1 Peter 2:23.

f 53:8 Or "who of his generation considered."

g 53:8 Or "He was cut off from the land of the living." See Dan. 9:26.

h 53:8 Or "my."

i 53:9 See Matt. 27:38; Mark 15:27; Luke 23:32; John 19:18.

j 53:9 See Matt. 27:57–60. The literal Hebrew is "and with the rich in his deaths (plural)." His death is our death too, for we have been co-crucified with Christ (Gal. 2:20). Jesus was born from a virgin womb and laid in a virgin tomb.

k 53:10 Or "disease."

he will be restored to favor.^a
After his soul becomes a guilt-offering,^b
he will gaze upon his many offspring and prolong his days.^c
And through him, Yahweh's deepest desires
will be fully accomplished.^d
¹¹After the great anguish of his soul,
he will see light^e and be fully satisfied.^f
By knowing him,^g the righteous one,
my servant will make many to be righteous,^h
because he, *their sin-bearer*, carried away their sins.ⁱ
¹²So I, *Yahweh*, will assign him a portion
among a great multitude,
and he will triumph
and divide the spoils of victory with *his* mighty ones—^j
all because he poured out his life-blood^k to death.
He was counted among the worst of sinners,
yet he carried sin's burden for many^l
and intercedes for those who are rebels.^m

---

a 53:10 This points to the resurrection of Jesus Christ, who died and rose again to the place of highest honor (Phil. 2:5–10).

b 53:10 See Mark 10:45; Eph. 5:2; Heb. 9:14.

c 53:10 Christ's sacrifice results in the birth of spiritual offspring. He will see his spiritual offspring and enjoy living his life through them; thus, it could be said he prolonged his days. The life we live is no longer our own, and in a way, we prolong his days as we walk in close fellowship with Christ. A people in his image is the joy that was set before him (Heb. 12:1–2).

d 53:10 Or "the will of the Lord will prosper in his hand."

e 53:11 This vision of light is the light of a new day, the resurrection morning light that flooded into the empty tomb.

f 53:11 Or "He will eat and drink his fill." See Song. 5:1.

g 53:11 Or "by his knowledge" or "by his sweat." The Hebrew word *knowledge* is taken from a homonymic root for "sweat." Perhaps this is an allusion to his sweat trickling from the cross or of the sweat of blood in the garden of Gethsemane, as well as the knowledge of life that comes to us when we believe in him. See also Gen. 2:9 and 3:17–19, which also connect knowledge (of good and evil) with Adam's sweat.

h 53:11 This is an intimate knowledge, or experience of him by faith, that imparts the righteousness of God to everyone who believes. To be declared righteous involves pardon and acceptance. We are fully pardoned and fully accepted in Christ. See Rom. 3:22–26, 8:1; 2 Cor. 5:21; Eph. 1:5–6; 1 John 4:10.

i 53:11 Jesus accepted the responsibility for the consequences of our sins. See Ps. 38:4; John 1:29; 1 John 3:5.

j 53:12 Jesus shares the spoils of his victory on the cross and resurrection with us, his mighty ones. He purchased your victory, your salvation, your emotional wholeness, your healing, your deliverance, and your triumph over every foe.

k 53:12 Or "himself."

l 53:12 See Matt. 11:28.

m 53:12 The work of a priest was to offer sacrifice for sin and intercede for the sinner. Our High Priest, Jesus, has done this for us. He became our sacrifice and now is interceding for us. See

God's Tender Love for Zion

54 "Rejoice*ᵃ with singing*, you barren one!
You who have never given birth,
burst into a song of joy and shout,
you who have never been in labor!*ᵇ*
For the deserted wife will have more children
than the married one," says Yahweh.*ᶜ*

²"*Increase is coming,* so enlarge your tent
and add extensions to your dwelling.*ᵈ*
Hold nothing back! Make the tent ropes longer and the pegs stronger.*ᵉ*
³You will increase and spread out in every direction.*ᶠ*
Your sons and daughters*ᵍ* will conquer nations
and revitalize desolate cities.
⁴Do not fear, for your shame is no more.
Do not be embarrassed,
for you will not be disgraced.
You will forget the inadequacy you felt in your youth
and will no longer remember the shame of your widowhood.
⁵For your Maker is your husband;
his name is Yahweh, Commander of Angel Armies!
Your Kinsman-Redeemer is the Holy One of Israel!
He has the title *Mighty* God of All the Earth!*ʰ*
⁶For I, Yahweh, have invited you to come back
like a depressed, deserted wife.
Like a young wife who has experienced rejection,
I am drawing you back to me," says Yahweh.
⁷"For just a brief moment I deserted you,
but with tender feelings of love
I will gather you *back to me.*
⁸In a surge of anger, for just the briefest moment,
I hid my face from you,

Luke 23:33–34; Rom. 8:34; Heb. 7:25, 27.

a 54:1 This verse begins with only two words in Hebrew: *barren* and *rejoice*. These are two ends of the emotional spectrum. Nothing brings sorrow like being barren. Yet God promises that even in our greatest sorrow there can be a song of joy.

b 54:1 This verse can be viewed as the remedy for spiritual barrenness—the song of triumph and the shout of joy! Spiritual barrenness is broken by the power of worship. Where God's people are held back in worship, spiritual barrenness soon follows. Our worship has the power to bring new birth (evangelism) into our congregations. Worship is a mighty force to influence the lost and bring new birth. See Gal. 4:27.

c 54:1 See Gal. 4:27.

d 54:2 Or "Stretch out the curtains of your dwelling."

e 54:2 Or "Lengthen your cords; make firm your tent pegs."

f 54:3 Or "to the right and to the left."

g 54:3 Or "your seed," the same Hebrew word found in 53:10 and Gen. 3:15.

h 54:5 This amazing verse gives us seven names of God.

but with everlasting kindness,
I will show you my cherishing love,"
says Yahweh, your Kinsman-Redeemer.

⁹"To me, this is like the time when I vowed
that the waters of Noah's flood
would never again cover the earth.
Now I vow to you that I will neither be angry with you
nor rebuke you.
¹⁰Even if the mountains were to crumble
and the hills disappear,
my heart of steadfast, faithful love
will never leave you,
and my covenant of peaceᵃ with you will never be shaken,"
says Yahweh,
whose love and compassionᵇ *will never give up on you.*

God Will Restore

¹¹"You unhappy one, storm-tossed and troubled,ᶜ
I am ready to rebuild you with precious stonesᵈ
and embed your foundation with sapphires.ᵉ
¹²I will make your towers of rubies,
your gates of sparkling jewels,ᶠ
and all your wallsᵍ of precious, delightful stones.
¹³All your children will be taught by Yahweh,ʰ
and great will be their peace and prosperity.
¹⁴You will be established in righteousness.
Oppression—be far from them!ⁱ
Fear—be far from them!ʲ
Yes, terror will not come near you, nor will you be afraid.
¹⁵If anyone dares to stir up strife against you,

---

a 54:10 This is the covenant of *shalom* that God has made with us, his people. God's covenant promise is that his *shalom* ("peace, prosperity, success, wholeness, and well-being") will be our portion all our days on earth. See Eph. 2:14.

b 54:10 The Hebrew word for "compassion" (*racham*) means "to love deeply, like a mother's love." *Racham* is a homonym for "womb," with an implication that God's love is like the love of a mother carrying a child in her womb.

c 54:11 See Eph. 4:14.

d 54:11 Or "I am about to set your stones in antimony."

e 54:11 The sapphire stone was the second stone of the high priest's breastplate and had engraved upon it the name Simeon ("he who hears").

f 54:12 Or "beryl."

g 54:12 Or "border."

h 54:13 See John 6:45.

i 54:14 See Acts 10:38.

j 54:14 See 2 Tim. 1:7.

it is not from me!
Those who challenge you will go down in defeat.
[16]See, I am the one who created the craftsman
who fans the coals into a fire
and forges a weapon fit for its purpose,
and I am the one who created the destroyer to destroy.
[17]*But I promise you*,
no weapon meant to hurt you will succeed,
and you will refute[a] every accusing word spoken against you.
This promise is the inheritance of Yahweh's servants,[b]
and their vindication[c] is from me," says Yahweh.

Invitation to an Abundant Life

55 "Listen! Are you thirsty *for more*?
Come to the *refreshing* waters *and drink*.[d]
Even if you have no money,
come, buy, and eat.[e]
Yes, come and buy all the wine[f] and milk[g] you desire—
it won't cost a thing.
[2]Why spend your hard-earned money
on something that can't nourish you[h]
or work so hard for something that can't satisfy?[i]
So listen carefully to me
and you'll enjoy a sumptuous feast,
delighting in the finest of food.[j]
[3]Pay attention and come closer to me,
and hear, that your total being may flourish.[k]
I will enter into an everlasting covenant with you,[l]
and I will show you the same faithful love
that I showed David.[m]

---

a 54:17 Or "condemn."
b 54:17 In ch. 53 we learn about the Servant of the Lord (Jesus Christ): his humiliation, his death, and the glory that followed. Here we find the Servant has become many servants (plural), a corporate body of believers. The Son has become sons. From this point on, Isaiah's focus finds its fulfillment with the corporate church and the glorious bride of Jesus Christ.
c 54:17 Or "righteousness."
d 55:1 See Ps. 23:2; John 4:14; 7:37–39; Rev. 22:17.
e 55:1 See Matt. 4:4.
f 55:1 See Song. 2:4; Neh. 8:10. This wine can symbolize the joy-filled blessings of God.
g 55:1 See 1 Peter 2:2. This milk can symbolize the spiritual nourishment we receive from God's Word.
h 55:2 See Ps. 107:9.
i 55:2 Matthew 11:28–30 is Jesus' commentary on this verse.
j 55:2 See John 6:48–63.
k 55:3 Or "Listen to me so that your soul may live."
l 55:3 See Heb. 13:20.
m 55:3 See Acts 13:34.

⁴"See! I made him a witness to the nations,
 an example of leadership,
 as prince and commander of peoples."

⁵Look! You will summon nations you've never heard of.
 Nations who have never heard of you
 will come running *to follow you*ᵃ
 because Yahweh, your God, the Holy One of Israel,
 has glorified you!

God's Mercy Greater than Man's
⁶Seek the Lord Yahweh when he makes himself approachable;ᵇ
 call upon him when *you sense* he is near.
⁷The wicked need to abandon their ways,
 and sinful ones need to banish every evil thought.ᶜ
 Let them return to Yahweh,
 and they will experience his compassionate mercy.
 Yes, let them return to God,
 for he will lavish forgiveness upon them.

⁸"For my thoughts *about mercy*ᵈ are not like your thoughts,
 and my ways are different from yours.
⁹As high as the heavens are above the earth,
 so my ways and my thoughts are higher than yours.

¹⁰"As the snow and rain that fall from heavenᵉ
 do not return until they have accomplished their purpose,
 soaking the earth and causing it to sprout with new life,
 providing seed to sow and bread to eat.
¹¹So also will be the wordᶠ that I speak;
 it does not return to me unfulfilled.ᵍ

---

a 55:5 See 2 Sam. 22:44–46; Song. 1:4; John 12:19.
b 55:6 Or "while he lets himself be found." See 1 Tim. 6:16: "the immortal God, living in the unapproachable light of divine glory!" It is "the true man, Jesus, the Anointed One" who makes himself approachable (1 Tim. 2:5).
c 55:7 See 2 Cor. 10:3–6.
d 55:8 In the context, the thoughts of God are in reference to compassion, mercy, and forgiveness. Man's thoughts of mercy are not God's. Man's mercy runs out, but God's mercy is higher than the heavens. God's mercy and forgiveness are generous and abundant.
e 55:10 In the language of biblical metaphor, snow is a picture of mercy blanketing the earth. Rain is a frequent symbol of revelation-teaching that soaks the heart (soil) and makes us fruitful. Note the seven terms for God's Word in vv. 8–10: thoughts, ways, snow, rain, water, seed, bread. These same terms can be used to describe the Lord Jesus. He is the seed of the woman, living bread, the way and the life that sprouts in us. He is the Word that was sent (as our Apostle, Heb. 3:1), and he will not return to heaven without accomplishing all God's pleasure.
f 55:11 In the context, God's word is his promise to show love, compassion, and forgiveness to all who turn to him. '
g 55:11 Or "empty."

My word performs my purpose
and fulfills the mission I sent it out to accomplish."[a]

[12]For you will leave *your exile* with joy[b]
and be led[c] *home wrapped* in peace.
The mountains and hills in front of you will burst into singing
and the trees of the field will applaud![d]
[13]Cypress trees will flourish where there were only thorns[e]
and myrtle trees instead of nettles.[f]
These will stand as a testimony to Yahweh's renown,
everlasting signs[g] that will not be cut off.

Joy for the Outcasts

56 Yahweh says *to his people*:

"Promote the cause of justice!
Do what is just and right,[h]
for soon my salvation will come
and my righteousness will be unveiled.
[2]Blessed is the one who will faithfully keep his commitment.
Yes, blessed is the one
who honors the Sabbath[i] and does not disregard it,
and the one who keeps their hands from doing evil."

[3]The foreigner who joins himself to Yahweh
should never say,
"*Because I'm a foreigner,*
Yahweh will exclude me from his people."
And the eunuchs should never say,
"*Because I can't have children,* I'm just a barren tree."[j]

---

a   55:11 The Septuagint adds a phrase not found in the Hebrew: "And I will make your way
    prosperous."
b   55:12 See Rom. 14:17.
c   55:12 See Rom. 8:14.
d   55:12 Isaiah was a master poet. With beautiful metaphors, he describes the return of God's
    people out of captivity. What once limited God's people as a barrier (mountains and hills) now
    celebrates with singing as the redeemed leave their captivity and come into God's full purpose
    for them. See Rom. 8:19–21.
e   55:13 Thorns are a symbol of the curse of sin. See Gen. 3:18; Matt. 27:29; Gal. 3:13–14.
f   55:13 There is a hint of the Lord Jesus in these trees. Jesus is the blessed man who is like a
    tree (Ps. 1); he replaces the briars and thorns of our flesh with the flourishing tree of life in us.
g   55:13 Or "memorial (as a reminder)."
h   56:1 Or "cultivate righteousness."
i   56:2 For believers today, our Sabbath is now a man, the Lord Jesus Christ. We have entered
    into the seventh day from Adam (2 Peter 3:8) and rest in the finished work of the cross. We
    cease from our own labors and enter into his Sabbath rest. See Heb. 4.
j   56:3 This is a figure of speech, comparing being unable to procreate to being like a withered

⁴For Yahweh says *to such a man*,
  "To the eunuchs who keep my Sabbaths,
  and choose the things that honor me,
  and remain true to my covenant, *I make this promise*:
⁵*I will bestow upon them within my household*ᵃ
  both an honored place*ᵇ* and an honored name,
  even better than the honor that comes from having children.
  I bestow upon them my everlasting favor;ᶜ
  you will never be forgotten.'
⁶And to the foreigners who join themselves to Yahweh
  to worship him, those who want to be his servants
  and love the name of Yahweh—
  all who honor the Sabbath and do not disregard it,
  and who remain true to my covenant—*I make this promise*:
⁷*I will welcome you into my holy mountain*ᵈ
  and make you joyful in my house of prayer.*ᵉ*
  I will accept every sacrifice and offering
  that you place on my altar,
  for my house *of worship* will be known
  as a house of prayer for all people.'"
⁸The Lord God Almighty,
  who brings home the outcasts of Israel, says,
  "There are many others I will gather,
  and I will add them to those who are already gathered."ᶠ

Corrupt Leaders

⁹All you wild beasts, come and devour,
  you wild animals of the forest.
¹⁰Blind watchmen, all of them!
  They have no revelation knowledge;
  they're like dumb dogs that don't even bark—
  dreaming, sleeping, devoted to slumber.
¹¹They're greedy dogs that never eat enough.

---

tree. Eunuchs were forbidden to worship with God's people (Deut. 23:1), but God's mercy triumphs over rejection.

a 56:5 Or "in my house and within my walls." This becomes a figure of speech for God's household or family, not a literal plaque in the temple. God is saying that grace is greater than our disqualifications. In spite of our imperfections, if we continue to honor God and his Word, favor will rest on our lives forever. This favor and name will endure longer than what comes from having children.

b 56:5 Or "monument (memorial)."

c 56:5 Or "with an everlasting name."

d 56:7 Yahweh's holy mountain is the Zion-realm. See Heb. 12:22–24.

e 56:7 God's desire has always been to gather his people into the house of prayer. See Matt. 21:13; Mark 11:17; Luke 19:46.

f 56:8 Or "to those who are already gathered." See John 17:20–24.

And the shepherds have no discernment;
they follow their own desires.
Every last one of them seeks his own profit.
[12]Each one says, "Let's get wine and liquor and have a party!
And tomorrow, more of the same, except even better!"[a]

Israel's Idolatry

57 The godly perish,
but no one seems to notice.
The faithful ones are taken away,
and no one understands.
It is because of evil
that they are preserved from calamity,
[2]and the godly ones enter into peace,
resting serenely upon their death beds.

[3]"But you—come here, you son of a sorceress!
You're nothing but an offspring
of an adulteress and a prostitute.[b]
[4]Who do you think you're mocking?
At whom do you sneer and stick out your tongue?
Why, you're a rebellious child, the offspring of liars!
[5]You burn with lust *for other gods*
among the oak groves and under every green tree.
You sacrifice your own children in the caves[c]
near the bed of a stream.
[6]From there you take smooth stones
and worship them as idols.
Yes, they become your idols!
You bring them grain offerings
and pour out wine as drink offerings.
Do you think I will not seek vengeance for this?
[7]On a high hill, you practice ritual sex[d]
and go up to the lofty place to offer sacrifice.
[8]Hidden inside your front doors
you have set up your obscene idols.[e]
Forsaking me, you went up
and uncovered yourself
and climbed into your wide bed.
You made covenant with them for yourselves,

---

a 56:12 The Septuagint omits this verse.

b 57:3 This is a vivid picture of those who practice idolatry. See James 4:4.

c 57:5 See 2 Chron. 28:3; 33:6.

d 57:7 Or "On high you set up your bed."

e 57:8 Or "(phallic) symbols."

you slept with them, and you gazed upon their nakedness.
⁹You journeyed to the king[a] with oil
  along with many perfumes.
  You sent your envoys to exotic lands,
  even down to the underworld.[b]
¹⁰Though all your wanderings wearied you,
  you never said, 'I give up.'
  Your strength was renewed
  so that you did not faint.

¹¹"Why were you so afraid of them that you told lies
  and did not remember me or even cared what I thought?
  Is it because I have been patient and long silent
  that you no longer fear me?
¹²I will denounce your presumed 'righteousness'
  and your 'good works,'
  so don't trust in your idols to help you.
¹³Let's see if your pantheon of idols can save you when you cry out!
  They will be blown away by the wind;[c]
  merely a breath will carry them off!
  But whoever makes me a hiding place
  will possess the land and inherit my holy mountain."[d]

A Promise of Revival and Healing

¹⁴*Yahweh says, "Let the people return to me.*
  Build! Build up the road, clear the way, and get it ready!
  Remove every obstacle from their path."
¹⁵For this is what the high and majestic one says,
  the one who fills the eternal realm with glory,[e]
  whose name is Holy:
  "I dwell in high and holy places
  but also with the bruised and lowly in spirit,
  those who are humble and quick to repent.
  I dwell with them to revive the spirit of the humble,
  to revive the heart of those who are broken over their sin.
¹⁶You will not find me continually accusing them[f]
  or holding anger against them,

---

a 57:9 Or "to the (Canaanite god) Molech."

b 57:9 Or "to Sheol."

c 57:13 Or "spirit."

d 57:13 That is, Mount Zion. The believer today inherits the kingdom of God, the Zion-realm.
    See Ps. 37:9, 11; 69:35, 36; Isa. 49:8; Matt. 5:5; Heb. 12:22.

e 57:15 The Hebrew word *shakan* (*shekinah*) means "to dwell or settle." The implication is that
    God inhabits eternity, filling it with his glory.

f 57:16 Or "continually striving with them."

lest they *feel defeated* and lose heart before me.
For I am the One who gave the breath of life to my people.
[17]It was their sin and greed that made me angry,
so I struck them and hid my face from them.
But they continued in rebellion, following their own desires.
[18]Even though I've seen their ways, I will heal them.*a*
I will guide them *forward* and repay them with comfort,*b*
giving mourners the language of praise.
[19]I offer peace to those who are far *from me,*
and I offer peace to those who are near,*c*
and I will heal *their deepest wounds,*" says Yahweh.
[20]"But the wicked are like the storm-tossed sea,
whose restless waves are never still,
stirring up mud and mire.
[21]There is no peace*d* for the wicked," says my God.

Ritual and Ceremony Is Not Enough

58 "Shout it loud *and clear*!
Don't hold back!
Let your voice be like a trumpet blast!
Declare to my people their rebellion
and to Jacob's tribes their sin!
[2]Yes, daily they seem to seek me,
pretending that they delight to know my ways,
as though they were a nation that does what is right
and had not rejected the law of their God.
They ask me to show them the right way,
acting as though they are eager to be close to me.
[3]They say, 'Why is it that when we fasted,
you did not see it?
We starved ourselves, and you didn't seem to notice.'

"Because on the day you fasted
you were seeking only your own desires,
and you continue to exploit your workers.*e*
[4]During your fasts, you quarrel and fight with others
and strike them with an angry fist.

---

a 57:18 This is the same Hebrew word found in 53:5. See Hos. 6:1–3.

b 57:18 It is possible to see in this verse the progression of the worshiper from the outer court (healing), forward into the Holy Place, until we are drenched with God's comforting presence in the Holy of Holies, where we release our language of praise.

c 57:19 See Eph. 2:11–22.

d 57:21 Or "well-being" or "prosperity."

e 58:3 See Lev. 16:29. It was clear that their fasting was an attempt to appear spiritual and manipulate God.

When you fast like that, your voice will not be heard on high.
[5]Do you think I'm impressed with that kind of fast?
  Is it just a day to starve your bodies,
  make others think you're humble,[a]
  and lie down in sackcloth and ashes?
  Do you call that a fast?
  Do you think I, Yahweh, will be pleased with that?[b]

Worship God in Truth
[6]"This is the kind of fast that I desire:
  Remove the heavy chains of oppression!
  Stop exploiting *your workers*![c]
  Set free the crushed and mistreated!
  Break off every yoke of bondage!
[7]Share your food with the hungry!
  Provide for the homeless
  and bring them into your home!
  Clothe the naked!
  Don't turn your back on your own flesh and blood!
[8]Then my favor will bathe you in sunlight
  until you are like the dawn bursting through a dark night.[d]
  And then suddenly your healing[e] will manifest.[f]
  You will see your righteousness march out before you,
  and the glory of Yahweh will protect you from all harm![g]
[9]Then Yahweh will answer you when you pray.
  When you cry out for help, he will say,
  'I am here.'

  "If you banish every form of oppression, the scornful accusations,[h]
  and vicious slander,
[10]and if you offer yourselves in compassion[i] for the hungry
  and relieve those in misery,[j]

---

a 58:5 Or "to bow your heads like (bent over) reeds."
b 58:5 Or "That is a day acceptable to Yahweh."
c 58:6 Or "Loose the ropes of the yoke."
d 58:8 Showing justice will bring the light of a new day. This sunrise pictures God's restored favor and blessing coming upon the people.
e 58:8 Or "health" or "restoration." This would include the body, soul, and spirit.
f 58:8 Or "sprout speedily, grow."
g 58:8 Or "will be your rear guard"; that is, God's glory covers us from our past and protects us today and forever, with glory going before us and following after as well.
h 58:9 Or "extending the finger."
i 58:10 Jesus offered himself to us, so we should offer ourselves in compassion for others. See Matt. 10:8; Acts 20:33–35; Gal. 1:4; Eph. 5:2, 25; 1 Tim. 2:6; Titus 2:14.
j 58:10 The five qualifications of last-days ministry are found in vv. 9–10: (1) Commit to banish every form of oppression in our lives, churches, and society. (2) Remove scornful accusation

then your dawning light will rise in the darkness
and your gloom will turn into noonday splendor![a]
[11]Yahweh will always guide you where to go and what to do.
He will fill you with refreshment
even when you are in a dry, difficult place.
He will continually restore strength to you,
so you will flourish like a well-watered garden
and like an ever-flowing, trustworthy spring *of blessing*.
[12]Your people will rebuild long-deserted ruins,
building anew on foundations laid long before you.[b]
You will be known as Repairers of the Cities[c]
and Restorers of Communities.[d]

[13]"If you stop pursuing your own desires on my holy day,
and refrain from disregarding the Sabbath,
if you call the Sabbath a delightful pleasure
and Yahweh's holy day honorable,
if you honor it properly by not chasing your own desires,
serving your own interests, and speaking empty words,
[14]then you will find the joyous bliss
that comes from serving Yahweh.
And I will cause you to prosper
and be carried triumphantly over the high places of the land.[e]
You will enjoy the heritage of Jacob, your ancestor."

Certainly the mouth of Yahweh has spoken it!

Conviction of Sin

59 Truly Yahweh's arm is not too powerless to save *you*
nor his ear too deaf to hear.

(criticism) of others and their ministries. (3) Forbid to spread malicious slander. (4) Have compassion for the poor and disenfranchised. (5) Comfort those enduring suffering and tragedy. Then God promises (vv. 10–12) that multiple blessings will come: (1) Our spiritual light (influence) will increase in our communities. (2) Discouragement and gloom will disappear from our lives. (3) God will give us specific guidance and counsel to know what to do and where to go. (4) He will fill us with renewing grace, even when we are surrounded by difficult situations. (5) Our spiritual lives will flourish like a lush garden with fruit and beauty. (6) We will not cease to be an ever-flowing source of blessing to others. (7) We will be given God's grace to rebuild lives and institutions in our cities, churches, and nations. (8) We will take up the legacy of our spiritual fathers and build on their foundations. (9) We will have a testimony of healing cities. (10) We will restore well-being to our communities.

a 58:10 Or "double light."
b 58:12 Or "on foundations of many generations."
c 58:12 Or "repairers of the gap."
d 58:12 Or "restorers of paths that lead you home." This is the Elijah ministry of restoration. See Neh. 1–4; Acts 3:21.
e 58:14 That is, God will raise you up and cause you to *prosper greatly*. See Deut. 32:13; Eph. 1:3; 2:6.

²Rather, your sinful deeds have built a barrier
  between you and your God.
  Your sins have made God turn his face from you
  so that he does not hear *your prayers*.
³For your hands are stained with blood
  and your fingers are dripping with the guilt of sin.
  Lies spill from your lips
  and your tongue mutters treachery.
⁴No one seeks true justice;
  no one pleads his case with honesty.
  They rely on their illusions and misleading lies;
  they conceive trouble and give birth to sin.
⁵They hatch *harmful plots* like snake's eggs
  and spin *their lies* like a spider spins its web.
  Whoever eats their "eggs" dies
  and a poisonous snake gets hatched!
⁶Their "webs" cannot substitute as clothing,
  they cannot cover themselves with the lies they spin,
  nor can their works cover themselves adequately.
  Their actions are evil,
  and the wages of violence is in their hands.
⁷Their feet eagerly run after evil,
  and they are swift to shed innocent blood.ᵃ
  Their imaginations are filled with evil;ᵇ
  destruction and desolation litter their paths.
⁸They know nothing of the way of peace,ᶜ
  and injustice is their way of life.
  Their paths are so crooked
  that no one who walks in them knows peace.

Confession of Sin

⁹For this reason, justice is far from us
  and righteousness doesn't reach us.
  We hope for light, but sadly, there is only darkness.ᵈ
  We wait for a bright light, but walk in darkness.
¹⁰We are like the blind groping along a wall,
  inching along in the dark like those who cannot see;
  we stumble around in broad daylight like it was night,
  like the walking dead.ᵉ
¹¹We are *frustrated*, growling like bears,

---

a 59:7 See Prov. 6:16–19; Rom. 3:15–16.

b 59:7 See Gen. 6:5.

c 59:8 See Rom. 3:17; Eph. 2:14.

d 59:9 See John 8:11–12.

e 59:10 The meaning of this Hebrew clause is uncertain. See Eph. 2:1.

like doves cooing mournfully.
We wait and wait for justice, but it never seems to come;
for salvation, but it remains distant.
[12]For our many rebellious deeds are stacked high before you;
our sins testify against us.
We are aware of our sins,
and we know our evil deeds all too well.
[13]We have rebelled and even tried to deny Yahweh;
we have forsaken our God.
Our speech stirs up oppression and revolt,
and our hearts conceive, then confess, lies.[a]
[14]Justice is driven away
and righteousness stands on the sidelines,
for truth has stumbled in the public square
and morality cannot enter.
[15]Yes, truth has disappeared,[b]
and those who turn from evil become the next victim.

Yahweh saw this and was greatly displeased
that there was no justice.

The Lord, Our Redeemer

[16]And then he was astonished to see that there was no champion,[c]
not even one, who would rescue the oppressed.[d]
So then his own mighty power[e] was released to deliver,
and his own righteousness supported him.
[17]He put on righteousness as his body armor,[f]
salvation for a helmet;
a garment of warring vengeance was his uniform
and passion, his cape.
[18]He will repay wrath to his enemies
and retribution to his foes,
according to what they have done.
Reckoning is coming to the islands for what is due them.
[19]From the west to the lands of the rising sun,
the glory and the name of Yahweh
will be held in highest reverence,

---

a 59:13 See Eph. 4:25.
b 59:15 Or "Truth is hidden" (Vulg.).
c 59:16 Or "intercessor."
d 59:16 Or "intercede."
e 59:16 Or "arm," a metaphor for his mighty power.
f 59:17 See Eph. 6:10–18.

for he will break in as a flooding, rushing[a] river
driven on by the breath of Yahweh![b]

God's Covenant with Zion

[20]"He will come to Zion as a Kinsman-Redeemer
to those of Jacob's tribes who repent of their rebellion,"
says Yahweh.
[21]"And this is my covenant promise with them,"[c]
says Lord Yahweh.
"From now on, my Holy Spirit will *rest on them*
and not depart from them,
and my *prophetic* words will fill their mouths
and will not depart from them, nor from their children,
nor from their descendants, from now on and forever,"
says Lord Yahweh.

The Glorious New Day

60 "Rise up in splendor and be radiant,[d] for your light has dawned,
and Yahweh's glory[e] now streams from you!
[2]Look carefully! Darkness blankets the earth,
and thick gloom[f] covers the nations,
but Yahweh arises[g] upon you
and the brightness of his glory appears over you![h]
[3]Nations will be attracted to your radiant light[i]
and kings to the sunrise-glory of your new day.[j]
[4]Lift up your eyes higher! Look all around you *and believe*,

---

a 59:19 God broke into the human condition as a man who died on the cross. His blood, like a flood of righteousness, washes away the sins of those who believe in him.

b 59:19 Or "When the enemy comes in, the Spirit of Yahweh, like a flood, will lift up a standard against him" or "When the enemy comes in like a flood, the breath of Yahweh will put him to flight."

c 59:21 See Jer. 31:33; Rom. 11:26–27; Gal. 3:29; Heb. 12:22–24.

d 60:1 Or "break forth with the light of (a new) day." See Eph. 5:27. Applying vv. 1–2 to the church, we see Jesus as the Light that shines upon us (John 8:12; 2 Cor. 4:6) and the light of the church shining upon the nations (Matt. 5:14–16).

e 60:1 Here Isaiah begins a new section in his masterpiece. The theme of these last seven chapters is The Glorious New Day, corresponding to the Feast of Tabernacles. The Hebrew word for "glory" appears twenty-three times in chs. 60–66. A possible outline of these chapters is: (60) A New Day. (61) A New Priesthood. (62) A New Wedding. (63) A New Mercy. (64) A New Prayer. (65) A New Heaven and a New Earth. (66) A New Jerusalem.

f 60:2 Or "thick clouds."

g 60:2 Or "breaks out over you."

h 60:2 See Isa. 60:19–22; Mal. 4:2; Rev. 21:2–3.

i 60:3 Or "Nations will walk by your light." Light is often seen as a biblical metaphor for understanding and revelation. See Eph. 1:18.

j 60:3 Or "to the brightness of your sunrise." The sunrise of our new day came at the resurrection of Jesus Christ.

for your sons are returning from far away
and your daughters are being tenderly carried home.
Watch as they all gather together, eager to come back to you!

Zion's Wealth

[5]"Then you will understand and be radiant.[a]
Your heart will be thrilled and swell with joy.
The fullness of the sea will flow to you[b]
and the wealth[c] of the nations will be transferred to you!
[6]Caravans of camels will cover your land,
young camels *loaded with goods* from Midian[d] and Ephah.[e]
All the *wealthy merchants* from Sheba will come,
bearing gold and frankincense
and singing the praises of Yahweh!
[7]All the flocks of Kedar[f] will be gathered to you,
and the rams[g] of Nebaioth[h] will be yours
as acceptable *sacrifices* on my altar,
and I will adorn with more glory my glorious temple.[i]

[8]"Who are these who soar like clouds,[j]
flying like doves[k] into their portals?[l]
[9]Indeed, the distant islands eagerly look for me,
with their large ships[m] leading the way.
They are bringing Zion's children from afar.
They come with *offerings of* silver and gold
to honor the name of Yahweh, your God, the Holy One of Israel,
for he has glorified you![n]

---

a 60:5 Or "As you understand you will sparkle." The Hebrew word (*nahar*) can also be translated "flow together"— "As you understand, you will *flow together*."
b 60:5 This is not simply fish, but the fullness of the nations, the sea of humanity. See Rom. 11:25.
c 60:5 Or "forces (armies), virtues, strength, might, power, riches, goods."
d 60:6 Midian was a son of Abraham and Keturah who settled near the Gulf of Elath.
e 60:6 Ephah was a grandson of Abraham and one of the five sons of Midian. Camels were seen as a symbol of wealth. See Judges 6:5.
f 60:7 Kedar was one of Ishmael's sons and his tribe became the dominant military power of the Ishmaelites in North Arabia (see Hitti, *History of the Arabs*, 42).
g 60:7 Rams were brought as "consecration offerings" for the ordination of priests. See Ex. 29.
h 60:7 Nebaioth was the firstborn son of Ishmael and Esau's brother-in-law and becomes a metonymy for the Ishmaelites. See Gen. 28:9; 36:3.
i 60:7 We are now the glorious temple of God, adorned with even more glory than we comprehend. See John 17:22; Rom. 8:30; 1 Cor. 3:16–17.
j 60:8 See 1 Kings 18:44; Heb. 12:1–2; Rev. 1:7.
k 60:8 See Song. 1:15; 2:14.
l 60:8 Or "windows" or "dovecotes."
m 60:9 Or "the ships of Tarshish."
n 60:9 See John 17:22; Rom. 8:30.

Zion's Restoration

¹⁰"Foreigners*ᵃ* will rebuild your walls
and their kings will serve you.
Even though I punished you in my anger,
I will restore you in my *gracious* favor
and show you my tender compassion.
¹¹Your gateways will always remain wide open*ᵇ*
around the clock to let in the procession of kings
bringing *their constant stream of* the riches of the nations.
¹²The nation or kingdom
that refuses to serve you will perish and be utterly ruined.*ᶜ*
¹³Lebanon's glory will be yours.
The cypress, fir, and pine will come to you
to beautify the site of my holy place.
And I will glorify the place where I rest my feet.*ᵈ*
¹⁴The descendants of your oppressors
will come bowing low before you,
and all who hated you will bow down at your feet.
They will call you The *Beautiful* City of Yahweh,
Glorious Zion of the Holy One of Israel.

Zion's Honor

¹⁵"Although once you were rejected and despised,
undesirable for anyone to pass through you,
I will make you majestic forever,*ᵉ*
a *source of* joy for every generation.*ᶠ*
¹⁶You will guzzle the milk of nations*ᵍ*
and suckle at the breast of kings.
You will know me intimately
that I am Yahweh, your Savior,
for I am the Mighty Hero *who rules over* Jacob's tribes,
your Kinsman-Redeemer!

Everything Made Better

¹⁷"I will replace your copper with gold,
your iron with silver,*ʰ*

---

a 60:10 Or "sons of foreigners."
b 60:11 See John 10:9–10. Jesus Christ is always ready to receive any who come to him.
c 60:12 See Ps. 2:12.
d 60:13 Or "I will make my footstool glorious."
e 60:15 Or "an eternal excellency."
f 60:15 Read this verse again with the understanding of its fulfillment in Jesus Christ.
g 60:16 This is a figure of speech for receiving the best from the nations and being enriched by kings.
h 60:17 These items are seen elsewhere in Scripture as symbols. Copper (brass) is a frequent symbol of judgment and gold a common symbol of the divine nature. God replaces our guilt

your wood with copper,
and your stone with iron.
I will install peace and prosperity as your government
and righteousness as your overseer.
[18]*Threats of* violence will no longer be heard in your land,
nor will destruction and ruin be found within your borders.
You will name your walls Salvation
and your gates Praise.

Zion's Glory

[19]"The sun will no longer be needed to brighten the day,
nor the moon to shine at night,
for Yahweh will be your unfailing light;
your God will be your glory![a]
[20]There will be no more sunsets or new moons,[b]
for Yahweh will be your everlasting light
and your days of sadness will be over.[c]
[21]All your people will be righteous
and will permanently possess the land.
I planted them there as a tender sapling,
the work of my own hands to display my glory.
[22]I will multiply the least of you into a thousand[d]
and the weakest one into a mighty nation.[e]
I am Yahweh, and when the right time comes,[f]
I will accomplish it swiftly!"

Messiah's Mission

61 The mighty Spirit of Lord Yahweh[g] is *wrapped* around[h] me
because Yahweh has anointed me,[i]

---

with godliness. Unyielding iron can be seen as a symbol of stubbornness and silver is a common symbol of redemption.

a 60:19 See 1 John 1:5; Rev. 21:23.

b 60:20 Or "the moon withdrawing itself."

c 60:20 The dark night of our sin and pain and grief are ended by the work of Jesus on the cross and the work of the Holy Spirit within us. See John 14–16; 19:30; Rom. 8:14–25.

d 60:22 Or "a tribe."

e 60:22 See Zech. 12:8.

f 60:22 See Eccl. 3:1–8; Acts 2:1–4; Gal. 4:4.

g 61:1 The Spirit of the Lord Yahweh is viewed by many scholars as a synonymical phrase for the Spirit of Prophecy.

h 61:1 Or "upon, in, on, over, above, by, for, through, throughout, around, beside."

i 61:1 The title of Messiah is taken from the Hebrew verb "to anoint." *Messiah* means the Anointed One in both Hebrew (*mashiach*) and Greek (*Christos*). Our Lord Jesus quoted this passage in Nazareth (Luke 4:16–21) and introduced his "jubilee" ministry to Israel (Lev. 25). The first three verses of this chapter describe the twofold mission of Jesus: (1) to open the door of the day of grace to the world; (2) to proclaim the day of vengeance coming on sin, darkness,

as a messenger to preach good news to the poor.[a]
He sent me to heal the wounds of the brokenhearted,
to tell captives, "You are free,"[b]
and to tell prisoners, "Be free from *your* darkness."[c]
[2]*I am sent* to announce a *new* season[d] of Yahweh's grace[e]
and a time of God's recompense *on his enemies,*[f]
to comfort all who are in sorrow,
[3]to strengthen those *crushed by despair* who mourn in Zion—
to give them a beautiful bouquet[g] in the place of ashes,
the oil of bliss[h] instead of tears,[i]
and the mantle of joyous praise[j]
instead of the spirit of heaviness.[k]
Because of this, they will be known as
Mighty Oaks[l] of Righteousness,
planted[m] by Yahweh as a *living* display of his glory.
[4]They will restore ruins from long ago
and rebuild what was long devastated.[n]

---

sickness, and eventually, the "goat" nations. As a prophet, he comes to preach the new season of grace; as a priest, he comes to heal; and as a king, he comes to decree and herald peace and freedom to the captives. See Luke 3:21–22; Acts 10:38.

a 61:1 Or "humble, lowly, depressed."

b 61:1 See Rom. 8:21; 2 Cor. 3:17; Gal. 5:1.

c 61:1 Or "to release the blind from darkness" (LXX).

d 61:2 Or "year"—not a literal year but a season of time.

e 61:2 Or "favor, good pleasure, acceptance."

f 61:2 Through the cross and the resurrection of Jesus, a time of recompense has come (Col. 2:15) to conquer sin, sickness, Satan, death, demonic power, and injustice—not just vengeance on humanity but on evil wherever it is found.

g 61:3 Or "beauty for ashes" or "a garland (of flowers) or headdress." There is an interesting wordplay in the Hebrew text. The word for "beauty" is *phe'er*, and the word for "ashes" is *epher*—simply the moving of one letter. God has the power to change and move things around in our lives to make them into something beautiful. See Rom. 8:28.

h 61:3 Or "joy, gladness." See Heb.1:9.

i 61:3 Or "(robes of) mourning."

j 61:3 Or "a splendor-garment."

k 61:3 Or "the spirit of failure." The Hebrew word for "heaviness" (*keheh*) comes from a root word for "dark, dim, obscure, colorless, gloom."

l 61:3 The oak, a hardwood tree, was used to make yokes for oxen and symbolizes strength, might (or mighty men), stability, conviction, uprightness, resoluteness. This could be the *Quercus calliprinos,* also known as the Palestine oak. There is a Palestine oak not far from Hebron that has been estimated to be 850 years old. "Oaks of Righteousness" points to a godly, spiritually mature people who will know the righteousness of God and walk in it. Jesus, the Tree of Life, multiplies himself in us so we become trees of righteousness. A Tree became a forest. See Ps. 1:3.

m 61:3 See Ps. 92:13; 1 Cor. 3:9.

n 61:4 These desolate places can also point to areas of our lives that are broken and to spiritual truths that have been lost and forgotten for generations, which are now being recovered. See

They will renew ruined cities
and desolations of past generations.
⁵Foreigners will be appointed to shepherd your *many* flocks;
strangers will cultivate your fields and tend your vines.

Messiah's Ministers
⁶But you will be known as Priests of Yahweh,ᵃ
and called Servants of our God.
You will feast on the wealth of nations
and revelᵇ in their riches!ᶜ
⁷Because you received a double dose
of shame and dishonor,
you will inherit a double portion
of endless joy and everlasting bliss!

⁸"For I, Yahweh, love fairness *and* justice,
and I hate stealing and sin.
I will rightly repay them because of my faithfulness
and enter into an everlasting covenant with them.
⁹Their seed will be famous among the nations,
and their descendants the center of attention of the people.
All who see them will recognize
that they are the seed that Yahweh has blessed *with favor!*"

Messiah's Music
¹⁰I will sing and greatly rejoice in Yahweh!
My whole being vibrates
with shouts *of joy* in my God!
For he has dressed me with salvationᵈ
and wrapped me in the robe of *his* righteousness!ᵉ
I appear like a bridegroom *on his wedding day,*
decked out with a beautiful sash,ᶠ
or like a radiant bride adorned with sparkling jewels.
¹¹In the same way the earth produces its crops
and seeds spring up in a garden,
so will the Lord Yahweh cause righteousness and praise
to blossom before all the nations!

Acts 3:21.

a 61:6 It has been the desire of God to make all of his people priests (Ex. 19:1–6; 1 Peter 2:1–10; Rev. 5:9–10). This far surpasses the priestly ministry of the Old Covenant (Heb. 8:6).

b 61:6 Or "glory."

c 61:6 Or "admired because of their wealth" (LXX).

d 61:10 See Rom. 13:11–14; 2 Cor. 5:1–5.

e 61:10 See Ex. 28:4; Luke 15:22; Rom. 14:17; Rev. 6:11; 7:9–14; 19:7–8.

f 61:10 Or "ornaments, (priestly) turban, garland."

God Delights in Zion

62 For Zion's sake, how can I keep silent?
For Jerusalem's sake, how can I remain quiet?
I will keep interceding until her righteousness
breaks forth like the blazing light of dawn
and her salvation like a burning torch!
²Nations will see your victory-vindication,
and every king will witness your *blinding* radiance!
You will be called by a brand-new name,ᵃ
given to you from the mouth of Yahweh himself.
³You will be a beautiful crown held *high* in the hand of Yahweh,
a royal crownᵇ of splendor
held in the open palm of your God!
⁴You will never again be called the Abandoned One,
nor will your land be called Deserted.
But you will be called My Delight Is in You,ᶜ
and your land My Beloved Wife,ᵈ
for Yahweh finds his delight in you
and he married your land.
⁵As a young man marries the young woman *he loves*,
so your builder-sonsᵉ will marry you.
As the bridegroom finds joy in *his union with* his bride,
so will your God take joy in *his union with* you!

Intercession

⁶Jerusalem, I have stationed intercessors on your walls
who will never be silent, day or night.
You "reminders"ᶠ of Yahweh, take no rest,
⁷and *tirelessly* give God no rest,
until he firmly establishes Jerusalem
and makes her the praise of all the earth!

⁸Yahweh swears an oath by the authority of his right hand
and by his mighty arm:
"I will never again give your new grain as food for your enemies,
nor will foreigners drink your new wine

---

a 62:2 A new name signifies a new nature, a new character, and a new authority. See Gen. 32:28; Rev. 2:17, 3:12.

b 62:3 Or "diadem."

c 62:4 Or "Hephzibah." See 2 Kings 21:1.

d 62:4 In an allegorical sense, Yahweh's wife foreshadows Christ's relationship with his bride, the church (2 Cor. 11:2; Eph. 5:22–23; Rev. 19:7–9).

e 62:5 Isaiah uses a homonym that can mean "builders or sons."

f 62:6 Or "rememberers"; that is, those who intercede continually to remind God of his promises. Like divine administrators, we remind God of the promises and appointments he must keep.

that you worked hard to produce.
⁹Instead, you who harvest it will eat it
 and offer your praise to Yahweh,
 and you who gather the grapes
 will drink the new wine in my holy courts."ᵃ

¹⁰Pass through, pass through the gates,
 and go from old to new.
 Prepare a new path for the people.
 Build! Build up a highway *for them to come to me*!
 Remove every hindranceᵇ
 and unfurl a banner for the nations!
¹¹See? Yahweh has proclaimed to the ends of the earth:
 Tell my daughter, Zion,
 "Look, here comes your Deliverer!
 See? He's bringing his reward,
 and his recompense goes before him."
¹²They will be called His Holy People,
 The Redeemed of Yahweh.
 And you will be known as Those Whom God Loves,ᶜ
 A City Not Abandoned.

The Day of Vengeance

63 Who is this coming from the city of Bozrahᵈ in Edom?ᵉ
 He is dressed in garments of bright scarlet,ᶠ
robed in a garment dyed bright red,
marching *like a champion* in his great power and might.

 "It is I! I am the one who announces righteousness,
 I am mighty *and ready* to save!"ᵍ

---

a 62:9 The grain and the new wine can be symbols of the Word and the Spirit, respectively.

b 62:10 Or "stone."

c 62:12 John identified himself as the one whom Jesus loved, and so can we. See John 13:23.

d 63:1 *Bozrah* means "sheepfold" or "fortress."

e 63:1 Although Edom was an ancient kingdom in Transjordan, the general consensus of scholars is that *Edom* here is a symbolic term for the enemies of God—a collective archetype of that which stands in God's way. It is possible, since Edom is a variant form of Adam, sharing the same Hebrew root, that we are seeing how God triumphs over "Adam" by the crimson blood of the Last Adam, Jesus Christ. Additionally, the Edomites were bitter enemies of the Jews and typify the warfare of flesh vs. the spirit (Gal. 5:17). Isaiah sees this mystery man coming on the road from Bozrah to Zion, clothed in crimson garments, having conquered his enemies, not weary or fainting. He comes in the greatness of his strength.

f 63:1 Or "majestic in attire."

g 63:1 This points to Jesus Christ, who is mighty to save those who come to him in faith. Alone, he conquered sin, death, Satan, sickness, fear, and the grave. Isaiah's focus seems to be on the finished work of Jesus on the cross. See John 19:30; Eph. 1:20–23; Col. 2:15; 1 John 2:14–18.

²Why are your robes so red,
   like those of one treading grapes?

³"I have been treading in the winepress alone,
   and there was no one there from the nations to help me.
   I stomped on *the nations* in my anger
   and trampled them down in my wrath.
   Their blood soaked my clothing and stained all my robes.
⁴For a day of vengeance*ᵃ* was in my heart,
   and the time for my redeeming work had come.
⁵I looked, but there was no one to help me.
   I was amazed that there was no one to support me.
   So my own power*ᵇ* accomplished salvation,
   and my wrath*ᶜ* sustained me.
⁶So I trampled down nations in my anger
   and shattered them*ᵈ* in my fury
   and spilled their blood on the ground."

God's Endless Mercy

⁷I will tell again of the faithful, gracious acts*ᵉ* of Yahweh
   and praise him for everything*ᶠ* he has done for us—
   the wonderful goodness,*ᵍ* the riches of his mercy,
   which he has shown to the house of Israel,
   and the abundance of his *endless* love.
⁸For he said,
   "Truly, they are my loyal children who will not act deceitfully."
   He became their Savior.*ʰ*
⁹When they suffered, he suffered with them.
   The Angel of His Presence*ⁱ* saved them.

---

a 63:4 A "day of vengeance" has multiple applications. It can refer to the release of the Jews from Babylon, the release of the church from the Dark Ages, the release of creation from the bondage of corruption brought by sin (Rom. 8:19–21), or, as some would claim, a future war of Armageddon. But the context favors a prophetic fulfillment when Jesus Christ was crucified and rendered judgment on principalities and powers by the blood of his cross and his triumphant resurrection.

b 63:5 Or "my own arm," a symbol of God power.

c 63:5 Some Hebrew manuscripts have (*weṣidqathi*): "My victorious [right hand] sustained me."

d 63:6 As translated from most Hebrew manuscripts and Targum (Aramaic); however, some manuscripts read "I made them drunk with my fury."

e 63:7 Literally "the loving-kindnesses."

f 63:7 Or "the praiseworthy deeds."

g 63:7 See Ps. 145:7.

h 63:8 See Matt. 1:21–23.

i 63:9 Or "Neither an elder or an angel, but the Lord himself saved them." See Ex. 23:20–23; 33:14–15; Deut. 4:37. The Angel of His Presence is literally "the Angel of His Faces." God has many faces that he reveals to his people. Most scholars conclude that this phrase, a hapax

Out of his enduring love and compassion
he redeemed them.
He lifted them up, carried them *in his arms,*[a]
and cared for them all the days of old.
[10]But they rebelled against him
and grieved his Holy Spirit.[b]
Only then did he turn against them.
He became their enemy and fought against them.

The Day of Remembrance
[11]Then they remembered *God's deeds* in days past,
the days of Moses and his people.
And they asked:
"Where now is Yahweh, who brought them *miraculously*
through the Red Sea
along with *Moses,* the shepherd-*leader*[c] of his flock,
and put his Holy Spirit among them?[d]
[12]*Where now is the one*
who linked his magnificent power to Moses,[e]
who divided the waters before them
to gain everlasting fame for himself?
[13]Who led them through the depths of the sea?
They were as sure-footed as horses on dry, level ground—
they did not stumble.
[14]As a herder leads his cattle to *find rest* in a fertile valley,
the Spirit of Yahweh led them into rest.[f]
In the same way, you led your people
to win for yourself a glorious name!"[g]

The Day of Prayer
[15]*Lord,* look down from heaven,
from your holy, glorious dwelling place, and see *us.*
What happened to your passion *for us*

---

legomenon, is not referring to one of the angelic host but to the Lord himself. Others see this
angel as Gabriel, for he is described as the angel who comes from the presence (face) of God
(Luke 1:19).

a 63:9 See Deut. 1:31; 32:10–12.

b 63:10 The Holy Spirit has feelings that can be hurt, leaving him grieved. See Gen. 6:6;
Ps. 78:40; Eph. 4:30.

c 63:11 Or "shepherds" (plural), indicating that it would be Moses, Aaron, and the leaders of Israel.

d 63:11 See Num. 11:17.

e 63:12 Or "who made his majestic arm march at the right hand of Moses." This may be a figurative way of saying that God put his power in Moses' right hand.

f 63:14 See Ps. 23:1–3.

g 63:14 See Eph. 1:20–23; Phil. 2:5–11.

and your mighty acts of power?
Why are you withholding from us
your feelings[a] of tender compassion?[b]
16For you are our loving Father.
Even if our ancestors, Abraham and Jacob,[c]
don't acknowledge us,
you, O Yahweh, are our loving Father![d]
From ancient times your name is our Redeemer.

17Yahweh, why do you allow us[e] to wander from your ways
and harden our hearts to be so stubborn
that we do not obey you?[f]
Please come back to us,
for the sake of those who serve you,
for the sake of your people,
the tribes that are your inheritance.
18For a short time
your holy people possessed *a holy place.*[g]
But now our enemies have *invaded and* trampled down
your sacred sanctuary.
19You treat us as though we had never been your people,
called by your name, or ruled by you.

A Cry for Revival

64 *God,* if only you would tear open
the heavenly realm and come down!
How the mountains would tremble[h]
in your *awesome* presence![i]
2In the same way that fire sets kindling to blaze
and causes water to boil,
let the fire of your presence[j] come down.

---

a 63:15 Or "yearnings." God has deep feelings toward us, for the Hebrew is literally "[Don't hold back] the agitation of your intestines."

b 63:15 The Hebrew word for compassion is a homonym that can also be translated "womb." They both speak of nurturing love, care, and tenderness.

c 63:16 Or "Israel."

d 63:16 See Deut. 32:6.

e 63:17 The Hebrew word is *tatenu* ("make us"). Similar to the tolerative form of the Hiphil of ta'ah in Jer. 50:6, it is best seen as "allow us" versus causative, in its usual form, "make us."

f 63:17 Or "fear you."

g 63:18 Or "Jerusalem."

h 64:1 See Judg. 5:5; Hab. 3:6. Mountains can also symbolize governments and kingdoms. There is one King and one kingdom that rises above every other mountain (Isa. 2:1–5).

i 64:1 Or "before your faces."

j 64:2 Fire is a frequent metaphor for the presence of God. See Gen. 3:24; Ex. 3:1–2; Isa. 4:5; 6:6; 10:16–17; 29:6; 30:27, 30; 31:9; 33:12, 14; 66:15–16, 24; Acts 2:3; Heb. 12:29.

Reveal to your enemies your mighty name
and cause the nations to tremble before you!
³When you did amazing wonders we didn't expect,
    you came down,
    and mountains shuddered in your presence!
⁴These amazing things had never been heard of before;
    you did things never dreamed of!
    No one perceived *your greatness.*
    No eye has ever seen a God like you,ᵃ
    who intervenes for thoseᵇ
    who wait and longᶜ for you!ᵈ
⁵Those who delight in doing what is right—
    you go out to meetᵉ them *with kindness.*
    They remember you and cherish your ways.
    You showed your anger
    when we sinned again and again,
    yet we can be saved.ᶠ

Sin Is Our Problem

⁶We have all become contaminated with sin,
    and you see our self-righteousness as nothing better
    than a menstrual rag.
    We are all like fallen leaves,
    and our sins sweep us away like the wind.ᵍ
⁷No one calls on your name
    or presses in to lay hold of you,
    for you have hidden your face from us.
    You have let us be ruinedʰ by our own sins.

The Master Potter

⁸Yet still, Yahweh, you are our Father.
    We are like clay and you are our Potter.
    Each one of us is the creative, *artistic* work of your hands.
⁹Yahweh, don't be angry with us!
    Don't remember our sins again forever!
    Please look at us; we are your people.

---

a 64:4 See 1 John 1:1–4.

b 64:4 Or "who works on behalf of those."

c 64:4 The Hebrew word *chakah* implies waiting with trusting anticipation (longing).

d 64:4 Or "him." See Isa. 40:31; 1 Cor. 2:9–10.

e 64:5 Or "You attack them [with kindness]."

f 64:5 Or, as a question, "How can we be saved?" There is no verse in Isaiah that is more perplexing and difficult to translate than this one. The exact Hebrew meaning is uncertain.

g 64:6 The implication is that we are whirled along by the wind of our sins.

h 64:7 Or "melted by our own sins."

¹⁰Your sacred cities are *abandoned* like a desert;
　Zion is a wasteland; Jerusalem sits in ruins.
¹¹Our holy temple, our source of pride,
　where our ancestors sang your praise,
　has been consumed by fire.
　All that we held dear has been destroyed.
¹²Now, Yahweh, after all this, are you still unmoved?
　Will you continue to stand silently by
　and afflict us so severely?

God's Righteous Judgment

65 "I revealed myself to those
　who didn't even ask to know me.
　Those who did not seek me found me.*ᵃ*
　I said to a nation that did not call on my name,*ᵇ*
　'Here I am! Here I am! *I will help you!*'
²Day after day I have *graciously* outstretched my hands*ᶜ*
　to a people who turned their backs to me,
　whose way of life is corrupt,
　who insist on going their own way.*ᵈ*
³They are a people who continually insult me to my face.
　They openly and defiantly offer sacrifices to their gods
　in their sacred groves
　and burn incense on pagan altars.*ᵉ*
⁴They sit inside tombs
　and spend the night in secret caves.*ᶠ*
　They eat pork*ᵍ*
　and their pots are polluted with the broth of unclean meat.
⁵They tell others,
　'Stay away! Don't come near; I'm too holy for you to touch.'
　These people are like a stench in my nostrils,
　a smoldering fire that doesn't go out!
⁶Their verdict is determined before me,
　and I will not keep silent:
　'I will repay them for what they have done;
　I will pay them back for what their sins deserve,*ʰ*

---

a 65:1 See Rom. 10:20–21.

b 65:1 See Matt. 21:42–43; 1 Peter 2:1–10.

c 65:2 There is at least a hint here of the outstretched hands of Jesus on the cross.

d 65:2 Or "after their own thoughts." See Judges 21:25; 2 Cor. 10:3–6.

e 65:3 Or "altars of bricks" or "(roof) tiles"; i.e. rooftops. See 2 Kings 23:12; Jer. 19:13; 32:29; Zeph. 1:5.

f 65:4 Possibly to receive messages from the dead. The Hebrew meaning is uncertain.

g 65:4 Pork was considered unclean according to Jewish dietary laws.

h 65:6 Or "I will repay them into their laps."

⁷for both their sins and the sins of their fathers.
  Because they burned incense on the high places
  and blasphemed me on the hills,
  I will punish them severely, as their actions deserve,'"
  says Yahweh.

A Chosen Remnant

⁸Here is what Yahweh says:
  "As new wine is found in the cluster,
  and someone says,
  'Don't destroy it, for there is a blessing in it,'
  that's what I will do for my servants' sake.ᵃ
  I will not destroy them all.
⁹I will raise up offspring from Jacob
  and from my chosen *ones* of Judah
  to possess my mountains,
  and my servants will settle there.
¹⁰For my people who seek me,
  I will make *the Plain of* Sharonᵇ
  a pasture for flocks *in the east*,
  and *in the west*, the Valley of Troubleᶜ
  will be a resting place for cattle,
  for my people who seek me *and no other god.*

¹¹"But you who forsake Yahweh
  and ignore my holy mountain,
  who celebrate a feast for the goddess called Lady Luckᵈ
  and fill cups of wine to toast the god Destiny,ᵉ
  know this: your luck has run out.
¹²For I will destine you for the sword!
  You will all kneel down to be slaughtered *like sheep*
  because when I called, you did not answer,
  and when I spoke, you did not listen!ᶠ
  You did evil before me and chose what I despise."
¹³Therefore, this is what the Lord God says:
  "My servants will eat,

---

a 65:8 The "Servant" of the Lord is now plural "servants," a term that is mentioned seven times in this chapter (vv. 8, 9, 13 three times, 14, 15). One has become many (Rom. 8:29; 1 Cor. 12:12–14; Heb. 2:6–13).

b 65:10 The Plain of Sharon extends north of the city of Joppa.

c 65:10 Or "Valley of Achor," commonly identified as Wadi el-Kelt, a deep ravine south of Jericho.

d 65:11 Or "Gad," the name of a Babylonian god, "the god of Fortune (Luck)."

e 65:11 Or "Meni," the name of a Babylonian god, "the god of Destiny."

f 65:12 See Prov. 1:24–33; Heb. 4:12–13.

but you will go hungry.
My servants will drink,
but you will go thirsty.
My servants will rejoice,
but you will be put to shame.
¹⁴My servants will sing joyfully with hearts of gladness,
but you will cry out from the pain deep inside,
and wail from a broken heart.
¹⁵When you die, your name will become a curse
used by my chosen ones.
The Lord God will put you to death,
but his *godly* servants
will leave behind the legacy of an honorable name.
¹⁶For whoever pronounces a blessing on the earth
will do so in the name of the God of Faithfulness.*ᵃ*
And whoever swears by an oath on the earth
will invoke the name of the God of Faithfulness.
The failures*ᵇ* of the past
will be forgotten;
they will be hidden from my eyes.

A New World Order

¹⁷"Look! I am creating
entirely new heavens and a new earth!*ᶜ*
They will be so wonderful
that no one will even think about the old ones anymore!
¹⁸*As you wait for the reality of* what I am creating,
be filled with joy and unending gladness!
Look! I am ready to create Jerusalem
as a source of *sheer* joy,
and her people, an *absolute* delight!
¹⁹I will rejoice in *this new* Jerusalem
and find *great* delight in my people.
You will no longer hear
the sound of weeping or cries of distress.
²⁰No baby will die in infancy there,
and everyone will live out their full lifespan.*ᵈ*
For when centenarians die,
they will be considered youngsters,
and anyone who dies earlier
will be considered of no account.

---

a 65:16 Or "the God of Truth" or "the God of Amen." See Gen. 12:2–3.
b 65:16 Or "troubles, emotional pain, guilt, anxieties, hardships, distresses, tribulations."
c 65:17 See Isa. 66:22; 2 Peter 3:12–13; Rev. 21:1.
d 65:20 See Ps. 21:4; 91:16; Prov. 3:1–14.

²¹⁻²²People will build their own houses to live in,
and they will not be taken over by someone else.
They will plant their own vineyards to enjoy,ᵃ
and they will not be *confiscated* by someone else.
They will live long lives, like age-old trees,ᵇ
and my chosen ones will enjoy to the fullest
the work of their hands throughout their lives.
²³They will neither work in vain *for someone else*,
nor will their children face disaster
for they will be childrenᶜ and grandchildrenᵈ
who are blessed by Yahweh.
²⁴Before they even call out to me,
I will answer them;ᵉ
before they've finished telling me what they need,
I'll have already heard.
²⁵The wolf and the lamb will graze side by sideᶠ
and the lion will eat straw like the ox,ᵍ
and the serpent's food will be dust.ʰ
There will be neither violence nor murder
on my entire holy mountain *of Zion*," says Yahweh.

God's Resting Place Is with the Humble

66 This is what Yahweh says:
"The heavens are my throneⁱ
and the earth is my footstool.
Where is the house you will build for me?ʲ
Where is the place where I will rest?
²My hand made these things so they all belong to me," declares Yahweh.

---

a 65:21–22 Or "eat (drink) their fruit." The implication of these two verses is that foreign invaders will not take over the land.

b 65:21–22 See Rev. 22:2.

c 65:23 Or "seed." See Isa. 53:10.

d 65:23 Or "descendants."

e 65:24 See Isa. 30:19; Jer. 33:3; Matt. 6:8; John 16:23–24.

f 65:25 See Isa. 11:6.

g 65:25 See Isa. 11:7.

h 65:25 See Gen. 3:14; 1 Cor. 15:47–49. Man was made from dust. The serpent feeds on whatever we withhold from God. The devil's dining room is the fallen human nature and the mind of a man who is not yielded to God. Over time, the serpent feeds and grows into the great dragon (Rev. 12:9).

i 66:1 The glorious God is too great to be limited to a literal chair-like throne. This *throne* is symbolic, a term meant to help us understand his great sovereignty and authority as ruler over all.

j 66:1 God rebukes the returning exiles for wanting to rebuild the temple and to restore the outward forms of worship with no intention of turning from their evil ways and having their hearts changed. God no longer dwells in man-made buildings but in God-shaped hearts of people who love, worship, and believe in him. See v. 2; 1 Kings 8:22–43; Acts 7:48; Eph. 2:19–22; Heb. 3:5–6.

"But there is one my eyes are drawn to:
the humble one, the tender one,[a] the trembling one
who lives in awe of all I say.
3But the one who offers a bull *with no humility*
is like one who kills a man.
The one who offers a lamb *without contrition*
is like one who breaks a dog's neck.
The one who brings grain offerings *with no heart-purity*
is like one who offers pig's blood!
The one who offers incense *with no sincerity*
is like one who kisses[b] an idol!
They have all chosen their own way, *not mine*,
and they take delight in these disgusting things!
4So I chose to punish[c] them
and to bring on them what they fear the most
because I called out to them and they ignored me.
I spoke and they did not listen
but did what is evil in my sight
and chose what I despise."

5Hear the words of Yahweh, you who tremble at what he says:
"Shame on your own people,
who reject you and hate you,
claiming they do it for my sake.
For they *mock you*, saying,
'May Yahweh be glorified; let us see you rejoice.'"

God Intervenes
6Listen! A sound of uproar is coming from the city
a sound from the temple!
It is the thunder[d] of Yahweh
as he completely punishes his enemies!

7*Zion* gave birth suddenly, even before going into labor.
She delivered a son without any painful contractions.
8Who has ever seen or heard of such a wonder?
Could a country be born in a day?
Can a nation be birthed so suddenly?[e]
Yet no sooner does Zion go into labor

---

a 66:2 Or "the one bruised (crushed) in spirit."

b 66:3 Or "blesses."

c 66:4 Or "mock."

d 66:6 Or "voice." Ch. 40 begins with a thunderous voice in the wilderness; Isaiah ends with a
voice like thunder in his *temple.*

e 66:8 This actually happened with Israel being "reborn" as a nation in 1948. And it happened
at Pentecost when the church, a holy nation, was birthed by the Holy Spirit. See Acts 2:1–4.

than she gives birth to sons!
⁹Yahweh, your God, says,
"Do I allow you to conceive and not to give birth?
Do I shut the womb when I'm the one who delivers?"

¹⁰So rejoice with Jerusalem and be glad for her!
All who love her, join in with her great joy,
especially those who remember her grief!
¹¹You, *her children,* will drink the milk of her prosperity
and nurse with delight from her glorious abundance!

¹²For Yahweh says:
"I will extend to her prosperity like a river
and the wealth of gentiles like a flooding river.
You will nurse from her breast, be cradled in her arms,
and *delightfully* bounced on her knees.
¹³As a mother tenderly comforts her child,
so will I tenderly comfort you,
and you will find comfort in Jerusalem."

Judgment by Fire and Sword
¹⁴When you feast your eyes on this,
your heart will leap for joy and be revived;
your *body* will flourish and sprout like grass.ᵃ
The mighty powerᵇ of Yahweh will be revealed,
resting on his servants,
but his fury will be shown to his enemies!
¹⁵Look! Yahweh is coming as a raging fire
and his chariots like a whirlwindᶜ
to unleash his anger with fiery fury
and with the fiery lightning of his rebuke!ᵈ
¹⁶For with fireᵉ and with his swordᶠ
Yahweh will judgeᵍ humanity—
many will be the slain of Yahweh!

¹⁷"The end is near for those who 'consecrate' and 'purify' themselves to enter their cultic groves! They go in procession one after another *into their ceremonies.*

---

a 66:14 Or "Your bones (a metaphor for your inner being) will sprout like grass (flourish)." Some commentators view this as physical health and well-being.

b 66:14 Or "hand," a metaphor for his power and anointing.

c 66:15 See 2 Kings 2:1–18; Ezek. 1:4–28.

d 66:15 See Zech. 9:14; Heb. 12:29.

e 66:16 See Jer. 23:29–32.

f 66:16 See Heb. 4:12.

g 66:16 Or "contend" or "plead." See Amos 7:4–6.

They eat *disgusting foods*—pork, mice, and rodents. [18]I *despise* their *evil works*[a] and their thoughts,"[b] says Yahweh.

God's Reign

"The time is coming for me to gather people together from all over the world,[c] and they will come and gaze on my radiance. [19]I will set an amazing sign[d] among them. I will send some of the remnant to other nations—to Tarshish, Put,[e] Lud[f] (known for its archers),[g] Tubal,[h] Javan,[i] and distant islands that have never heard of my fame nor gazed on my glory. They will declare my glory among the gentiles! [20]And they will bring back from the nations your own people as an offering to me," says Yahweh.

"They will come on horseback, in chariots, in wagons, on mules and camels to my holy mountain, Jerusalem," says Yahweh. "In the same way my people bring a grain offering in a sacred vessel to the temple, they will be brought as grain offerings to my holy mountain, Jerusalem, as a holy offering to me. [21]And some of them I will appoint as Levitical priests," says Yahweh.

[22]This is what Yahweh declares: "The new heavens and the new earth that I am making will remain and endure before me in the same way your offspring[j] and your name will endure. [23]From one Sabbath to the next, one month to the next, one year to the next, all humanity will come to worship me!

[24]"They will go out *of the city* and see the dead bodies of those who rebelled against me. For their worm will not die[k] and their fire will never go out.[l] And they will be abhorrent to humanity."[m]

---

a 66:18 See Gal. 5:19–21.

b 66:18 Or "imaginations." The works and thoughts of fallen humanity can be compared to the "mark (character) of the beast" on the hands (works) and the foreheads (thoughts, mind-sets) of people. See Acts 17:29; Rev. 13:13–18.

c 66:18 Or "nations and tongues." See Acts 2:5–12.

d 66:19 To "set a sign" is likely a figure of speech for "to display a mighty miracle." This Hebrew phrase is also found in Ps. 78:43 and Jer. 32:20. In the book of Acts, the miracle sign God set among his people was the Holy Spirit, who sent out laborers into the harvest fields of the nations.

e 66:19 Or "Pul." Put is modern-day Libya.

f 66:19 Lud is Lydia in modern-day western Turkey.

g 66:19 Or possibly Meshech, a region frequently associated with Tubal, which could be a reference to Russia (Moscow).

h 66:19 Ancient Tubal is comprised of much of modern-day Turkey.

i 66:19 Javan was the son of Japheth and the grandson of Noah. This is a likely metonymy referring to modern-day Greece.

j 66:22 Or "seed."

k 66:24 This is likely a figure of speech for unending suffering. Some equate the worm with the guilty conscience. See Mark 9:48.

l 66:24 It is possible that this refers to a mass burial site where maggots continue to eat flesh and fire burns continually with corpses. Some see this as having been fulfilled by the slaughter of the enemies during the time of the Maccabees, others as a view toward a future slaughter, and still others as a description of hell.

m 66:24 Or "all flesh," the last words of Isaiah. It is a long-held Jewish tradition that Isaiah was placed inside a hollow tree and sawn in two, by the order of King Manasseh. The book of Isaiah is likewise "sawn in two" by theologians with theories of two or more authors.

YOUR PERSONAL INVITATION

TO FOLLOW JESUS

We can all find ourselves in dark places, needing some light—light that brings direction, healing, vision, warmth, and hope. Jesus said, "I am light to the world and those who embrace me will experience life-giving light, and they will never walk in darkness" (John 8:12). Without the light and love of Jesus, this world is truly a dark place and we are lost forever.

Love unlocks mysteries. As we love Jesus, our hearts are unlocked to see more of his beauty and glory. When we stop defining ourselves by our failures, but rather as the ones whom Jesus loves, our hearts begin to open to the breathtaking discovery of the wonder of Jesus Christ.

All that is recorded in the Scriptures is there so that you will fully believe that Jesus is the Son of God, and that through your faith in him you will experience eternal life by the power of his name (see John 20:31).

If you want this light and love in your life, say a prayer like this—whether for the first time or to express again your passionate desire to follow Jesus:

Jesus, you are the light of the world. I want to follow you, passionately and wholeheartedly. But my sins have separated me from you. Thank you for your love for me. Thank you for paying the price for my sins, and I trust your finished work on the cross for my rescue. I turn away from the thoughts and deeds that have separated me from you. Forgive me and awaken me to love you with all my heart, mind, soul, and strength. I believe God raised you from the dead, and I want that new life to flow through me each day and for eternity. God, I give you my life. Now fill me with your Spirit so that my life will honor you and I can fulfill your purpose for me. Amen.

You can be assured that what Jesus said about those who choose to follow him is true: "If you embrace my message and believe in the One who sent me, you will never face condemnation, for in me, you have already passed from the realm of death into the realm of eternal life!" (John 5:24). But there's more! Not only are you declared "not guilty" by God because of Jesus, you are also considered his most intimate friend (John 15:15).

As you grow in your relationship with Jesus, continue to read the Bible, communicate with God through prayer, spend time with others who follow Jesus, and live out your faith daily and passionately. God bless you!

ABOUT THE TRANSLATOR

Dr. Brian Simmons is known as a passionate lover of God. After a dramatic conversion to Christ, Brian knew that God was calling him to go to the unreached people of the world and present the gospel of God's grace to all who would listen. With his wife, Candice, and their three children, he spent nearly eight years in the tropical rain forest of the Darien Province of Panama as a church planter, translator, and consultant. Brian was involved in the Paya-Kuna New Testament translation project. He studied linguistics and Bible translation principles with New Tribes Mission. After their ministry in the jungle, Brian was instrumental in planting a thriving church in New England (USA) and now travels full-time as a speaker and Bible teacher. He has been happily married to Candice since 1971 and boasts regularly of his three children and eight grandchildren.

Follow The Passion Translation at:

Facebook.com/passiontranslation

Twitter.com/tPtBible

Instagram.com/passiontranslation

For more information about the translation project please visit:

ThePassionTranslation.com

NOTES

ThePassionTranslation.com